"This is a fine collection of essays by experts in ecclesiology and pastoral theology and is a true gift for the church as we journey together in the synod on synodality. Experts from around the world explain the barriers to systemic reform and the call to deep listening, attunement to the Holy Spirit, and accompaniment required of the faithful in this time of renewal. Readers will encounter honest and pragmatic analysis of complex and conflict-ridden questions. The authors' suggestions for dialogue and discernment take seriously the contributions of lay people, especially women, to the ongoing work of the church now and in the future. A must read for pastors, theologians, and all who are participating in the global synod."

— Emily Reimer-Barry, PhD, Associate Professor of Theology and Religious Studies, University of San Diego

"These essays are part of the 'mutual listening' that Pope Francis wants to characterize the 2023–2024 synodal process. But it is more than that. For the first time in centuries Catholics are calling for reform—it is a theme in the air we breathe. This is more than 'renewal' or some 'updating' procedures: we are talking of *reform*, which means admitting we have problems, have made serious mistakes in past centuries, and now we must look the problems in the eye. These eleven essays—each expert and from a different perspective and from across the globe—are a snapshot of our problems; and they are a guide to what we must confront if the synodal process is to be more than fine words."

— Thomas O'Loughlin, Professor Emeritus of Historical Theology, The University of Nottingham

"In *Reforming the Church*, Declan Marmion and Salvador Ryan present a miniature 'synod on synodality,' with clear voices from Australia, Europe, India, South America, and the United States, each presenting a different perspective on the processes and the facts of synodality— past, present, and future. The work is invaluable for the ongoing work of fruitful change in the Church."

— Phyllis Zagano, PhD, Hofstra University, New York

"Far from ultimatums from impatient reformers, the essays in *Reforming the Church: Global Perspectives* promote thoughtful consideration on how the entire people of God together can become 'actors of discernment.' In going out to the peripheries, by genuinely listening to one another's stories with 'a hermeneutic of compassion,' Declan Marmion and Salvador Ryan have chosen a trajectory of synodal paths that not only enlarge our tent, but create space for true communion, participation, and a solid foundation for carrying out Christ's mission for the future."

— Mary Ann Hinsdale, IHM, Boston College

"Significant church reform is the unfulfilled promise of Vatican II. Pope Francis has now taken up this promise by setting the Church on a synodal path of listening and genuine dialogue. This collection of papers, from theologians and scholars around the world, provides an excellent roadmap for the range of issues needing attention: the role of women; clericalism; the sexual abuse crisis; and so on. May their voices bear fruit in the reforms the Church so urgently needs."

— Neil Ormerod, Honorary Professor, Alphacrucis University College, Sydney, Australia

"The eminent authors of these essays together offer a substantial contribution to the theology of ecclesial reform, here in the key of 'synodality'. From multiple perspectives, such as the length of the Catholic tradition or present crises in the church, we are given a refreshing challenge for change. Envisaging the church primarily as all the people of God, this vision for reform demands a listening especially to those on 'the peripheries' and an enabling for mission through participation of all in the church's sacramental and teaching life, as well as its governance. This book will be widely welcomed."

— Ormond Rush, Australian Catholic University

" 'Synodality' and 'reform' go together seamlessly. Both terms hold out a vision of a community receptive to the diverse voices and gifts of all the baptized. As ever, translating vision into everyday realities is a challenging task, one that requires resources as well as creativity. *Reforming the Church* provides resources—historical, theological, and pastoral—to stimulate and support creativity. The chapters of *Reforming the Church*, drawn from academic research and experiences across the global church, will nourish the mission of the pilgrim community."

— Richard Lennan, Professor of Systematic Theology,
Boston College—School of Theology and Ministry

"In this compelling collection, issued as Catholics celebrate the sixtieth anniversary of Vatican II and prepare for an upcoming synod on synodality, theologians around the world take up key issues that must be addressed in order to advance needed reform in the church. Crafted for a wide audience, these insightful essays will benefit seasoned theologians, pastoral agents, lay and ordained in the church and in society, as well as students who are trying to find their ways during a contentious age."

— Bradford E. Hinze, Fordham University

"This terrific collection of essays foregrounds the current synod on synodality but is not confined to it, offering us keys to understanding the synod against the broad backdrop of church reform. Scholarly yet vivid, *Reforming the Church* is just what is needed right now: insights and reflections that allow the ordinary faithful to grasp the most important Catholic event since Vatican II."

— Austen Ivereigh, DPhil, author, journalist, and fellow in
contemporary church history at Campion Hall,
University of Oxford

Reforming the Church

Global Perspectives

Edited by
Declan Marmion
and
Salvador Ryan

Epilogue by
Kristin Colberg

LITURGICAL PRESS
ACADEMIC

Collegeville, Minnesota
www.litpress.org

Cover design by Monica Bokinskie.
Pentecost by Mark Wiggins. Image courtesy of Veritasse.

Scripture quotations are from New Revised Standard Version Bible © 1989 National Council of the Churches of Christ in the United States of America. Used by permission. All rights reserved worldwide.

Excerpts of Pope Francis, "Ceremony Commemorating the 50th Anniversary of the Institution of the Synod of Bishops" (October 17, 2015), © Dicastero per la Comunicazione-Libreria Editrice Vaticana. Used with permission.

1	2	3	4	5	6	7	8	9

Library of Congress Cataloging-in-Publication Data

Names: Marmion, Declan, editor. | Ryan, Salvador, editor.
Title: Reforming the church : global perspectives / edited by Declan Marmion and Salvador Ryan.
Description: Collegeville, Minnesota : Liturgical Press, [2023] | Summary: "The long-term ecclesiological trajectory of Pope Francis is toward a reformed church along synodal lines. This volume traces not only the historical roots of synodality but also examines the shape of synodal processes currently underway in different contexts and continents"— Provided by publisher.
Identifiers: LCCN 2023003730 (print) | LCCN 2023003731 (ebook) | ISBN 9780814668641 (paperback) | ISBN 9780814668658 (epub) | ISBN 9780814668658 (pdf) | ISBN 9780814668665 (pdf)
Subjects: LCSH: Catholic Church--Doctrines. | Church renewal. | Councils and synods (Canon law)
Classification: LCC BX9.5.C65 R35 2023 (print) | LCC BX9.5.C65 (ebook) | DDC 262.001/7—dc23/eng/20230606
LC record available at https://lccn.loc.gov/2023003730
LC ebook record available at https://lccn.loc.gov/2023003731

Contents

Acknowledgments

We would like to express our gratitude to all who made this publication possible. We are grateful to Rev. Prof. Michael Mullaney, President of St. Patrick's Pontifical University, Maynooth, and our faculty colleagues, for their encouragement and support in preparing this volume. We would also like to especially thank Dr. Astrid Schilling, Katholische Akademie in Bayern, for her translation of Prof. Dr. Julia Knop's chapter and for the support of *Irish Theological Quarterly* in sponsoring the translation. We are also grateful to Prof. Rafael Luciani for his translation of Prof. Pedro Trigo's chapter. Finally, we wish to thank Peter Dwyer, Hans Christoffersen, and the entire team at Liturgical Press for their courtesy and professionalism during the preparation of this volume.

Introduction

This volume was inspired by the call of Pope Francis on October 10, 2021, for a two-year consultation process leading to a synod on synodality in Rome in October 2023. In doing so, he invited Catholics to "look others in the eye and listen to what they have to say" and to "become experts in the art of encounter."[1] More recently, the pope announced that the final phase of what has been described as "the greatest consultation effort in human history," attempting "to listen to the world's 1.36 billion Catholics," would now be spread over two synodal meetings in Rome, in October 2023 and October 2024 respectively.[2]

Although this collection of essays takes its cue from the ongoing synodal processes, it also addresses wider issues relating to church reform while situating these in their historical context. While all contributions discuss themes that have relevance to the universal church, several chapters address issues of more local, or culturally specific, significance, in this way mirroring the results of synodal consultations conducted worldwide. This is especially evident

---

[1] Catholic News Agency, "2023 Synod on Synodality: Pope Francis Launches 2-year Synodal Path with Call to 'Encounter, Listen, and Discern,'" October 10, 2021, https://www.catholicnewsagency.com/news/249241/2023-synod-on-synodality-pope-francis-launches-2-year-synodal-path-with-call-to-encounter-listen-and-discern.

[2] Christopher Lamb, "Pope Francis Announces Global Synod Meeting Will Occur over Two Years," *Chicago Catholic*, October 19, 2022, https://www.chicagocatholic.com/vatican/-/article/2022/10/19/pope-francis-announces-global-synod-meeting-will-occur-over-two-years.

when one compares the chapters herein with the *Document for the Continental Stage* published on October 25, 2022.[3] This is a single global synthesis of all the submissions from countries around the world, which comprised 112 bishops' conferences and 15 Oriental Catholic Churches, in addition to reflections from 17 out of 23 dicasteries of the Roman Curia, from the men's and women's international unions of superiors general, and from Catholic lay associations and movements.[4] Its call for greater inclusion for many people who feel marginalized or unwelcome in the church is encapsulated in the main title of the document itself: "Enlarge the Space of Your Tent," a quotation from Isaiah 54:2. The tent is identified as "a space of *communion*, a place of *participation*, and a foundation for *mission*" (DCS 11).

This volume begins with placing the synodal process and current efforts to renew and reform the church and its structures in a historical context. Christopher Bellitto opens his chapter by acknowledging that reforming the church is "the attempt to fill the gap between what is preached and what is practiced" and that this also asks of the church no small degree of honesty and authenticity: "The key to reform is to be honest about what needs to be fixed." He notes that reforms work best "when arising from real-life circumstances and not theoretically or ideologically." This point is also taken up by a number of other contributors. Bellitto emphasizes the significance of the peripheries in generating movements of reform, noting that "history has repeatedly shown how effectual reform action travels from the periphery to the center and then out to other peripheries." He also cautions against the temptation to regard critics of the church as the church's enemies; rather, he notes that critics of the church are very often those who deeply love the church. It is all too easy for those who would rather resist reform to dismiss reform-minded individuals as "malcontents or heretics," and the history of the church is replete with examples of such much-too-hasty brandings. An observation of

<hr/>

[3] General Secretariat for the Synod, *Working Document for the Continental Stage*, https://www.synod.va/content/dam/synod/common/phases/continental-stage/dcs/Documento-Tappa-Continentale-EN.pdf. Hereafter cited as DCS.

[4] Vatican News, "Synod: Church Leaders Welcome Document for Continental Stage," October 28, 2022, https://www.vaticannews.va/en/church/news/2022-10/church-leaders-welcome-document-for-continental-stage-of-synod.html.

the late church historian John W. O'Malley, who spent a great part of his career writing about conciliar reform, is instructive here. In an interview in 2020, O'Malley advocated the adoption of a "hermeneutic of compassion," which would allow for the fact that "people basically want to be good," and to thereby resist "approaching every human expression as simply badly motivated or self-serving."[5]

The deep fissures within the church that such approaches can lead to are discussed by Shaun Blanchard in his essay on true and false reformers in the church. Here Blanchard problematizes the term *reform* itself as being "too pliable, too general, and too ideologically situated to really mean much by itself." After all, it's not enough to regard church reform as simply "a change for the better" if there are wildly diverging views of what constitutes "better." Indeed, for some, truly reforming the church involves nothing less than a reversal of a whole series of previous "reforms" that are considered to have been ultimately damaging and, therefore, need to be jettisoned. Considering the nature of the true reformer, Blanchard turns to the work of Yves Congar (1904–1995), a key inspiration of John XXIII and Vatican II. Congar acknowledged that it was often difficult for reformers to be patient "as their intentions are usually so good, even sometimes utopian," especially when they encounter the magisterium as guardian, "charged with gravely weighing new paths," an idea echoed in the sentiments of Bellitto and O'Malley noted above. Nonetheless, Blanchard notes, Congar was wary of "the powerful prophetic impulse. When unrealized, it can become destructive, sectarian, and ultimately schismatic." In the previously noted essay, Bellitto remarks that "evolutionary change is better than revolutionary change" and, as Blanchard reminds us, Congar stated that the church does not like ultimatums from reformers. The process of reform is thus a very finely balanced enterprise.

Living with tensions and conflicts and allowing mature solutions to emerge over time rather than yielding to the temptation of the quick fix is also a theme that emerges in Declan Marmion's contribution, which examines the 2018 document of the International

---

[5] Emanuele Colombo, " 'So What?': A Conversation with John W. O'Malley," *Journal of Jesuit Studies* 7, no. 1 (2020): 117–133.

Theological Commission, *Synodality in the Life and Mission of the Church*, in which synodality is identified as the specific *modus vivendi et operandi* of the church, the people of God.[6] Synodality represents a move away from an older model in which the pope and the bishops represented the *ecclesia docens* (the "teaching church") and the rest of the people of God, the *ecclesia discens* (the "learning church"). Synodality, by contrast, recognizes that the *sensus fidei* pertains to *all* the faithful and, indeed, that the church has much to learn from the experience of its skeptical and alienated members. The move to a more synodal *modus operandi* in the church will involve bishops and theologians listening to how the faithful have faced dilemmas, namely, listening to them "tell their stories." Christopher Bellitto quotes the ecclesiologist Dario Vitali, who identifies this as a process "where the faithful are not extras but actors of discernment through a listening that really wants to recognize in their voices the voice of the Spirit." Yet the wheels of change often turn slowly, and older ways of doing things can sometimes persist. Francis Gonsalves, writing on the context of the church in India, relates how the "pray, pay, obey" axiom for the laity seems apt to a fairly large extent even today. Gonsalves notes that an excuse often given to keep the lay faithful out of decision-making is that "they do not have sufficient training," but goes on to ask, "If this is true, then, while so much time and money is spent on training candidates for priesthood, why is there such hesitancy to train promising lay faithful to be leaders in the church?"

Moving away from a model of the *ecclesia docens* and the *ecclesia discens* also involves a reimagining of the dynamic between bishops and lay faithful. In his chapter, Rafael Luciani regards synodality as "a whole process of ecclesial transfiguration that finds its foundation in the *essential*—and not auxiliary—commitment of *co-responsibility* proper to the model of the church as the people of God" with an emphasis on the "ecclesial *we*." He notes that "it is not the people of God that must be integrated into the hierarchy by participating in episcopal structures . . . but the hierarchy that

---

[6] International Theological Commission, *Synodality in the Life and Mission of the Church*, March 2, 2018, https://www.vatican.va/roman_curia/congregations/cfaith/cti_documents/rc_cti_20180302_sinodalita_en.html.

must place itself . . . within the people of God, listening to the voice of all the faithful."

Massimo Faggioli examines another aspect of this listening to the voice of the faithful when he addresses issues surrounding the process of episcopal appointments. He argues that the issue of the reform of the appointment of bishops "must be seen from an ecclesiological point of view, that is, the need for the procedure to reflect more the idea of the church as the people of God, participating in the selection of their pastors, in ways that foster the unity of the church but also accountability and responsibility." Meanwhile, taking inspiration from Pope Francis's reference to the need for a "conversion of the papacy," Francis Gonsalves suggests that "if more bishops strove for a 'conversion of the episcopacy,' things would change and more people would be active in church life and mission."

The synodal process has inevitably cast further light on the catastrophic effects of the abuse of power within the church and the ongoing legacy of clerical sex abuse, which the *Document for the Continental Stage* terms "an open wound that continues to inflict pain on victims and survivors, on their families, and on their communities" (DCS 20). Agnès Desmazières reminds us that, in line with his conception of a "servant church," Yves Congar maintained that "the first service that the church gives to the world is to tell the truth" and that "the shift from an essentialist conception of the church, as perfect and thus pure, to a more historical one" has led to a greater focus on an institution tainted by human sinfulness. Thus, if the synodal process is to mean anything, it must also involve the church facing up to some uncomfortable truths.

In her contribution on the Synodal Path in Germany, Julia Knop points to power structures within the Roman Catholic Church that support a system that "has massively damaged, still damages, and can further damage the physical and psychological integrity of boys, girls, women, and female members of religious orders," and she notes that many who "are excluded and discriminated against by the church's teaching and practice" perceive the institution to be more interested in guarding its doctrine than in protecting its faithful from harm, even at the hands of the church itself.

Reflecting, in turn, on the parables of the good shepherd and the good housekeeper, Ethna Regan suggests that "the revelations of recent years have shown us that an overreliance on shepherd leadership and flock-followers has brought great human damage and ecclesial corruption." She sees the reforms of Pope Francis, albeit moving too slowly for some, as "reaching into the darkest and least accessible parts of the *ecclesia*, illuminating these spaces, and searching for what is lost under the accumulated dirt of abuse, clericalism, and hierarchicalism." Regan, invoking the post-synodal document of 1971, *Justice in the World,* highlights two objectives of the synod on synodality, "the challenge of congruence between teaching about justice and the practice of justice *ad intra,* and the question of credibility." The report from superiors of institutes of consecrated life, as found in the *Document for the Continental Stage,* explicitly names this: "Sexism in decision-making and Church language is prevalent in the Church. . . . As a result, women are excluded from meaningful roles in the life of the Church, discriminated against by not receiving a fair wage for their ministries and services. Women religious are often regarded as cheap labour" (DCS 63). Regan identifies justice *ad intra* as "one of the church's most pressing responsibilities in order to regain credibility," and she recommends the further development of the field of ecclesial ethics "to enable a more accountable and participative church."

In his chapter, Bishop Vincent Long, reflecting on the theme of synodality in light of the experience of the Australian church, contends, "The church cannot have a better future if it persists in the old paradigm of triumphalism, self-reference, and male dominance. So long as we continue to exclude women from the church's governance structures, decision-making processes, and institutional functions, we deprive ourselves of the richness of our full humanity. So long as we continue to make women invisible and inferior in the church's language, liturgy, theology, and law, we impoverish ourselves." Bishop Long also calls for a much more inclusive engagement with those on the margins, noting that "the future of ecclesial synodality is much more in the peripheries than in the synod hall at the Vatican," which echoes a point made by Christopher Bellitto in his contribution.

This plea for an engagement with those on the margins is, perhaps, made most emphatically by Pedro Trigo when he reminds us that "synodality with the poor . . . marks the measure of our fidelity to the path of Jesus." He challenges Christian theologians by stating that they often fail to "understand that conceptual knowledge of realities has nothing to do with experiencing them in life and living by them. Until they grasp that difference and realize that knowledge is an invitation to live, they will hardly be Christian." Such realities were starkly highlighted by the report from the Bolivian church, cited in the *Document for the Continental Stage*. It expressed regret that so many remained unrepresented in the synodal process, namely "the poorest, the lonely elderly, indigenous peoples, migrants without any affiliation and who lead a precarious existence, street children, alcoholics and drug addicts, those who have fallen into the plots of criminality and those for whom prostitution seems their only chance of survival, victims of trafficking, survivors of abuse (in the Church and beyond), prisoners, groups who suffer discrimination and violence because of race, ethnicity, gender, culture and sexuality" (DCS 40). Of course, this list of the marginalized might equally apply to any one of the responding regions globally, reminding us that beyond the welcome language of "enlarging the tent," there are harsh realities that are much more difficult to navigate in real life. The assertion of the Italian report, cited in the *Document for the Continental Stage*, that "the Church-home does not have doors that close, but a perimeter that continually widens" (DCS 29), hits the right synodal note, but it remains a considerable challenge to translate such inclusive rhetoric into concrete action. For Julia Knop, synodality needs to go beyond a synodal culture and mindset. "It also needs synodal structures; otherwise, arbitrariness will ultimately win out." The search for what Ethna Regan terms "the loss of the *imago Christi* in our structures and systems" will, indeed, take time, patience, and a deep, respectful listening. For Regan, the parable of the good housekeeper "reminds us that the recovery of memory of the forgotten, the finding of what is lost, and the hard, dirty work of cleaning the house is primarily God's work. Our efforts at reform are a participation in this." It is our hope that the essays that follow will be helpful in reflecting on the theme of reform within the church—what it has meant in the past, what it means for us now, and what it might mean in the future.

Declan Marmion & Salvador Ryan

Synods, Reform, and Pope Francis: A Historical Perspective

Christopher M. Bellitto

Reforming the church is the attempt to fill the gap between what is preached and what is practiced. There has never been a time in church history when that gap has not existed—not even in the earliest communities, despite later generations' attempts to turn the *ecclesia primitiva* into an exemplum. Paul's letters give evidence of believers divided by loyalties and conflicts; several can be paraphrased as pleading, "Would you please stop fighting?" While there never was a golden age in church history, that does not mean that at least some in the church have not attempted to travel in a better way along the pilgrim journey.

The key to reform is to be honest about what needs to be fixed. The phrase *ecclesia semper reformanda* might have its origins in the sixteenth century, within John Calvin's circle.[1] There are two ways to translate it: "the church will always be reformed" (future passive) and "the church is always reforming" (present active). The

---

[1] Hans Küng, *The Council, Reform, and Reunion*, trans. Cecily Hastings (New York: Sheed and Ward, 1962), 9; for other candidates for the phrase's origin, see Giancarlo Pani, *"Ecclesia Semper Reformanda*: From the Fourteenth to the Sixteenth Century," in *For a Missionary Reform of the Church: The* Civiltà Cattolica *Seminar*, ed. Antonio Spadaro and Carlos María Galli (New York: Paulist Press, 2017), 120–22, especially nn. 1–9.

first supposes an outside person or force (presumably God) will perform the reform; the second supposes that humans are acting and doing so now. What we presuppose is that the only constant in church history is change and the need for reform.

That open-eyed attitude has not always been in evidence. The impressive Carthusian order had medieval supporters who boasted, "*Non deformata, non reformata.*" In 1832, Pope Gregory XVI scoffed, "It is obviously absurd and injurious to propose a certain 'restoration and regeneration' for [the church] as though necessary for her safety and growth, as if she could be considered subject to defect or obscuration or other misfortune."[2] The very idea of reforming the church was impossible because you could only reform what is deformed; for this pope, that notion was simply impossible. Closer to our own era, the intransigent Cardinal Alfredo Ottaviani (1890–1979) chose as his episcopal motto *Semper Idem*—Always the Same. All three examples shut down reform as something inconceivable. Socrates, preaching the Delphic oracle's message to "know thyself," would have disagreed. There is always room for improvement.

Reform from the Periphery to the Center

Historically, reforms work best when arising from real-life circumstances and not theoretically or ideologically. If reform ideas come from the people at the periphery and not the prelates at the center, they tend to be practical and engaging. Relevance resonates. There is, to use modern business terms, input from the end-users and buy-in from the stakeholders because those at the bottom of the pyramid are included in meaningful ways. A modern illustration: Mother Teresa's effective and authentic ministry in Calcutta, far from the Roman nexus of power, resonated because a BBC documentary in 1969 brought her message from the periphery to the center at a global moment when the focus was on those in society who are left behind. There it gained notice, energy, and papal support that propelled it back outward to new peripheries.

---

[2] Pope Gregory XVI, encyclical letter *Mirari Vos*, August 15, 1832, 10, https://www.papalencyclicals.net/Greg16/g16mirar.htm.

Reformers within the church's body rarely want to overturn the entire system; they seek to fix what is broken within their communities. Critics of clericalism who do not wish to abolish priesthood or the episcopacy but to reform them are still distrusted. Witness Francis of Assisi, whose modern reputation as an über-saint forgets that this medieval man was at first suspected of being part of a wandering band of *pauperes Christi* criticizing the worldliness of the church—outsiders who annoyed hierarchical insiders. Geert Groote (1340–1384), a deacon and leader of the Dutch *devotio moderna* movement, once preached to priests, "I honor and greatly love the priest. I hate and properly abominate the fornicator." These are signs of rising expectations and standards by people in the church's body calling the heads of their church to order.[3]

As more people engaging in reform efforts on the ground are heard and supported, the chance of good results increases. First-millennium faithful pursuing *metanoia* in early communities that became convents and monasteries give evidence that concerns with personal reform predate institutional efforts. John Howe has argued convincingly that the institutionalized, top-down Gregorian revolution of the eleventh and twelfth centuries began with reform efforts in the church's body in the centuries before. An example would be the Cluny Abbey's charter of 909 that refused to accept lay interference in the monks' free election of their abbot as prescribed in Benedict's *Rule*. This successful declaration of independence was a model for the Gregorian goal of *libertas ecclesiae* to free the church from its cozy relationship with civil rulers seeking to impose bishops, abbots, and abbesses. That goal was codified (if imperfectly) at the Concordat of Worms in 1122 and then spread throughout the church at Lateran I the next year. Howe demonstrates that the ground for Gregorian centralization and success was already fertile because of reform efforts and effective practices away from Rome. A good idea from outside Rome was embraced and then promulgated by Rome; effectual reform

---

[3] John Van Engen, "Late Medieval Anticlericalism: The Case of the New Devout," in *Anticlericalism in Late Medieval and Early Modern Europe*, ed. Peter A. Dykema and Heiko A. Oberman (Leiden: Brill, 1993), 29.

action traveled from the periphery to the center and then out to other peripheries.[4]

Simultaneous reform efforts in peripheries and the center can push against each other. In the church's body, reformers took the phrase *libertas ecclesiae* differently than did the hierarchy, which used the slogan to assert the church's independence to name its own leaders. But twelfth-century Waldensians and other poor people's groups understood *libertas ecclesiae* to mean cleansing the church of the worldliness that infected it as popes and bishops built curias and bureaucracies to rival secular courts. These reformers also objected to the many new centralized church rules and procedures that were intended to free the church from outside interference but were seen from the peripheries as legalistic rules that choked the free exercise of the faith. In the twelfth century, Peter the Chanter at Paris warned: "When traditions are numerous they weigh heavily upon those who uphold them and upon those who transgress them. . . . They restrict the freedom of the church. . . . We are oppressively burdened with a multitude of contrived practices, although authority speaks, because even some useful things have to be tossed aside or we get borne down by them. We ought rather to teach and work to get the gospel observed, since so few now observe it."[5] The means and the ends of reform can overlap and even contradict: one curialist's idea of reform is a parishioner's experience of oppression. The act of reforming should entail creative tension between reform and renewal, conservation and innovation, tradition and progress, as well as among institutional strata. It is not always so.[6]

---

[4] John Howe, *Before the Gregorian Reform: The Latin Church at the Turn of the First Millennium* (Ithaca: Cornell University Press, 2016).

[5] As found in M.-D. Chenu, *Nature, Man, and Society in the Twelfth Century: Essays on New Theological Perspectives in the Latin West*, ed. and trans. Jerome Taylor and Lester K. Little (Toronto: University of Toronto Press, 1997), 256–57.

[6] Chenu, *Nature, Man, and Society*, 310–330; Heiko A. Oberman speaks of the "pregnant plurality" of religious ideas in "Fourteenth-Century Religious Thought: A Premature Profile," *Speculum* 53 (1978): 80–93 at 80; see also John Van Engen, "Multiple Options: The World of the Fifteenth-Century Church" *Church History* 77 (2008): 257–84, and Natalia Nowakowska, "Reform Before Reform? Religious Currents in Central Europe, c. 1500," in *A Companion to the Reformation in Central Europe*, ed. Howard Louthan and Graeme Murdock (Leiden: Brill, 2015), 121–26, 140–42.

Reform's resisters deflect criticism and defend their power by dismissing reformers as malcontents or heretics. Critics of the church love the church; they do not hate the church. To protect themselves, the Waldensians sought approval from Pope Alexander III at Lateran III in 1179. That pope appreciated their calls for poverty and clerical morality, allowing them to preach in an exhortatory manner but not doctrinally—a distinction that some in the movement surely did not understand. Five years later, Alexander's successor Lucius III condemned Waldensians as heretics, an act that radicalized them to reject many devotions and practices. Their fair criticisms were destroyed instead of embraced. This result set the stage for a more extremist movement susceptible to zealotry and a holier-than-thou mindset. Reformers in the peripheries were pushed aside by the center.

Timing and method are crucial. Reformers who have championed right ideas in the wrong moment or expressed them in unwelcome language and action have been condemned like the Waldensians: John Wycliffe, Jan Hus, and their followers come to mind. As Martin Luther learned—for all his characteristic impatience and bombast—evolutionary change is better than revolutionary change. The man who in 1520 decried the papacy as the Antichrist was soon himself painted with that same label by radical and violent reformers like Andreas Karlstadt, who thought Luther sluggish and tentative. Luther, for his part, said his followers should move slowly in changing the Mass into the vernacular, refrain from ripping down statues, and explain why Communion should be received often and in both species. He feared that if reformers changed too much too quickly, people who might be disposed to their side would instead be scared off. "The cause is good," Luther preached in 1522, "but there has been too much haste."[7]

Reformers also attempt to free the church from its own mistakes. We hear this approach in recent history in the comments the Argentinian Jorge Mario Bergoglio offered in a March 2013 meeting of his fellow cardinals as they prepared for the conclave that followed Pope Benedict XVI's resignation. In brief remarks that

---

[7] John W. Doberstein, ed. and trans., *Luther's Works* (Philadelphia: Muhlenberg Press, 1959), 51:72.

likely helped him get elected pope four days later, he urged the church to act boldly and to evangelize among the geographic and existential peripheries (those suffering in sin, pain, injustice, and so on). "I think," he said, "about the times in which Jesus knocks from within so that we let him out. The self-referential Church seeks to keep Jesus Christ within herself and does not let him out." He added that there are two competing images of the church: one evangelizing outward and the other concerned only with and for itself. "This should shed light on the possible changes and reforms which must be done for the salvation of souls."[8]

Synods and Reform

An efficient way to draw reform ideas from the peripheries to the center and then to send them out again is to hold a synod or council—words used interchangeably in the historical record. The church's twenty-one general councils are the largest instances of this type of consolidation and dissemination, but they are quite extraordinary events. Far more common have been the local, regional, or provincial synods, and then, in modern times, national synods and episcopal conferences. In the simplest terms, it makes sense to gather decision-makers and experts together to identify common problems, to assess which solutions have worked and which have not, and then to construct a system to address those problems on a larger scale. Challenges, of course, include cultural differences and social, economic, and political contexts that must be permitted to affect local implementation. One reform size does not fit all.

The church in a synod undertakes a process of listening and talking together. Process is key. The participants must listen before speaking, then think together before coming to consensus and acting. Such a process is, in essence, an action of ecclesiology: living the faith as a communion of believers. Examples of such group discernment are not hard to find among religious orders. Benedictines, Dominicans, and Jesuits have for centuries written

---

[8] As recounted in Gerard O'Connell, *The Election of Pope Francis: An Inside Account of the Conclave That Changed History* (Maryknoll, NY: Orbis, 2019), 153–54.

into their regulations such processes, which can easily be adapted to diocesan synods, while admitting that the participatory nature of the latter have been easily and often abridged by authoritarian bishops.[9]

Synods have long been essential to the church's life. John Colet, a friend of Erasmus and the dean of London's St. Paul Cathedral, proclaimed confidently that convocations like the one at which he was preaching in 1512 were vital for reform: "For nothing ever happens more detrimental to the church of Christ than the omission of councils, both general and provincial."[10] Although he was speaking of a general council, Pope Paul VI agreed in his 1964 encyclical:

> How often in past centuries has the determination to instigate reforms been associated with the holding of ecumenical councils! Let it be so once more; but this time not with a view to removing any specific heresies concerning the Church, or to remedying any public disorders—for disorders of this sort have not, thank God, raised their head in our midst—but rather with a view to infusing fresh spiritual vigor into Christ's Mystical Body considered as a visible society, and to purifying it from the defects of many of its members and urging it on to the attainment of new virtue.[11]

In its 2018 document, *Synodality in the Life and Mission of the Church*, reflecting Pope Francis's focus on the topic, the International Theological Commission (ITC) observed, "Although synodality is not explicitly found as a term or as a concept in the teaching of Vatican II, it is fair to say that synodality is at the heart of the work of renewal the Council was encouraging." ITC members concluded that renewing a sense of synodality, working out synodal structures,

[9] Giuseppe Ruggieri, "I sinodi tra storia e teologia," *Cristianesimo nella storia* 27 (2006): 365–92; Eugene Duffy, "Processes for Communal Discernment: Diocesan Synods and Assemblies," *The Jurist* 71 (2011): 77–90.

[10] For an analysis of this sermon, see Jonathan Arnold, *Dean John Colet of St. Paul's: Humanism and Reform in Early Tudor England* (London: I. B. Tauris, 2007), 108–35.

[11] Pope Paul VI, encyclical letter *Ecclesiam Suam*, August 6, 1964, 44, https://www.vatican.va/content/paul-vi/en/encyclicals/documents/hf_p-vi_enc_06081964_ecclesiam.html.

and moving toward reform processes were actions grounded in listening, dialogue, and communal discernment.[12]

The point of a synod is to gather the *sensus fidelium*, an act that John Henry Newman explained by discussing the fourth-century Arian heresy. One of the things to be determined is the nature of participation in order to ascertain that *sensus*. As the ecclesiologist Dario Vitali, consultor to the Secretariat of the Synod of Bishops, explains: "If we do not activate processes of participation, where the faithful are not extras, but actors of discernment through a listening that really wants to recognize in their voices the voice of the Spirit, where and how can the holy people of God learn to express their consent?" Who will vote: female and male, laity and clergy and vowed? Will voters be proportionately allocated according to their regions' gross population of Catholics or the percentage of Catholics in that region relative to national or global figures? Will votes be consultative or deliberative? Will a non-bishop's vote count the same as a bishop's vote in determining recommendations to send to the pope for the required validation?[13] In 2014, the ITC addressed some of these issues in the document Sensus Fidei *in the Life of the Church*, noting that synods are a way of consulting the faithful in line with the principle *"quod omnes tangit ab omnibus approbari debet"*: what touches all ought to be approved by all. It noted, too, an essential element of consulting the faithful: "Humble listening at all levels and proper consultation of those concerned are integral aspects of a living and lively Church."[14] But this ITC document did not address the necessary and practical questions about voting.

[12] International Theological Commission, *Synodality in the Life and Mission of the Church*, March 2, 2018, 6, 103–19, https://www.vatican.va/roman_curia/congregations/cfaith/cti_documents/rc_cti_20180302_sinodalita_en.html. Hereafter cited as SLMC.

[13] Dario Vitali, "The Circularity between *Sensus Fidei* and Magisterium as a Criterion for the Exercise of Synodality in the Church," in *For a Missionary Reform of the Church*, 211; on issues of fair representation, see Kenneth Pennington, "Representation in Medieval Canon Law," in *Repraesentatio: Mapping a Keyword for Churches and Governance*, ed. Massimo Faggioli and Alberto Melloni (Berlin: LIT Verlag, 2006), 21–40.

[14] International Theological Commission, Sensus Fidei *in the Life of the Church* (2014), 126, https://www.vatican.va/roman_curia/congregations/cfaith/cti_documents/rc_cti_20140610_sensus-fidei_en.html.

Synods and Reform in Church History

In studying the ancient church, much attention is paid to the first six general councils, which were in effect one very long council in stages: answers in creeds and doctrinal statements led to other questions, which in turn had to be addressed. These general councils were the products of local and regional or provincial councils (or synods) that helped the general councils deal with the fallout of a prior one and prepare the way for the next. Ramsay Macmullen identified 255 between Nicaea I (the first general council, in 325) and Constantinople II (the fifth, in 553). He optimistically reckons there may have been as many as 15,000 among the 120 provinces whose bishops were supposed to meet twice a year. Other estimates are far more conservative but still indicate that synods were common: Paolo Bernadini counts 62, about half of which he calls plenary, in north Africa from 220 to 535. Even taking a middle ground among those numbers, it is clear that synods were a regular way to consult among leaders (if not a broader public) and to make decisions. While much has been made of how the church adopted Roman imperial trappings and methods of centralized administration, it is also true that the empire permitted a fair degree of local self-rule. In its document on synodality, the ITC noted local cultural models, including the Roman senate, provincial administration, and municipal councils in north Africa, the Italian peninsula, and territories under Visigothic and Frankish rule. These civic mechanisms included viva voce votes in trials, elections, and debates. For an ecclesiastical cognate, consider the legend of Ambrose's election by acclamation in Milan: once the crowd quieted down, a boy's voice was said to call out, "Ambrose for bishop!" and was taken up by the crowd.[15]

In the Middle Ages, we find rulers like Charlemagne and popes using local councils and synods to promulgate their agendas, which included reform of church and civil matters. There were about sixty synods in central Europe between 500 and 900, typically

---

[15] Ramsay Macmullen, *Voting about God in Early Church Councils* (New Haven: Yale University Press, 2006), 1–23; Paolo Bernardini, "Sinodolità e concili africani del terzo secolo: vent'anni di studi," in *Synod and Synodality: Theology, History, Canon Law and Ecumenism in New Contact*, ed. Alberto Melloni and Sylvia Scatena (Münster: LIT Verlag, 2005), 115–42; SLMC 30, 32.

led by secular authorities, then dozens of episcopal and papal synods in Rome and elsewhere between 1050 and 1150. Pope Paschal II alone held sixteen synods during his nineteen-year pontificate (1099–1118). In addition, each general council could not succeed unless local and regional investigation and assessment had first taken place. In calling Lateran IV for November 1215, Innocent III announced in April 1213: "Meantime, both personally and by discreet agents, you will inquire precisely about all matters which seem to call for energetic correction of reform and, conscientiously writing a report, you will deliver it for the scrutiny of the sacred council."[16] We have, then, examples of ancient and medieval synods with a fair degree of participation and process built into their structures.

Not every pope trusted that the *vox populi* was the *vox Dei*. The church historian Norman Tanner asked whether the church's synodal history was too democratic for ecclesiology played in the papally-led key. Synodality as a regular part of the church's life lasted more than a millennium, but then late medieval conciliarists posited in their strongest versions that a general council's authority exceeded that of the pope as a delegated executive. Although most everyone in the late Middle Ages knew the church, from the papacy as its head, down to its constituent parts, needed reform, fifteenth-century popes were too preoccupied with recovering their authority from the internal threat of conciliarism to spend concerted effort in leading programmatic reform. Synods and councils fell under Roman mistrust as vehicles for governance and reform. Once Martin Luther and other reformers repeatedly called for a council to reform the church, popes were unwilling to do so immediately because it would seem to be conceding that a church gathering focused on reform was required—though just such a gathering ultimately occurred, as it had to, with the Council of Trent. Luther offered caustic marginal comments in a German translation of a leaked copy of the *Consilium de emendanda ecclesia* (1537), an honest reform memo commissioned by Pope Paul III. In his preface,

---

[16] C. R. Cheney and W. H. Semple, eds., *Selected Letters of Pope Innocent III Concerning England, 1198–1216* (London: Thomas Nelson & Sons, 1953), 146–47. For examples of how these synods functioned, see Uta-Renate Blumenthal, *The Early Councils of Pope Paschal II, 1100–1110* (Toronto: Pontifical Institute of Mediaeval Studies, 1978).

Luther commented, "If all this filth were to be shaken up in a free council, can you imagine what a stink would rise?" The relative dearth of regional councils that followed spelled trouble for the church's governance and reform. Tanner calls this decline "one of the greatest blows" and "one of the gravest wounds" in church history. Open, healthy, and respectful debate and dialogue were lost, which hampered reform efforts and vitality.[17]

The church responded to the rise of nationalism and secular democracies by retreating further from its own heritage of synods as modernity progressed. Early modern popes tended to be administrators rather than charismatic leaders; they presided in place of innovating. The claims of papal authority and allegiance reached their highest form in the nineteenth century with ultramontanism. Loyalty to Rome beat out imperial Febronianism, French Gallicanism, or any other expression of a national church or regional synods. Concerned with nationalism, popes took on a more monarchical *modus procedendi*. As the historian Francis Oakley has recounted, papalists and curialists supporting an "imperial papacy" deliberately consigned conciliarism to the proverbial ash heap of history by exercising a "politics of oblivion."[18] Certainly Vatican I's definition of the infallibility of the teaching authority of the pope made some wonder whether any general council or consultation would ever be needed again.

An example of what might have been had synods persisted as agents of reform during the early modern period comes from Pistoia in 1786. A synod both grounded in church history and ahead of its time, the meeting discussed developments that were rejected then but ultimately would come over the centuries, especially at and since Vatican II. It was the civil leader and not the bishop who called the synod. Duke Peter Leopold oversaw the first diocesan synod in sixty-five years in partnership with Bishop

---

[17] Norman Tanner, *The Church in Council: Conciliar Movements, Religious Practice and the Papacy from Nicaea to Vatican II* (London: I. B. Tauris, 2011), 55–86, especially 71–72, 76; Lewis W. Spitz, ed., *Luther's Works* (Philadelphia: Muhlenberg Press, 1960), 34:238.

[18] Francis Oakley, "The Conciliar Heritage and the Politics of Oblivion," in *The Church, the Councils, and Reform: The Legacy of the Fifteenth Century*, ed. Gerald Christianson, Thomas M. Izbicki, and Christopher M. Bellitto (Washington, DC: The Catholic University of America Press, 2008), 82–97.

Scipione de'Ricci. The agenda consisted of fifty-seven points. Participants recommended the laity receive the Eucharist at every Mass and that churches include only one altar on which to focus. They called for vernacular translations of Scripture and prayers along with simplified rites and lay Bible study. They foresaw a decentralized church with greater authority and liberty for the diocesan bishop, who should be involved in local consultation and not act in an imperious manner. They wanted improved education and standards for priests, greater lay involvement, and informed devotional practices to combat superstition. Trapped within power struggles among bishops, however, and tainted by links with Jansenism, the synod was condemned by Rome.[19]

Synods and Reform Today

Paul VI made the synod of bishops a permanent gathering to continue Vatican II's reform efforts. His synods' discussions led to a revised canon law code and the International Theological Commission; they also promoted justice and social teaching, evangelization, and catechesis. John Paul II, who held fifteen synods in his twenty-seven-year pontificate, often focused on regions (Europe, Africa, Lebanon, the Americas, Asia, and Oceania). The five synods during Benedict XVI's eight-year papacy considered the Eucharist, Scripture, and evangelization, as well as the church in Africa and the Middle East. Under John Paul II and Benedict XVI, synods were increasingly criticized, if quietly, as exercises in ratifying decisions Rome had already made, which undercut reforms moving from the periphery to the center. Occasional synods and regular *ad limina* visits became exercises in which bishops received Vatican directives rather than brought issues and solutions to Rome for mutual consultation.

Synods under Pope Francis robustly returned to the historical marriage of synods and reform where bishops collaborate, bringing ideas from their peripheries to the Roman center for common cause. There was some resistance. In a statement remarkable for

---

[19] Shaun Blanchard, *The Synod of Pistoia and Vatican II: Jansenism and the Struggle for Catholic Reform* (Oxford: Oxford University Press, 2020), 197–258.

its lack of historical understanding and ecumenical respect, Bishop Thomas Tobin of Providence, Rhode Island, commented about the October 2014 synod on the family, "The concept of having a representative body of the Church voting on doctrinal applications and pastoral solutions strikes me as being rather Protestant."[20] In his opening address to the October 2021 synod, Francis made clear what the synod was not: "I want to say again that the Synod is not a parliament or an opinion poll; the Synod is an ecclesial event and its protagonist is the Holy Spirit. If the Spirit is not present, there will be no Synod." This very concept of what a synod is fits neatly with Francis's conception of reform, which starts with people and processes—an open square and a listening church, as he said in that address, that starts not with the center's plan for reform but with the periphery's need and experience. This means that bishops and Rome must "listen to our brothers and sisters speak of their hopes and of the crises of faith present in different parts of the world, of the need for a renewed pastoral life and of the signals we are receiving from those on the ground."[21]

Francis retrieved the concept of collaborative decision-making that has been the church's norm for most of its life, but for him individual conversion comes first. As he said in his first extensive interview after his election, "The structure and organizational reforms are secondary—that is, they come afterward. The first reform must be the attitude."[22] His three sharp addresses to the Roman Curia around Christmas of 2014, 2015, and 2016 were also based on the need for personal reform. In 2014, he catalogued curial "diseases," then in 2015 he listed virtues to counter them. In 2016, he offered twelve guiding principles for systemic reform, starting with personal and pastoral conversion and including

[20] Michael O'Loughlin, "RI Bishop: Synod Process is 'Rather Protestant,'" *Crux*, October 21, 2014, https://cruxnow.com/church/2014/10/ri-bishop-synod-process-is-rather-protestant. The bishop's essay, "Random Thoughts about the Synod of the Family," appeared originally on his diocesan website.

[21] Pope Francis, "Address of His Holiness Pope Francis for the Opening of the Synod," October 9, 2021, https://www.vatican.va/content/francesco/en/speeches/2021/october/documents/20211009-apertura-camminosinodale.html.

[22] Antonio Spadaro, SJ, "A Big Heart Open to God: An Interview with Pope Francis," *America*, September 30, 2013, https://www.americamagazine.org/faith/2013/09/30/big-heart-open-god-interview-pope-francis.

subsidiarity, synodality, and discernment. Ever the Jesuit, Francis asked the church in synod to engage in a global discernment of spirits and examination of conscience from the peripheries to the center. The ITC's *Synodality in the Life and Mission of the Church* stressed this point: "Actually, dialogue offers the opportunity to acquire new perspectives and points of view in order to shed light on the solution of the matter in question. . . . Exercising discernment is at the heart of synodal processes and events" (SLMC 110–13). Discernment moves from the personal to the communal and, for Francis, is rooted in the Ignatian way of doing things. Process and patience produce good decisions and programs. Conversation leads to consensus, which occurs during the Jesuit *murmurationes* built into the election of the order's general, where delegates listen and talk for four days before voting.[23]

For a synod to produce lasting and authentic reform, there must be genuine openness and balance: witnessing and listening, the center drawing on and synthesizing peripheries. To accomplish this, Francis's reform stance drew on the work of the Dominican Yves Congar, who envisioned a middle, moderate path of reform that steered between tradition and progress, conservation and innovation. Congar, in his *Vraie et fausse réforme dans l'Église* (1950), also warned against opposing temptations: rigorism of religious formalism and obligation on the one side and wholesale rejection of the church's traditions on the other. Seeing the need to look inside first, Congar presented four characteristics of critical self-examination: frankness and candor without rancor, consideration of serious core issues and not nostalgia, a focus on the impact on the church's members, and a grounding in church history and tradition. He also prescribed four conditions of reform without schism: an attitude of charity and service, dialogue, patience, and an appreciation of authentic development.[24]

---

[23] Antonio Spadaro, "The Reform of the Church according to Pope Francis: The Ignatian Roots," in *For a Missionary Reform of the Church*, 3–23; a slightly revised and updated version appears as Spadaro, "Francis' Government: What Is the Driving Force of His Pontificate?" *La Civiltà Cattolica*, October 14, 2020, https://www.laciviltacattolica.com/francis-government-what-is-the-driving-force-of-his-pontificate/.

[24] Yves M.-J. Congar, *Vraie et fausse réforme dans l'Église* (Paris: Les Éditions du Cerf, 1950, 1968). Most of the second edition is now available as *True and False Reform in the Church*, trans. Paul Philibert (Collegeville MN: Liturgical Press, 2010). See also

In pursuing church reform, Francis has taken up Congar's guidance. Given the way synods progressed under John Paul II especially, bishops and church observers were quite taken by Francis's statement at the start of the October 2014 synod. Using the Greek concept of *parrhesia*, he declared that participants must speak boldly, candidly, and collaboratively:

> One general and basic condition is this: speaking honestly. Let no one say: "I cannot say this, they will think this or this of me. . . ." It is necessary to say with *parrhesia* all that one feels. After the last Consistory (February 2014), in which the family was discussed, a Cardinal wrote to me, saying: what a shame that several Cardinals did not have the courage to say certain things out of respect for the Pope, perhaps believing that the Pope might think something else. This is not good, this is not *synodality*, because it is necessary to say all that, in the Lord, one feels the need to say: without polite deference, without hesitation. And, at the same time, one must listen with humility and welcome, with an open heart, what your brothers say. *Synodality* is exercised with these two approaches.
>
> For this reason I ask of you, please, to employ these approaches as brothers in the Lord: speaking with *parrhesia* and listening with humility.[25]

An additional disruptive element stems from the fact that Francis's reform agenda for the synod on synodality did not exist. Rather than directing participants to inquire about a particular topic or region, Francis asked them to bring to Rome what they are thinking about—a clear case of the periphery directing the center. He made just this point when meeting with Italian bishops in Florence in November 2015: "You would say, 'What is the pope asking of us?'

Joseph Famerée, "True or False Reform: What are the Criteria? The Reflections of Y. Congar," *The Jurist* 71 (2011): 7–19. Christopher Ruddy examined how Congar applied his own system at Vatican II. "Yves Congar and Hans Küng at Vatican II: Different Paths of Church Reform," *Ecclesiology* 10 (2014): 161–70.

[25] Pope Francis, "Greeting of Pope Francis to the Synod Fathers during the First General Congregation of the Third Extraordinary General Assembly of the Synod of Bishops," October 6, 2014, https://www.vatican.va/content/francesco/en/speeches/2014/october/documents/papa-francesco_20141006_padri-sinodali.html (emphasis in the original).

It is up to you to decide: people and pastors together."[26] Francis intended that those people especially included voices that had not been heard enough or at all: women, minority and marginalized groups, and populations in smaller locales.

Reform works best when it is a joint and patient effort engaged by communities in the peripheries and the center. As the July 2021 preparatory document for the synod on synodality described the task: "This journey, which follows in the wake of the Church's 'renewal' proposed by the Second Vatican Council, is both a gift and a task: by journeying together and reflecting together on the journey that has been made, the Church will be able to learn through Her experience which processes can help Her to live communion, to achieve participation, to open Herself to mission. Our 'journeying together' is, in fact, what most effectively enacts and manifests the nature of the Church as the pilgrim and missionary People of God."[27] This passage engages best practices for seeking reform: the Greek sense of gathering, Vatican II's recovery of the idea that the church is a pilgrim and therefore imperfect, and the Latino method of working together (*en conjunto*) to draw on everyone's individual skills for a common good. How successfully the twenty-first-century church measures up to prior moments where synods and reform met fruitfully must be for later generations of historians to judge.

---

[26] Pope Francis, "Meeting with the Participants in the Fifth Convention of the Italian Church," November 10, 2015, https://www.vatican.va/content/francesco/en/speeches/2015/november/documents/papa-francesco_20151110_firenze-convegno-chiesa-italiana.html.

[27] *For a Synodal Church: Communion, Participation, and Mission*, Secretary General of the Synod of Bishops, 1, https://press.vatican.va/content/salastampa/en/bollettino/pubblico/2021/09/07/210907a.html.

True and False Reformers in the Church: Congarian Lessons for Today

Shaun Blanchard

One of my favorite anecdotes in all of church history is a story about the man who became Pope John XXIII. While serving as papal nuncio in Paris in the early 1950s, Archbishop Angelo Roncalli (1881–1958) came across a copy of Yves Congar's book *True and False Reform in the Church*. "A reform of the church?" Roncalli asked. "Is such a thing possible?"[1] A comment like this is interesting enough as an indication of the attitudes of Catholic prelates in the 1950s. But the comment takes on a humorous, even ironic, coloring since after he became Pope John XXIII in 1958, Roncalli initiated one of the most sweeping reforms in the history of Christianity by convening the Second Vatican Council (1962–1965). Canonized by Pope Francis in 2014, "good pope John" is now remembered as a kind of patron saint of Catholic reform. After Papa Roncalli's death in 1963, Congar and others, including the future pope, Joseph Ratzinger, answered the question of whether reforming the church was possible with a resounding *yes*.

---

[1] Paul Philibert, "Translator's Introduction," in Yves Congar, *True and False Reform in the Church*, trans. Paul Philibert (Collegeville, MN: Liturgical Press, 2010 [1968 ed.]), xi.

But in the early 1950s, Roncalli had good reason to be pessimistic about reform. Creatively faithful thinkers like Congar were often under clouds of suspicion for pushing beyond the narrow boundaries for thought and action that were set by many church leaders. At times, those who called for reform were even persecuted. The Holy Office, the Vatican congregation charged with policing doctrine, banned translations of Congar's book and subjected him to censorship. We Americans remember well the story of the Jesuit John Courtney Murray's silencing for teaching something that now seems blindingly obvious: that human beings have a right to religious liberty and should be free from coercion. A decade later, at Vatican II, Murray's "error" became the official teaching of the church and is now taken for granted by all Catholics, "liberal" and "conservative" alike, save a tiny handful of reactionaries (Catholic "integralists"). At the time, however, Roncalli's pessimism about reform was entirely justifiable, perhaps especially so since he had seen the inner workings of the Vatican first-hand. Despite all this, the great energy, zeal, and dynamism of postwar Catholicism was like a dam ready to break. Funnily enough, given his comment, it was Roncalli himself who moved the first pebble (perhaps it was more like pushing a giant boulder) that caused the avalanche of conciliar reform at and after Vatican II.

Since Vatican II, talk of the "reform of the church" has been incessant. More recently, Pope Benedict XVI (Joseph Ratzinger) reiterated a papal preoccupation with distinguishing between true and false reform. In one of the first major statements of his pontificate, a Christmas address to the Roman Curia in 2005, Ratzinger sketched a hermeneutic of true reform that sought to avoid the pitfalls of manic progressivism and static traditionalism. Francis's pontificate has put discussions of church reform even more front and center, especially with his championing of synodality and, with it, deliberative consultations from parishes to synods of bishops. The latter have not been without notable controversy and painful divisions. And the former do not exactly shy away from controversy, either, if the norm is anything like the session I sat through in one diocese in the American deep south.

Especially since the shocking resignation of Benedict XVI and the election of Jorge Bergoglio as Pope Francis in 2013, the church has seen a great deal of discussion about the nature of true (or false) reform. Reform agendas and contested issues (the liturgy, divorce and remarriage, the death penalty, priestly celibacy, same-sex relationships) are regularly centerpieces of discussion. Those concerned with the way the ecclesial winds are blowing often ominously contrast valid "developments of doctrine" with invalid doctrinal "corruptions," following the language of John Henry Newman. "Continuity" is pitted against "discontinuity," usually unhelpfully and ahistorically. The line between the pastoral and the disciplinary, on one hand, and the doctrinal and dogmatic, on the other, is elided by some and carefully parsed by others.

In this essay, I will argue that missing from many of these discussions of true or false reform (that is, of ideas and agendas) is an account of true and false *reformers* (that is, of people). First, I will try to show a need for this by considering the ways in which contemporary Catholics might be talking past each other when the topic of "reform" is raised. Next, I consider the nature of the true reformer, turning to the work of Yves Congar (1904–1995), a key inspiration of John XXIII and Vatican II.[2] Congar laid out four principles that must be considered normative in the life and work of the true reformer. He called them four "conditions for authentic reform without schism."[3] They are: 1) the primacy of charity and of pastoral concerns; 2) remaining in communion with the whole church; 3) patience with the time that reform takes; and 4) renewal through a return to the principle of tradition. In conclusion, I will examine the relevance of these four conditions in the context of fraught discussions regarding reform in the Catholic Church today.

---

[2] Some excellent recent sources on Congar in English include Gabriel Flynn, ed., *Yves Congar: Theologian of the Church* (Leuven: Peeters, 2005); Paul Murray, "Expanding Catholicity through Ecumenicity in the Work of Yves Congar: *Ressourcement, Receptive Ecumenism, and Catholic Reform*," in Gabriel Flynn and Paul Murray, eds, *Ressourcement: A Movement for Renewal in Twentieth-Century Catholic Theology* (Oxford: Oxford University Press, 2012), 457–81; Gabriel Flynn, "*Ressourcement*, Ecumenism, and Pneumatology: The Contribution of Yves Congar to *Nouvelle Théologie*," in Flynn and Murray, *Ressourcement*, 219–35; Andrew Meszaros, *The Prophetic Church: History and Doctrinal Development in John Henry Newman and Yves Congar* (Oxford: Oxford University Press, 2016).

[3] Congar, *True and False Reform*, 197.

The Term *Reform*: Are We Talking Past Each Other?

The word *reform* has a long and complex history in the Catholic Church. Frank acknowledgements of the need for reform at every level ("in head and members") were commonplace during the great crises of fifteenth and sixteenth centuries. But by the twentieth century, Catholics felt significant reluctance to apply the term to the church itself. One could reform a lax religious order, certainly, and sinners could be reformed. But could the church—the infallible Bride of Christ, the Mystical Body, the one Ark of Salvation—really *herself* need reform? The close link between the word *reform* and the Protestant Reformation contributed to this cooling in the frequency and vehemence of Catholic calls for the "reform of the church."[4] The attitudes identified with the slogan *Ecclesia semper reformanda* ("the church, always in need of reforming") had to be rejected, despite the presence of undeniable truth behind such sentiments.[5] If Protestants made a practice (like vernacular Bible reading) or a belief (like rejection of faith and works) central to their identity, then the "Catholic" position had to be articulated in terms of stark contrast, if not in direct contradiction. The ability for "self-critique" (to use Congar's word) was, consequently, severely limited, at least in certain contexts.

Even in the documents of Vatican II, the Latin term *reformatio* is only once applied directly to the church.[6] Rather notably, it is in the Decree on Ecumenism (*Unitatis Redintegratio*), the text that came the closest to an attitude of frankness regarding past Catholic sins and institutional failures. But despite Vatican II's reluctance to directly apply the term *reformatio* to the church itself, the Council had, undoubtedly, radically changed the church. This was clear to all, whether they celebrated that change or bemoaned it. In adopting the reformist principles of *aggiornamento* ("updating"), *ressourcement* ("return to the sources"—that is, Scripture and the church fathers), and the development of doctrine, Catholicism

---

[4] For a helpful sketch of this history, see John O'Malley, SJ, "'The Hermeneutic of Reform': A Historical Analysis," *Theological Studies* 73 (2012): 517–46.

[5] On this term, which in fact rose to prominence in the twentieth century (not the sixteenth), see Richard A. Muller, *Dictionary of Latin and Greek Theological Terms* (Grand Rapids, MI: Baker Academic, 2017), 102–103.

[6] O'Malley, "The Hermeneutic of Reform," 520.

had undergone a reform at Vatican II that was profound and far-reaching. After the council, calls for reform of the church mushroomed. Reform was a Catholic buzzword in the 1960s and 70s, and it remains so in the church today.

Unfortunately, it is difficult not to conclude that, on the whole, the term *reform* has degenerated into a platitude. If reform means something like "change for the better" (the word's definition at the most basic level), who could be against it? The problem, of course—and "problem" here is something of an understatement—is that we Catholics are sometimes not in agreement about *what* should change, whether it even *can* change, and what kind of changes qualify as "better." Thus, the word *reform*, at least as it functions in contemporary Catholic conversation, is simultaneously too pliable, too general, and too ideologically situated to really mean much by itself. A Catholic who tells me they want to see the "reform of the church" tells me nothing more than that they are a serious, committed Catholic who is paying attention or perhaps that they are a wounded Catholic who is honest about their alienation from the church, an alienation which could have any variety of causes.

To take a concrete example: if someone talks about "the reform of the liturgy," they could mean a kind of restorationism, a "reform of the reform," which posits that a huge amount of beauty, reverence, and mystery in Catholic worship and devotion has been lost over the last sixty years and must be recovered by returning to prior (perennial?) forms. But one who calls for "reform of the liturgy" could have the opposite orientation, a progressive perspective that sees the positive momentum of Vatican II as stifled or at least not fully implemented. These Catholics tend to advocate for fuller inclusion of women and lay people in the liturgy, or for further and deeper "inculturation." Almost always, such people want a worship that is less clerically focused or dominated. They probably feel that a number of good reforms were implemented after the council, but in many cases these have ground to a halt or even been reversed, often by young clergy girded in birettas and cassocks.

Or consider the disparate "reforms" called for in response to the sex abuse and cover-up crisis, one of the most grievous ethical and spiritual failures in the history of Christianity. All morally serious Catholics with any knowledge of these events recognize that the abuse crisis demands far-reaching church reform. More conservative Catholics tend to blame a familiar set of problems, issues that they have always identified as afflicting the postconciliar church: the influence of the sexual revolution, the breakdown of traditional ecclesial discipline and enforcement of canon law, and, most of all, homosexuality and homosexual clergy. More progressive Catholics tend to blame clericalism, which has generated a culture of secrecy and fear that prefers power and prestige to actual people. This reached a nadir when the institution was protected at any cost, even if that cost was the safety of vulnerable people. The latter see the greater inclusion of women in leadership as a sine qua non for reform in this area, while the former focus on turning the priesthood (back) into an institution of "real men" who fearlessly protect the sheep from the wolves.

On a more macro level, those who speak passionately about the "reform of the church" could hold precisely *opposite* agendas.[7] This is especially true in the deeply polarized ecclesial context that I inhabit in the United States. For many Catholic traditionalists, allied with those (far more numerous) conservatives who were very comfortable in Benedict XVI's pontificate but feel betrayed by Francis, "the reform of the church" seems to primarily mean a kind of rolling back of *bad reforms*. That is, true reform is principally the reversal of bad change, usually connected with Vatican II or at least its "spirit." This kind of reform is thus primarily about returning to a status quo ante, at least in theory. For these people, reform might not always be easy to implement, but the substance of true reform is quite simple and clear: teach what the church *actually* teaches (and, implicitly, *has always* taught), and use these truths to boldly confront a toxic secular culture outside the church and the "liberal" or "Modernist" Catholic rot within. Pope Francis is usually, at the very least, seen as unhelpful to such reform attempts. At most, the pope is cast as actively undermining or even attacking such an agenda and consequently grievously harming the church through myriad sins of commission or omission.

---

[7] This sometimes becomes clear only once one gets beyond terms that, unfortunately, too often function as vague slogans, like *discipleship, eucharistic renewal, Christocentrism*, and *evangelization*.

On the other hand, for more progressive Catholics, *reform* usually means pushing further the very agenda that their opponents wish to reverse (because these opponents see such reversal as itself "reform"!). Progressive reformers want a more dialogical church, a church that fully includes women and sexual minorities and that celebrates the baptismal dignity of the laity and the rights of local churches and communities vis-à-vis Rome. These ecclesiological agenda points are rather more convoluted now, however, due to the rise of a "liberal ultramontanism"[8] under Francis. Criticisms of "ultramontanism" (papal-centrism) and a consequent right to disagree with papal teaching or dissent from it were once the purview of liberal postconciliar Catholicism. Ironically, such positions have now become a central identity marker for traditional-leaning Catholics, who denounce Francis in terms that would scandalize the most vitriolic progressive critics of the pontificates of Benedict XVI and John Paul II.

Unfortunately, it is difficult to see how, apart from the action of the Holy Spirit, these deadlocks over reform can be broken. Feelings of defeat and resignation can be especially strong in toxic contexts like the United States, where bipartisan strife is the ever-present backdrop for the ecclesial situation. Often, this makes American Catholics feel as if the political tail is wagging the ecclesial dog. However, the good news is that the Holy Spirit seems to always work through people—his vessels—and not through agenda points, ad campaigns, or slogans. Any true reform in twenty-first-century Catholicism will be the organic, messy, Spirit-led work of true reformers, not the triumph of one agenda over another.

The True Reformer: Congar's Four Conditions

Yves Congar is one of the greatest theologians of the last hundred years, and his work is relevant for all kinds of reasons. His sustained reflections on the nature of the true reformer are particularly germane for us today. What is such a person like? What

---

[8] For the apt term *liberal ultramontanism* to describe our current context, see William L. Portier, "Unintended Ultramontanism," *Theological Studies* 83, no. 1 (2022): 54–69.

kind of life do they lead? How do they react to the (inevitable) criticism or even rejection of their ideas?

For Congar, the true reformer does not seek to change "dogma," but he or she is not just interested in the reform of abuses either. Wide-reaching reform seeks to change or improve the prevailing "state of affairs" (*l'état des choses*) in the church.[9] Changing *l'état des choses* sets the church on a new path, albeit one in essential continuity with its divine constitution and its dogmatic affirmations.[10] The opposite of this reformist spirit, which is the resistance to all change, even necessary change, Congar calls the "temptation of the synagogue."[11] In using this unfortunate phrase, Congar contrasts a regressive defensiveness with a healthy recognition that the church grows and develops until the eschaton—that is, that the church changes.[12]

Even though it is historical fact that the church changes, actually *seeking* to change *l'état des choses* is a dangerous business for the reformer. It is much easier to go with the flow. Congar does not really have much to say to the lukewarm or the apathetic. *True and False Reform*, on the contrary, is an important meditation for the passionate, deeply committed Catholic. It contains plenty of cautionary tales for would-be zealots of any ideological persuasion.

Congar's four conditions are habits of mind and action that the reformer must abide in to keep their reform from spinning out of control and harming the church, rather than helping build her up. Since these conditions are only actually helpful when they are brought from the realm of theory and into practice, Congar gives

[9] Portier, "Unintended Ultramontanism," 160–69.

[10] See Joseph G. Mueller, "Blindness and Forgetting: The Prophet-Reformer in Yves Congar's *Vraie et fausse réforme dans l'Église*," *Communio* 34 (Winter 2007): 640–56, esp. 643.

[11] Congar, *True and False Reform*, 124. Congar offers an explanation of what he meant by this phrase, a phrase that certainly could be interpreted in an anti-Semitic fashion. See 147–160.

[12] Congar, *True and False Reform*, 147. Writing in 1950 (rev. ed. in 1968), Congar did not yet have the full benefit of the development in historical scholarship and Catholic theological perspectives on ancient and modern Judaism. See, for example, the recent volume: Joseph Sievers and Amy-Jill Levine, eds., *The Pharisees* (Grand Rapids: Eerdmans, 2021).

numerous examples of reformers from church history who exhibit or fail to exhibit these qualities. He usually chose examples, naturally, from the time periods he knew best—the early church, the sixteenth and early seventeenth centuries (the ages of Reformation and Counter-Reformation), the nineteenth century that closed right before his birth, and the twentieth century in which he lived and wrote.

As in so much Catholic theological reflection, the eighteenth century—the Age of Enlightenment and Revolution—is relatively neglected. When I first read *True and False Reform* in graduate school, I was examining a number of exciting reform movements and figures in the eighteenth century, phenomena that shed a great deal of light on our own day and are too little known. The subject of my dissertation was one of the most spectacular failures in the history of Catholic reform: the Jansenist-inspired Synod of Pistoia of 1786. The conditions that Congar sketched were strikingly applicable to the characters in this story: the good, the bad, and the ugly.[13] As we go through his four conditions below, I will note some ways that Congar's conditions are eminently applicable to our own day, as much as they are to his own reflections on the Reformation era or my appropriation of his work for the eighteenth century.

The First Condition:
The Primacy of Charity and of Pastoral Concerns

According to Congar, every true reformer must seek to recenter the church on Christ and the paschal mystery. This is impossible to do without keeping *love* at the center, because Christ is love. This charity of the true reformer cannot be a love devoted to an abstraction—the "love of orthodoxy," for example, or of the truth, or even of the people of God. Christians must love all these things, but this charity must be made manifest in love for the concrete church. The true reformer must love the fellow Christians they are in community with, whatever challenges, disappointments,

[13] Blanchard, *The Synod of Pistoia and Vatican II*. See especially 237–58 for a "Congarian evaluation" of Pistoian reform.

and defeats may come. If any constant has held across twenty centuries of Christian life, it is that the life of the reformer is a life of hardship and sometimes of rejection and betrayal. True reformers are often subjected to slander and calumny. Some, maybe most, don't live to see the fruit of their life's work. None have easy lives.

The reformer's role as a "prophet" is central to Congar's scheme. He was wary, however, of the powerful prophetic impulse. When unrealized, it can become destructive, sectarian, and ultimately schismatic.[14] "The Prophetic initiative," Congar wrote, "should not develop into a System."[15] By a "System," Congar meant a moral, theological, or ecclesiastical state of affairs that becomes too separate from or opposed to the concrete Catholic Church. It is a great challenge for prophetic figures to avoid such a situation, because, "aware of [their] mission" and "captivated by [their] idea," prophets are often "solitary, opposed to the given state of affairs" and "not fully at home in the concrete church."[16]

"Great reformers generally are simplifiers" who become obsessed with one thing.[17] This obsession can be a strength, for it can yield a singular determination of the will, but such simplification can also be a great weakness, since it can lead to schism or even heresy. Without much explication, Congar mentions the great Dominican firebrand Savonarola and his opposition to the extravagantly corrupt Borgia pope, Alexander VI (pope from 1492 to 1503). Savonarola was ultimately executed, and the many positive elements of his reform agenda were spoiled by his extremism and self-righteousness. Congar sees the danger of such prophetic tendencies in reformers overcome, however, in a figure like St. Francis of Assisi.

In this chapter and many others, Congar contrasts two of the greatest French Catholics of the previous century. He endorses as a model reformer the famous Dominican preacher, Jean-Baptiste Henri-Dominique Lacordaire (1802–1861). Congar contrasts Lacordaire, who was bold yet patient and obedient, with the brilliant yet ultimately apostate Hugues Félicité Robert de Lamennais

---

[14] See Congar, *True and False Reform*, 169–95.
[15] Congar, *True and False Reform*, 215.
[16] Congar, *True and False Reform*, 215.
[17] Congar, *True and False Reform*, 215.

(1782–1854). For Congar, Jansenism epitomized the failure to meet this condition of charitable pastoral solicitude for the church as it concretely is, for this movement veered from authentic reform into the "spirit of an alternative 'system.'"[18]

The Second Condition:
Remaining in Communion with the Whole Church

The second condition, at face value, is a tautology: in order to enact an authentic Catholic reform, the reformer must remain a Catholic. While Congar is making this obvious point, he is also arguing for a certain style and mindset that avoids isolation, pride, and sectarianism, which are the pathways to schism. Remaining in communion with the whole church is necessary for one's theological ideas themselves to be authentically reforming because "the whole truth is only grasped in communion," which is essentially the theme of this second condition.[19] This condition overlaps substantially with the first, since both are intimately concerned with not allowing positive, needed reform to develop into the spirit of a "system."[20]

Of course, not all heretics, schismatics, or failed reformers actually had bad ideas per se. Many had, at least in part, very good ideas. Congar notes that "Pelagius had an authentically Catholic insight,"[21] and he rightly praises some central elements of the thought of leading Jansenists like Blaise Pascal, Antoine Arnauld, and the Abbé Saint-Cyran.[22]

Congar sees Jansenists as especially apt illustrations of dynamic Catholic reformers who failed to maintain adequate communion with the whole church. He focuses on the famous case of Pascal, a genius who was also one of the most sublime spiritual authors in the history of Christianity. In his bitter disappointment at Roman condemnations of Jansenism, Pascal came "close to a spirit

---

[18] Congar, *True and False Reform*, 226.
[19] Congar, *True and False Reform*, 229.
[20] Congar, *True and False Reform*, 226.
[21] Congar, *True and False Reform*, 233.
[22] Congar, *True and False Reform*, 226–27, 234, 250–60.

of schism."[23] "Sublime and prophetic" as he was, his attitude was "not entirely pure," for Pascal was certain that it was his enemies (especially Jesuits) and the pope who had erred, not he and his circle.[24] He appealed, then, from the earthly church to heaven, which he was sure held a different opinion of his writings than did Vatican committees: "If my letters are condemned in Rome, what I condemn in my letters has been condemned in heaven. *Ad tuum, Domine Jesu, tribunal appello*—Lord Jesus, I appeal to your tribunal."[25]

The Third Condition:
Patience with the Time That Reform Takes

Congar's third condition is simple and eminently practical, in light of the many frustrating setbacks and the reluctance to change that reformers always deal with.[26] Given the profile of the prophets and reformers that Congar has given us,[27] such inevitable delays and frustrations are especially trying because of the temptation of adopting a "boastful spirit."[28] Another reason it is so difficult for reformers to be patient is that their intentions are usually so good, even sometimes utopian. Often, however, reformers must submit their "intellectual" or "systematic" reforms to the pastoral reality that the church faces.[29] This submission can be very painful, especially since it almost always imposes a period of waiting and inaction, sometimes for the rest of the reformer's life.

[23] Congar, *True and False Reform*, 260.

[24] Congar, *True and False Reform*, 260.

[25] Quoted in Congar, *True and False Reform*, 260.

[26] Philibert's English translation of the 1968 edition has the third condition as: "Have patience with delays." While that formula certainly conveys part of Congar's meaning, the French that he wrote is closer to "have patience with the time reform takes" (Congar's formula was "La patience, le respect des délais"). See *Vrai et fausse réforme dans l'Église* (Paris: Cerf, 1950), 306–32. The section in *True and False Reform* is from 265–89. I am grateful to Joseph Mueller for pointing this out.

[27] Congar, *True and False Reform*, 169–95.

[28] Congar, *True and False Reform*, 269.

[29] Congar, *True and False Reform*, 267.

Reformers can then feel themselves "persecuted" if their reforms are "blocked" by the church.[30] Sometimes, the church has succumbed to the pitfalls of the "Synagogue" or "Pharisaism," but at other times it is rightly hesitant in the face of calls for change, preferring caution in order to safeguard "the unity of the flock."[31] The church, Congar rightly notes, does not like ultimatums from reformers.[32] A reformer can exhort, write, and preach, but one cannot demand action by the church on any particular timeframe. The reformer is thus called not only to submission and patience, but sometimes to a kind of self-abnegation.

The Fourth Condition:
Renewal through a Return to the Principle of Tradition

Congar's fourth condition is "genuine renewal through a return to the principle of tradition (not through the forced introduction of some novelty)."[33] First, it is important to point out that Congar does not say a "return to tradition" but rather a return to "the principle of tradition." I will explore the implications of this subtle phrase in the conclusion.

This condition warns against the tendencies of manic progressivism on the one hand and static traditionalism on the other. Concerning the former, Congar criticizes "mechanical adaptation," which is the attempt to uncritically incorporate something extrinsic to the church into Catholic life. On the other end of the spectrum, Congar also critiques "mechanical fidelity," which risks becoming "like the 'Synagogue'" or the "Pharisees."

Nevertheless, Congar argues that what might seem like intransigence at an early stage can in fact clear the way for the later acceptance of the good fruit of a more mature movement shorn of earlier, "hasty" ideas. In Congar's view, the earlier, firmly negative attitude of the Holy See toward ecumenism in fact bore good fruit. He argues that the pope (Pius XI) was right, in 1928, to reject

---

[30] Congar, *True and False Reform*, 276.

[31] Congar, *True and False Reform*, 276. For why these terms are problematic, see Sievers and Levine, *The Pharisees* (2021).

[32] Congar, *True and False Reform*, 277.

[33] Congar, *True and False Reform*, 291.

a form of ecumenism that would have only ended in "syncretism" or a kind of blending. The Catholic Church in fact served the early ecumenical movement by challenging it to reconsider what Christian unity actually is. Congar believed that by 1950 (the first edition of *True and False Reform*) the time was ripe for the Catholic Church to formally enter a movement which now understood unity along lines that Catholics not only could accept but were called to pursue: that is, full, visible unity in faith.[34] Again, Congar affirms the necessity of bold, reformist thinking that considers new solutions to new problems, provided these solutions are grounded in the principle of tradition and drawn from reflection upon revelation. But he also recognizes the role of the magisterium as a guardian, charged with gravely weighing new paths. Sometimes this role puts it in sharp conflict with the most fervent reformers. In and of itself, this is not to be bemoaned.

Conclusion: Congarian Reformers and Today

When I began research on eighteenth-century Catholicism, a fascinating and tumultuous period of church history that Congar (relatively) neglects, I was struck by how relevant his four conditions were to the characters I encountered. The descriptions of the true and false reformers that they enumerate were easily applied to passionate eighteenth-century pastors and theologians like Lodovico Muratori (1672–1750) and Bishop Scipione de' Ricci (1741–1810). I recently returned to Congar's great work as a companion for thinking about our contemporary situation, one full of hope and energy but also polarized and not infrequently painful. Congar's general prescriptions, as well as his four conditions for the true reformer, are as prescient and applicable to the present day as they are to the year 1950, 1750, or 1550.

Regarding the first two conditions—the primacy of charity and of pastoral concerns, and remaining in communion with the whole church—we might ask: How often have we seen fervent Catholics allow their zealous drive for reform isolate them in a "System" that is parallel to or even opposed to the concrete church? The

---

[34] Congar, *True and False Reform*, 305.

most powerful forces for change in the church today are often passionately traditional in approach or passionately progressive in approach (moderates—and I would include myself in this category—are too often afflicted with lethargy or even apathy). Both tendencies, in their liturgies, in the way they build institutional cultures, and, most of all, in the way they position themselves vis-à-vis the rest of the church easily become susceptible to the spirit of the "System." How often does an obsession with one's own party and one's own agenda cause fervent Catholics to forget to keep love and concern for the concrete pastoral life of the church at the center? Such concern is obviously applicable to traditionalist enclaves and conservative "Benedict Option"–style communities and cliques, but Congar would also have a lot to say today to more progressive Catholics as well. For example, in the American context, completely legitimate concern for reverence or beauty in liturgy by young people and especially young clergy is too often harshly stigmatized as a rejection of Vatican II or even as a holistic and reactionary ideological statement. In such situations, self-proclaimed dedications to "listening," "tolerance," the "voice of the people of God," and the "sense of the faithful" are revealed to be rather conditional commitments.

In 1950, when Congar warned of having patience "for the time that reform takes" (the third condition), he had numerous reformist initiatives before his eyes. Many were soon after taken up by the Second Vatican Council. Congar was absolutely right to warn against demanding ultimatums from church leadership on these points. Today, some of the most fervent Catholics are losing patience. Progressive Catholics, especially in places like Germany, make veiled (or not so veiled) allusions to walking a synodal way onto paths uncharted by the rest of the church and unapproved by the center of unity. On the other end of the spectrum, many on the "right"—again, especially in the United States—wonder aloud if the point has come for open defiance of a pope that they believe is in grievous error.

Finally, Congar's fourth condition is something all would-be Catholic reformers would do well to meditate upon. Catholic renewal comes "through a return to the principle of tradition." It does not come, against a progressivist paradigm, from "the forced introduction of some novelty" (Congar's words), especially not from some novelty that breaks communion with the rest of the Catholic world. On the other hand, Congar does not say renewal comes from a *return to tradition* but from a return to the *principle* of tradition.[35] Again using the Jansenist crisis as an example, it is not enough to merely repeat *what* past authorities said, however venerable (e.g., St. Augustine in the case of the Jansenists and nineteenth-century popes in the case of modern-day traditionalists). As part of a living tradition, Catholics are called not to simply repeat past formulas but to meet new situations and challenges by thinking *with* and *in* the tradition. Pope Francis articulated this point clearly when he formally developed doctrine on the death penalty. Anticipating the same methodological strategy taken by opponents of other developments of doctrine (e.g., on religious liberty), Francis said that theological debate "cannot be reduced to a mere résumé of traditional teaching without taking into account not only the doctrine as it has developed" and "the change in the awareness of the Christian people" on the issue.[36] In Congarian terms, Francis is striving to return to the *principle* of tradition even when a concrete reform position (total repudiation of the death penalty in all cases) places him in clear discontinuity with a consistent strand of the tradition, considered discretely.

The wisdom that Congar offers us does not primarily concern ideas but rather attitudes, actions, and patterns of living and relating to others in the church. Any agenda, policy, or movement must be carried out by actual historical actors, real life people who are formed in specific ecclesial, cultural, and familial environments. Of course, such people must debate the issues themselves. That is unavoidable, as is the conflict that arises from it. But if such debate is conducted in a healthy manner, it is an aid both to the church and to the world, even when a position advanced is later judged to have been "wrong" (although, more often, such positions are incomplete or partial grasps of the truth). In light of the

---

[35] "Return to Tradition" is the name, incidentally, of a prominent anti-Francis traditionalist YouTube channel.

[36] See Pope Francis, "Address of His Holiness Pope Francis to Participants in the Meeting Promoted by the Pontifical Council for Promoting the New Evangelization," October 11, 2017, https://www.vatican.va/content/francesco/en/speeches/2017/october/documents/papa-francesco_20171011_convegno-nuova-evangelizzazione.html.

polarization that seems to dominate ecclesial life, Catholics committed to the reform of the church must adopt the kind of posture advocated in difficult ecumenical dialogues. When ecumenical positions seem deadlocked and any progress seems impossible, all we can do is still move forward by drawing closer to Christ as individuals and communities. By walking ever closer to the Lord (or maybe leaning more helplessly on him!), we will, despite our deep and seemingly unbridgeable differences, draw closer to one another. In this limited but absolutely irreplaceable sense, we are all called to be true reformers.

"A Church That Listens": Synodality in the Life and Mission of the Church

Declan Marmion

Introduction: What Is Synodality?

At a ceremony commemorating the fiftieth anniversary of the institution of the Synod of Bishops in 2015, Pope Francis spoke of a synodal church as "a Church which listens, [and] which realises that listening 'is more than simply hearing.'" It is a mutual listening in which everyone has something to learn. The faithful people, the college of bishops, the bishop of Rome: all listening to each other and all listening to the Holy Spirit, the "Spirit of truth" (John 14:17), in order to know what he "says to the Churches" (Rev 2:7).[1] This is Francis's vision: "It is precisely this path of synodality which God expects of the Church of the third millennium."[2]

---

[1] Pope Francis, "Ceremony Commemorating the 50th Anniversary of the Institution of the Synod of Bishops," October 17, 2015, http://w2.vatican.va/content /francesco/en/speeches/2015/october/documents/papa-francesco_20151017_50 -anniversario-sinodo.html.

[2] Pope Francis, "Ceremony Commemorating the 50th Anniversary." A month later, speaking to the Convention of the Italian Church in Florence, he said that "our times require a deeply merciful Catholicism that is unafraid of change." Joshua J. McElwee,

34

Synodality, however, is a contested topic. While, on the one hand, it is hard to be "against" synodality, given its roots in our tradition, on the other hand, there are voices within the church who believe the term can be misinterpreted and presented as a kind of parallel authority, separate from the hierarchy, which leads to a "flattening" of the church. Instead of the diversity of charisms, where each person has his or her proper role, we end up with a majoritarian mass that undermines the proper functioning of the church. In a recent criticism of aspects of the German Synodal Path, Cardinal Walter Kasper underlined how controversial issues and questions (e.g., the church's sexual morality, the role of women in the church, priestly celibacy, etc.) could not be answered with "ideologically predefined answers which one then pushes through with a majority vote."[3]

So, what is synodality? Between 2014 and 2017, the International Theological Commission undertook a study of synodality in the life and mission of the church. The final text of the commission was published in 2018 with the approval of the Congregation for the Doctrine of the Faith and received a favourable response from Pope Francis. It speaks of the "programmatic commitment" of the pope to synodality as "an essential dimension of the Church" in the sense that "what the Lord is asking of us is already in some sense present in the very word 'synod.'"[4]

Synod, the document says, "is an ancient and venerable word in the Tradition of the Church. . . . Composed of a preposition

---

"Catholicism Can and Must Change, Francis Forcefully Tells Italian Church Gathering," *National Catholic Reporter*, November 10, 2015, https://www.ncronline.org /news/vatican/catholicism-can-and-must-change-francis-forcefully-tells-italian -church-gathering. Since 2013, Francis has organised four synods: the first two in 2014 and 2015 were on the family, the third in 2018 focussed on youth, and the most recent in 2019 on the challenges facing the Amazon region. He has also chosen synodality as the theme for the next world meeting of bishops that will conclude in 2023.

[3] See Christa Pongratz-Lippitt, "Kasper Warns German Synodal Path on Wrong Track," *The Tablet*, June 30, 2022, https://www.thetablet.co.uk/news/15632/kasper -warns-german-synodal-path-on-wrong-track.

[4] International Theological Commission, *Synodality in the Life and Mission of the Church*, March 2, 2018, 1, https://www.vatican.va/roman_curia/congregations /cfaith/cti_documents/rc_cti_20180302_sinodalita_en.html. Hereafter cited as SLMC. In the following I am summarising, paraphrasing, and quoting specific points and orientations of the ITC document.

συν (with) and the noun ὁδός (path), it indicates the path along which the People of God walk together. . . . In ecclesiastical Greek it expresses how the disciples of Jesus were called together as an assembly and in some cases it is a synonym for the ecclesial community." The document then quotes St. John Chrysostom, who said the church is a "name standing for 'walking together' (σύνοδος)" (SLMC 3).

Since the first centuries, the word *synod* has been applied, with a specific meaning, to ecclesial assemblies convoked on various levels (diocesan, provincial, regional, patriarchal, or universal). The distinction between *council* and *synod* is a recent one. At Vatican II, the terms were synonymous—both referring to a council session. The term *synodality* is a neologism that has appeared since Vatican II and is something that has been maturing in the ecclesial consciousness ever since (SLMC 5).

The ecclesiology of Vatican II stressed "the common dignity and mission of all the baptised" in exercising the variety and richness of their charisms, vocations, and ministries. It is an ecclesiology of communion. In this context, synodality is the specific *modus vivendi et operandi* of the church, the people of God. Such communion is manifest "when all her members journey together, gather in assembly and take an active part in her evangelising mission" (SLMC 6).

The document presents the apostolic Council of Jerusalem (see Acts 15 and also Galatians 2:1-10) as the paradigm for synods celebrated by the church: "By all listening to the Holy Spirit through the witness given of God's action and by each giving his own judgment, initially divergent opinions move towards consensus and unanimity (ὁμοθυμαδόν: see 15.25)" (SLMC 21). Such communal discernment bears fruit in the evangelizing mission of the church. The way the Council of Jerusalem operated is an excellent example of how the people of God moves forward—in an orderly and well thought out manner—and where each person has a specific position and role (SLMC 22).

When it comes to the witness of the fathers and tradition in the first millennium, the document refers to Ignatius of Antioch and Cyprian of Carthage. The former spoke of how all members (of the various local churches) are σύνοδοι or "companions on the journey" by virtue of the dignity of their baptism and friendship with Christ, while the latter formulated the episcopal and synodal principle that should rule the life and mission of the church locally and at a universal level: "While nothing should be done in the local Church without the Bishop—*nihil sine episcopo*—it is equally true that nothing should be done without your council (the Presbyters & Deacons)—*nihil sine consilio vestro*—or without the consensus of the people—*et sine consensu plebis*" (SLMC 25).

With the development of the synodal procedure, two points would be stressed: (1) the specific primacy of the church of Rome, and (2) the importance of communion between the churches or, put differently, that "each local Church is an expression of the one Catholic Church" (SLMC 28).

The synodal procedure was kept alive in the second millennium through cathedral chapters, while the Council of Trent established the norm that diocesan or local synods should take place annually and provincial synods every three years as a way of implementing the council's reforms in the wider church. St. Charles Borromeo, for example, as archbishop of Milan, convoked five provincial and eleven diocesan Synods. However, such synods did not involve the participation of the whole people of God. Rather, in the polemical and apologetical Counter-Reformation culture of the time, the hierarchical nature of the church was accentuated: the pope and the bishops represented the *ecclesia docens*, the rest of the people of God, the *ecclesia discens* (SLMC 35). The First Vatican Council (1869–70) would endorse this position, emphasizing the primacy and infallibility of the pope (see SLMC 37).[5] Nevertheless, "there was a growing awareness that 'the Church is not identical with her pastors . . . and that lay people have an active role in the transmission of the apostolic faith'" (SLMC 39).

Vatican II would relaunch the notion of synodality in its dogmatic constitution *Lumen Gentium* (1964) with its vision of the church as communion and as the "People of God on pilgrimage through history towards the heavenly homeland, in which all

---

[5] However, the document notes, "The formula according to which *ex cathedra* definitions of the Pope are irreformable 'in themselves and not in virtue of the consensus of the Church' 'does not make the *consensus Ecclesiae* superfluous.' . . . This is borne out by consultation carried out through the Bishops among the whole People of God . . . in view of the definition of the dogma of the Immaculate Conception . . . [and] the dogma of the Assumption of Mary" (SLMC 37).

members are by virtue of baptism honoured with the same dignity and appointed to the same mission" (SLMC 40). The decree *Christus Dominus* (1965) encouraged the establishment of a pastoral council in every diocese, the reinvigoration of synods and councils between churches in a region, and the promotion of episcopal conferences.

Toward a Theology of Synodality

In its second chapter, the document develops a theology of synodality. Its starting point is synodality as "an essential dimension of the Church" exemplified in the paradigmatic Council of Jerusalem (Acts 15:4-29) and its "method of communitarian and apostolic discernment. . . . *Synodality is not simply a working procedure, but the particular form in which the Church lives and operates*" (SLMC 42, italics mine). It denotes the particular style that qualifies the life and mission of the church, expressing her nature as the people of God journeying together, gathering in assembly, and putting into practice ways of fulfilling its mission.

Synodality is also an expression of the ecclesiology of communion and the pilgrim character of the church. "The faithful are σύνοδοι, companions on the journey" (SLMC 55), "the People of God gathered from among the nations (Acts 2:1-9; 15:14)" (SLMC 49). Indeed, all the faithful have been gifted with an instinct of faith—*sensus fidei*—which helps them discern what is truly of God. The *sensus fidei* is the presence of the Spirit in the lives of Christians, endowing them with "a certain connaturality with divine realities, and a wisdom which enables them to grasp those realities intuitively."[6]

If synodality is an essential dimension of the church, then it ought to be expressed in the church's ordinary way of living and working. The three phases of synodal development are listening, deciding, and acting. This happens "through the community listening to the Word and celebrating the Eucharist, the brotherhood

[6] Pope Francis, apostolic exhortation *Evangelii Gaudium* (November 24, 2014), 119, https://www.vatican.va/content/francesco/en/apost_exhortations/documents/papa-francesco_esortazione-ap_20131124_evangelii-gaudium.html. Hereafter cited as EG.

of communion and the co-responsibility and participation of the whole People of God in its life and mission, on all levels and distinguishing between various ministries and roles." Specifically, synodality "denotes those *structures* and *ecclesial processes* . . . involving the whole People of God in various ways on local, regional and universal levels, . . . to discern the way forward . . . and to take particular decisions and directions with the aim of fulfilling its evangelising mission" (SLMC 70).

Implementing Synodality

The third chapter reflects on ways of putting synodality into practice. This involves not only consultation of the faithful but their active participation. The previous chapter had described a synodal church as "a Church of participation and co-responsibility. In exercising synodality she is called to give expression to the participation of all, according to each one's calling. . . . Participation is based on the fact that all the faithful are qualified and called to serve each other through the gifts they have all received from the Holy Spirit" (SLMC 67). Thus, any renewal of the church's synodal life "demands that we initiate processes for consulting the entire people of God" (SLMC 65). Distinguishing between consultative and deliberative votes should not detract from the profound synodal dynamic of the whole community "called together to pray, listen, analyse, dialogue, discern and offer advice on taking pastoral decisions" (SLMC 68) for their particular situation. At the same time, the document underlines the *"function of governing proper to Pastors:* The synodal process must take place at the heart of a hierarchically structured community" (SLMC 69), while the "authority of Pastors is a specific gift of the Spirit of Christ the Head for the upbuilding of the entire Body, not a delegated and representative function of the people" (SLMC 67).

An obstacle to the participation of the lay faithful is "a clerical mindset which runs the risk of keeping them on the edges of ecclesial life" and away from decision making (SLMC 73, which makes reference to EG 102). *The opposite of synodality is clericalism.*[7] This

---

[7] For Francis, clericalism is another "mistaken way of living out the ecclesiology proposed by Vatican II. . . . Clericalism forgets that the visibility and sacramentality

manifests itself in a refusal to be open to the creation of synodal structures, inspired by Vatican II, where the lay faithful can express themselves. After all the first level in which synodality operates is at the local level—it begins in the parish (SLMC 83–84).[8] The chapter speaks not only of synodal structures—diocesan, regional, and universal—but of a "synodal style" that facilitates discernment of pastoral challenges and seeks together new ways of mission (SLMC 77). And this same synodal style applies on a national and universal level—from episcopal conferences to the college of bishops to ecumenical councils. Such a style is reflected in processes of consultation that aim to reach "all the voices that are an expression of the People of God in the local Church" (SLMC 79).

Chapter 4 speaks of the pastoral conversion required for the implementation of synodality: "Some paradigms . . . still present in ecclesiastical culture need to be quashed, because they express an understanding of the Church that has not been renewed by the ecclesiology of communion. These include: the concentration of responsibility for mission in the ministry of Pastors; insufficient appreciation of the consecrated life and charismatic gifts; rarely making use of the specific and qualified contribution of the lay faithful, including women, in their areas of expertise" (SLMC 105). On the other hand, "an ecclesial mentality shaped by synodal thinking joyfully welcomes and promotes the grace in virtue of which all the baptised are qualified and called to be missionary disciples" (SLMC 104). This is the circular dynamic of synodality referred to a number of times in the document "between the ministry of Pastors, the participation and co-responsibility of lay people, [and] the stimulus coming from the charismatic gifts" (SLMC 106a).

The "synodal spirit" or paradigm shift outlined above can only emerge from a profound conversion to what the document de-

---

of the Church belong to all the People of God (see *Lumen Gentium* 9–14), not only to the few chosen and enlightened." "Letter of His Holiness Pope Francis to His Eminence Cardinal Marc Armand Ouellet, PSS, President of the Pontifical Commission for Latin America," March 19, 2016, http://w2.vatican.va/content/francesco/en/letters/2016/documents/papa-francesco_20160319_pont-comm-america-latina.html.

[8] These paragraphs refer to "two structures which have a synodal character: the parish pastoral council and the financial council" and suggests the former should be obligatory.

scribes as a "spirituality of communion," where there is a transition from an " 'I' understood in a self-centred way to the ecclesial 'we,' " where every Christian understands him/herself as living and journeying "with his or her brothers and sisters as a responsible and active agent of the one mission of the People of God" (SLMC 107). This synodal spirit requires certain dispositions: a trust and openness, a mature sense of faith (*sensus fidei*) and a thinking with the church (*sentire cum ecclesia*) (SLMC 107–108). Specific elements that nourish the *affectus synodalis* include: creating and fostering a eucharistic communion which is a reflection of the trinitarian communion; acknowledging our failures and a desire for reconciliation; listening to the word of God in order to illuminate our path; and mission, for synodality exists for the sake of mission and every synodal event prompts the church to move outwards "towards everyone in order to go together towards God" (SLMC 109).

The document concludes with an emphasis on dialogue and discernment. "Synodal dialogue depends on courage both in speaking and in listening. It is not about engaging in a debate where one speaker tries to get the better of the others or counters their positions with brusque arguments" (SLMC 111). An attitude of humility and the principle that "unity prevails over conflict" can help build communion amid tensions and disagreement. Finally, it insists that "exercising discernment is at the heart of synodal processes and events" (SLMC 113). While not spelling out the principle and methods of such discernment, it is clear these must go beyond the personal level to include communal discernment processes that help us "discover God's call in a particular historical situation" (SLMC 113).

Appraisal and Reflection: The Challenge of Synodality

There is much to commend in the document: a helpful overview of the development of the term *synodality*—its historical development in the East and West and how synodality is not restricted to the *modus operandi* of the synods of bishops or episcopal conferences but applies to all the baptised exercising differing vocations within the Christian community. It correctly identifies a synodal dynamic on three levels: the local, national, and universal. Clearly, the commission is drawing inspiration from Pope Francis, who has revived the term and is committed to building a more synodal church. The document is trying to capture the idea that synodality represents *a new way of being church*, more participatory and dialogical, more merciful and listening, more decentralised and with greater involvement of people at the local level and the periphery,[9] and more aware of the diversity of charisms at the service of mission and evangelisation. Synodality, for Francis, not only implies fraternity, listening, and collaboration, but is part of a wider agenda of reform—including reform of the Roman Curia, of bishops' synods, and of the papacy itself.

As with many Vatican documents, this one too remains at the more general and aspirational level. The practical implications for the various national churches will need to be teased out at the local level. In other words, the document will have to be "translated" into different ecclesial contexts. *Synodality begins at home.* An analogy might be made with the recent document on priestly formation, *The Gift of Priestly Vocation*, published by the Vatican's Congregation for the Clergy in 2016. On the basis of this charter, each country or jurisdiction will devise its own national plan or *Ratio*, taking into account its particular situation and challenges.

A commitment to synodal transformation requires journeying, creativity, and responsibility. On this journey, Francis reminds us, the "organs of communion" in the local church (e.g., the presbyteral council, the college of consultors, chapters of canons, and the pastoral council) must "keep connected to the 'base' and start from people and their daily problems."[10] Only then can a synodal church begin to take place. This reflects Francis's ecclesiology of the "inverted pyramid," where "the top is located beneath the base," and where the "only authority is the authority of service."[11] It is in line too with the fundamental reorientation of ecclesiology

---

[9] Francis does not believe in a synodality "from above" disconnected from the base, that is, without a synodality "from below." See Pope Francis, "Address to the Italian Bishops' Conference," May 20, 2019, http://w2.vatican.va/content/francesco/de/speeches/2019/may/documents/papa-francesco_20190520_cei.html.

[10] Pope Francis, "Ceremony Commemorating the 50th Anniversary."

[11] Pope Francis, "Ceremony Commemorating the 50th Anniversary." See also Ormond Rush, "Inverting the Pyramid: The *Sensus Fidelium* in a Synodal Church," *Theological Studies* 78 (2017): 299–325, at 307.

at Vatican II (*Lumen Gentium*, chapter 2) that put an end to the pyramidal vision of the church, stressing instead the fundamental equality of all believers by virtue of their baptism. In short, synodal transformation is a commitment of dioceses to co-responsibility and action. As one US bishop put it:

> This future will ask much of us. . . . We will need to collaborate and work together in new ways, come to a much deeper level of co-responsibility for the life of the whole diocese, surrender any parochialism, competition or isolation that keeps us divided, break out of the torpor that often says, "We've always done it this way," shatter the complacency that can keep us in a spiritual rut, and be more proactive and inviting in our evangelization efforts. If we do not embrace such a vision, our local Church will simply continue a slow and steady slide towards a painful diminishment of the faith in our people.[12]

In promoting the synodal calling of the whole people of God, the ITC document speaks much of the consultation and participation of the laity, who "are the immense majority of the People of God" (SLMC 73). Drawing on section 12 of Vatican II's *Lumen Gentium*, it encourages synodal assemblies "to listen more broadly and more attentively" to the *sensus fidei* or *instinct of faith* of the people of God (SLMC 100). This instinct of faith is a gift of the Spirit helping Christians discern what is truly of God. It "gives Christians a certain connaturality with divine realities, and a wisdom which enables them to grasp those realities intuitively" (SLMC 56, citing EG 119). This connaturality, or interior affinity with the object of faith, shows itself in a *"sentire cum ecclesia,"* a capacity to feel, sense, and perceive in harmony with the church.

Sensus Fidei

The theme of *sensus fidei* has been a disputed topic since Vatican II. The phrase used in Vatican II's *Lumen Gentium* 12 was *"sensus fidei totius populi."* If synodal processes desire to consult as widely

---

[12] Bishop Donald J. Hying, "Go, Therefore, and Make Disciples of All Nations . . .," February 25, 2016, 23, https://dcgary.org/sites/default/files/2020-02/NWIC 2017Synod_English.pdf.

as possible, then the sense of faith not only of committed believers but also of those who are on the periphery, the ecclesially liminal, needs to be heard. These include: the poor, those who are ambivalent toward or dissent from aspects of church teaching, the separated and divorced, and LGBTQI+ persons. Like Yves Congar, Francis is aware that many reforms come from the periphery.[13] The qualifier *totius* is now being taken with greater seriousness by theologians and pastors alike, acknowledging that the *sensus fidei* pertains to *all* the faithful, and that the church has much to learn from the experience of its skeptical and alienated members. In short, the *sensus fidei* is present in every Christian who struggles to make sense of, and practice, her faith. To this extent, the document could have done with more of a cutting edge, but like most such documents it reflects a theological compromise. Its authors would have been aware that the *sensus fidelium*, not unlike synodality, can be used as a kind of lobbying or pressure tactic pitting the laity against the hierarchy. But bishops also share in the *sensus fidelium*. Nevertheless, the process of discerning and determining the *sensus* or *consensus fidei* involves a degree of tension, disagreement, and conflict—even among bishops themselves, as recent synods have shown. Francis is unfazed by this. He encouraged and approved of the open discussions and debates at the 2014 and 2015 synods.[14] He believes in the synodal process as a collective search for the truth, not one where majority rules, but where the aim is to allow a common will to emerge in the church.

Ecclesial conflicts are not new. The ITC document referred to the Council of Jerusalem (see Acts 15:7) as an example of an early hermeneutical conflict where, after much debate, a *consensus fidelium* was reached. In the words of Australian theologian Ormond Rush, "Dialogue is the means through which the Spirit commu-

[13] Yves Congar, *Vraie et fausse réforme dans l'Église* (Paris: Cerf, 1951), 277.

[14] At the conclusion of the 2014 synod, he said, "I have seen and I have heard—with joy and appreciation—speeches and interventions full of faith, of pastoral and doctrinal zeal, of wisdom, of frankness and of courage: and of *parrhesia*." "Address of His Holiness Pope Francis for the Conclusion of the Third Extraordinary General Assembly of the Synod of Bishops," October 8, 2014, http://w2.vatican.va/content/francesco/en/speeches/2014/october/documents/papa-francesco_20141018_conclusione-sinodo-dei-vescovi.html.

nicates."[15] Helpful, too, is the distinction made by Cardinal Luis Tagle between problems and dilemmas: Problems can be solved but dilemmas don't have clear and universal solutions.[16] Part of the journey toward a more synodal *modus operandi* in the church will involve bishops and theologians listening to how the faithful have faced dilemmas, namely, listening to them "tell their stories," how they are trying to make sense of the Gospel, their *sensus fidei*, as it were. In such situations, people are not looking for solutions but for meaning, encouragement, and hope.

It is regrettable that in discussing the implementation of synodality, the ITC document did not give more explicit attention to the issue of *women's* participation and leadership in the church. In Francis's battle to overcome clericalism and the culture of abuse to which it gave rise—abuse of power, abuse of conscience, and sexual abuse—women and young people have a key role to play. Developing synodal and collegial practices in the church implies the active participation of laity in its decision-making processes.[17] Specifically, there have been growing calls for the ordination of women to the diaconate and for the presence of more women in leadership positions in dioceses and curial congregations.

The importance of listening to new and different voices, of trying to understand them rather than to reject or censor them, will be crucial if synodal processes are to have a reforming impact on church teaching and practice. Engaging with a multitude of

[15] Ormond Rush, "A Synodal Church: On Being a Hermeneutical Community," in Anthony Godzieba and Bradford Hinze, eds., *Beyond Dogmatism and Innocence: Hermeneutics, Critique, and Catholic Theology* (Collegeville, MN: Liturgical Press, 2017), 169.

[16] Joshua J. McElwee, "Cardinal Tagle: Church Should Not Look to 'Idealized Past' with Nostalgia," *National Catholic Reporter*, May 22, 2015, https://www.ncronline.org/news/world/cardinal-tagle-church-should-not-look-idealized-past-nostalgia.

[17] "Naturally women—who immediately introduce otherness into the clerical system and bring a desire for collaboration in reciprocity with men for greater pastoral fecundity, and also women religious, because of their experience of fraternal life in community, of community discernment and of an obedience experienced as 'listening together' to the Spirit—have a fundamental role to play in promoting, together with many lay people who want to belong to this synodal Church, new ecclesial practices whose new expressions are 'listening,' 'serving all,' humility and conversion, participation and co-responsibility." Nathalie Becquart, "The Role of Women in Repairing the Church," *L'Osservatore Romano*, July 27, 2019, http://www.osservatoreromano.va/en/news/role-women-repairing-church.

perspectives and voices is to acknowledge that "the *sensus fidelium* can be an important factor in the development of doctrine" and that "the magisterium as a whole does not have responsibility for [the faith]."[18] It is to see in the *sensus fidelium* a true *locus theologicus,* or "conscience of the church," as Greek theology puts it, that has not only pastoral value but a formal authority that can lead to shifts in magisterial discourse and teaching. For example, this would mean listening to the experience and testimony of committed gay and lesbian believers, to their *sensus fidei.*[19] While Francis has moved away from the policy of anathematizing the dissenter and has acknowledged how leadership has erred, the official church teaching on the gay issue still borders on a "theology of contempt."[20] In its 2014 document Sensus Fidei *in the Life of the Church,* the International Theological Commission recognized that the majority of the faithful can be indifferent to or reject particular doctrinal or moral teachings but they might not always be to blame: "In some cases it may indicate that certain decisions have been taken by those in authority without due consideration of the experience and the *sensus fidei* of the faithful, or without sufficient consultation of the faithful by the magisterium" (SFLC 123).

The neuralgic issue is how to determine the *sensus fidei.* Whose *sensus?* Which *fidelium?* Synodality tells us that this is a process that takes time and demands patience. It cannot be forced or rushed. While the *sensus fidei* is not a synonym for public opinion—it must be the truth rather than majority opinion that prevails—synodality commits the church to real engagement with all members of the church. We do this "by discerning with our people and never for

[18] International Theological Commission, Sensus Fidei *in the Life of the Church* (2014), 73, http://www.vatican.va/roman_curia/congregations/cfaith/cti_documents/rc_cti_20140610_sensus-fidei_en.html. Hereafter cited as SFLC.

[19] See Brian N. Massingale, "Beyond 'Who Am I to Judge?' The *Sensus Fidelium,* LGBT Experience, and Truth-Telling in the Church," in *Learning from All the Faithful: A Contemporary Theology of the* Sensus Fidei, ed. Bradford E. Hinze and Peter C. Phan (Eugene, OR: Wipf and Stock, 2016), 170–183.

[20] The phrase is from Archbishop Rembert G. Weakland, OSB, in his *A Pilgrim in a Pilgrim Church: Memoirs of a Catholic Archbishop* (Grand Rapids, MI: Eerdmans, 2009), 18.

our people or without our people."[21] It entails a processive, participative, and dialogical search for truth, acknowledging there is not one uniform *sensus fidelium* but many—the *sensus fidelium* can exist in the plural.[22] The Spirit, Francis believes, conducts and unifies this symphony of different sounds and harmonies.

But is this picture too idealistic? Yes and no. Yes, in that the document on synodality does not refer to the current reality of polarization within the church, to what has been described as "the newly fractured Catholicism, at least in the Euro-Western hemisphere."[23] This intra-Catholic polarization often mirrors a political polarization and tends to revolve around issues like abortion and same-sex marriage. How is the *sensus fidelium* determined against a backdrop of opposing understandings of Catholicism? No, in that the synodal process offers a way forward beyond polarization, a journey that, as Francis described at the conclusion of the 2014 synod, has "moments of consolation and grace" but "also moments of desolation, of tensions and temptations."[24] For him, the synodal process is the concrete form of a decentralised ecclesiology of communion marked by a participatory style and real debate. It is not about finding "exhaustive solutions for all the difficulties" facing the church; nor is it about demonizing those with whom we disagree, for "even people who can be considered dubious on account of their errors have something to offer which must not be

---

[21] Pope Francis, "Letter of His Holiness Pope Francis to His Eminence Cardinal Marc Armand Ouellet, PSS, President of the Pontifical Commission for Latin America," March 19, 2016. See Pope Francis, "Address to the Italian Bishops' Conference," May 20, 2019.

[22] Cristina L. H. Traina, "Whose *Sensus*? Which *Fidelium*?" in Hinze and Phan, *Learning from All the Faithful*, 155–169.

[23] Massimo Faggioli, "Polarization in the Church and the Crisis of the Catholic Mind," *La Croix International*, November 27, 2017, https://international.la-croix.com/news/polarization-in-the-church-and-the-crisis-of-the-catholic-mind/6444. Elsewhere Faggioli suggests that the document could have acknowledged the sense of frustration at the paucity of national or local synodal processes over the last forty years and more. See Massimo Faggioli, "The Uncertain Future of Synodality: Polarization and Ecclesial Paralysis," *La Croix International*, August 21, 2019, https://international.la-croix.com/news/the-uncertain-future-of-synodality/7790.

[24] Pope Francis, "Address of His Holiness Pope Francis for the Conclusion of the Third Extraordinary General Assembly of the Synod of Bishops."

overlooked" (EG 236).[25] This means living with the tensions and conflicts and allowing mature solutions to emerge over time rather than yielding to the temptation of the quick fix. In the final document of the Amazon synod, Francis laid the groundwork for reform. If he disappointed some by sidestepping (for now) the hot-button issues of women deacons and the ordination of married men, neither did he silence the discussion. He puts greater faith in the local church and does not insist the magisterium must intervene to settle every doctrinal, moral, and pastoral dispute. At the same time, in a letter to the German bishops, who have been engaged for some time in a synodal process, he underlined two points:

1. The synodal path of personal and ecclesial renewal must be linked to the church's central task of evangelisation and be guided by the Holy Spirit.

2. Any process of synodal renewal must guard against the twin dangers of polarization and fragmentation by means of a strong *sensus ecclesiae* and connectedness to the universal church.[26]

"Realities are greater than ideas" is an oft-quoted line of Pope Francis. Archbishop Blaise Cupich of Chicago sees in this statement an invitation to "a new epistemology, a new way of learning, of knowing—another way in which we are informed. . . . It's important not to have just a 30,000 feet perspective on life but to really be there in the reality of the situation and pay attention to the observables right now around you."[27] This is an appeal to link

[25] See also Pope Francis, "Conclusion of the Synod of Bishops: Address of His Holiness Pope Francis," October 24, 2015, http://w2.vatican.va/content/francesco/en/speeches/2015/october/documents/papa-francesco_20151024_sinodo-conclusione-lavori.html.

[26] Pope Francis, "Schreiben von papst franziskus an das pilgernde volk gottes in deutschland," June 29, 2019, 11, https://www.dbk.de/fileadmin/redaktion/diverse_downloads/presse_2019/2019-108a-Brief-Papst-Franziskus-an-das-pilgernde-Volk-Gottes-in-Deutschland-29.06.2019.pdf.

[27] Joshua J. McElwee, "Exclusive: Chicago's New Archbishop Talks about 'Stepping into the Unknown," *National Catholic Reporter*, September 21, 2014, https://www.ncronline.org/news/people/exclusive-chicagos-new-archbishop-talks-about-stepping-unknown.

the doctrinal with the pastoral, a hermeneutical circle or spiral, whereby "we get a sense of the whole (in theological terms, the doctrinal perspective) by getting down into the detail (the pastoral perspective); and from the perspective of the detail, we have to form a revised and more 'real' sense of the whole."[28] This dynamic is well known in the church: from earliest times it has had to creatively interpret the Gospel for new times and contexts.

Ireland

In March 2021, the bishops of Ireland announced a new Synodal Path for the Catholic Church leading to a national synodal assembly within five years.[29] In preparing for this assembly, the bishops posed the question: "What does God want from the Church in Ireland at this time?" They envisaged the subsequent two years as a time of prayer, listening, and discernment, involving a nationwide consultative conversation on this theme. It was an attempt to listen to what the Holy Spirit is saying to the church in an Ireland faced with rapid transformation that includes a marked decline in religious practice; shocking revelations in published reports on institutional and clerical abuse; a plea for greater transparency, participation, and accountability in the church; and the critical need to honor the contribution of women, to hear their deep concerns, to formally recognize their roles and articulate new models of co-responsibility and leadership involving all lay people—women and men. The bishops acknowledge that many people have left the church behind and in some cases feel ignored, excluded, or forgotten. Their voices, too, need to be heard.

A synthesis of the national consultation in Ireland was published in August 2022 on behalf of the Irish Catholic Bishops'

---

[28] It is a "back and forth process of questioning, from whole to part and back again, from general to particular and back again to general knowledge." Rush, "A Synodal Church," 164–65.

[29] See Irish Catholic Bishops' Conference, "Statement of the Spring 2021 General Meeting of the Irish Catholic Bishops' Conference," March 10, 2021, https://www.catholicbishops.ie/2021/03/10/statement-of-the-spring-2021-general-meeting-of-the-irish-catholic-bishops-conference/.

Conference.[30] It included not just the familiar themes of lay ministry, adult faith formation, and so on, but also the issue of physical, sexual, and emotional abuse and its concealment by the church in Ireland. There was a clear call for women to be given equal treatment within church structures in terms of leadership and decision-making. Another call was for the full inclusion of LGBTQI+ people in the church and for less judgemental language in church teaching. The overall tenor was to engage with the wider Irish culture, to build bridges to connect with people, even if this is not easy in a society where a secular, liberal mindset predominates.

While there are reasons for hope, the challenge remains how to put the synodal theory into practice. The laity's enthusiasm for synodal processes is not always matched by that of clerics. In Ireland we still retain a clerical model of church and a service model of parish. Some bishops realize that this model is no longer appropriate nor in line with Pope Francis's synodal vision. One bishop put it starkly: "The Catholic Church in Ireland is in the maelstrom of its gravest crisis in centuries," and it is a crisis from within.[31] Yet Francis does not believe the solution to the church's problems lies exclusively with structural, organisational, and administrative reform. He sees in this a concession to the current *Zeitgeist*—a "technocratic mentality" or contemporary form of Pelagianism, whereas his stress is on spiritual renewal and evangelisation.[32] On the one hand, he aims to "promote a sound 'decentralisation'"[33] and bolster the governing and teaching authority of regional conferences of bishops; on the other, he reminds local

---

[30] The Association of Catholics in Ireland, "The Irish National Synodal Synthesis," August 16, 2021, https://acireland.ie/the-irish-national-synodal-synthesis-august-16th-2022/.

[31] Bishop Dermot Farrell, "Speaking Notes of Bishop Dermot Farrell for Conference with Laity and Priests in the Diocese of Ossory," November 28, 2018, https://associationofcatholicpriests.ie/exploring-our-parishes-today-conference-of-laity-and-priests-of-the-diocese-of-ossory/.

[32] See, for example, Pope Francis, "Schreiben von papst franziskus an das pilgernde volk gottes in deutschland," 5, and Pope Francis, apostolic exhortation *Gaudete et Exsultate*, March 19, 2018, 57–59, https://www.vatican.va/content/francesco/en/apost_exhortations/documents/papa-francesco_esortazione-ap_20180319_gaudete-et-exsultate.html.

[33] Pope Francis, *Evangelii Gaudium*, 16.

churches that they are part of a bigger body—the church universal. Church reform does not come overnight, he continues, but takes time to mature; it is a question of holding the tensions and imbalances together.[34] But should the spiritual and the structural be played off against each other? Church reform is systemic, not simply personal. Do we need not only a consultative but also a deliberative model of synodality?[35] The fruits of synodality are still to be seen—hopefully it is not an impossible dream but a genuine impulse of the Spirit that "a synodal Church is the Church of the future."[36]

[34] Pope Francis, "Schreiben von papst franziskus an das pilgernde volk gottes in deutschland," 5, 9.

[35] Even at the most recent pan-Amazon synod, while there were religious sisters and indigenous laity participating, not one had voting rights. Women continue to be excluded from decision-making processes in the church. See Sheila Curran, RSM, "Struggling Together after the Pan-Amazon Synod," *Doctrine & Life* 70 (2020), 2–3.

[36] Gerry O'Hanlon, SJ, *The Quiet Revolution of Pope Francis: A Synodal Catholic Church in Ireland?* (Dublin: Messenger Publications, 2018), 159.

Synodality and the Appointment of Bishops: Issues and Proposals from Vatican II to Global Catholicism Today

Massimo Faggioli

The Appointment of Bishops from Christendom to Vatican II

The issue of the appointment of bishops demonstrates how mutable some key aspects in the institutional life of the church are—and how much ecclesial institutions and structures have changed in history. An early church model that affirmed the right of the people of God to participate in the selection of their bishops gave way to a Christendom church whose political power grew enormously—including in the election of the bishop of Rome, hence the invention of the conclave between the eleventh and thirteenth centuries. Beginning in the sixteenth century, the joint participation of the papacy and political leaders in the choice of bishops led to the development of the institution of concordats, bilateral juridical agreements of international relevance. This continued up to the golden age of the concordats in the nineteenth and twentieth centuries, which cemented the concept of the appointment of bishops as a mutable procedure, according to particular local traditions, but with two key elements in play: first, the need to take into account the demands of national governments (kings, presidents) and empires in terms of participation in the procedure, and second, the recognition of the gold standard (according to the papacy) of the way in which a bishop should be appointed, that is, by free decision of the pope without external interference from lay authorities.

The latter was the ideal model described and legislated by the Code of Canon Law of 1917, in which for the first time the free appointment by the pope was established according to a common rule, in canon 329: "The Roman pontiff freely appoints bishops."[1] The reference to elections and other kinds of appointments and presentations remained, but only as an exception (see canon 332 §1).

This set the stage for Vatican II, when some council fathers raised the issue of the reform of the appointment of bishops in the context of the discussion of the draft of the schema for the decree on the pastoral ministry of bishops, which later became *Christus Dominus*.[2] The overall theological structure of the discussion and of the decree reflected the need to address two macro-questions that emerged between the preconciliar period and the approval of *Lumen Gentium*. The first was the legitimacy of the ecclesiastical institution in its Tridentine elements (papacy and episcopate; diocese; parishes) and in its nineteenth- and twentieth-century developments (papal primacy and episcopal ministry in the diocese; governance of the universal church; the local and national dimension of episcopal conferences; the relationship with the new nation states)—all questions that the ecclesiological constitution presupposes but deferred to postconciliar texts. Secondly, there was the

---

[1] See Jean Gaudemet, *Les élections dans l'église latine des origines au XVIe siècle* (Paris: Lanore, 1979); Klaus Ganzer, "Bischofswahl, Bischofsernennung," in *Lexicon für Theologie und Kirche* (Freiburg-Basel-Wien: Herder, 1994), ed. Walter Kasper, vol. 2, 504–507; E. Roland, "Élection des évêques," in *Dictionnaire de théologie catholique*, ed. A. Vacant and E. Mangenot (Paris: Letouzey et Ané, 1911), vol. IV, 2256–2281; Robert L. Benson, *The Bishop-Elect: A Study in Medieval Ecclesiastical Office* (Princeton: Princeton University Press, 1968).

[2] For the history of the document, see Massimo Faggioli, *Il vescovo e il concilio: Modello episcopale e aggiornamento al Vaticano II* (Bologna: Il Mulino, 2005), especially chapters 4 and 5 on the issue of the reform of the appointment of bishops by Vatican II.

question of the relationship between episcopal ministry and pastoral care in the light of the experience of the council and the pontificate of John XXIII, and in particular the shift from a concept of ministry functional to the minister (linked to the institution of the *beneficium*, on which Vatican II turns the page and moves forward) to a conception of ministry as a service to the people of God.

From the preparation period to the conciliar debate in the second session of 1963, in the context of the discussion on the schema on pastoral ministry of bishops, very few council fathers proposed a reform of the procedure of the appointment of bishops that was compatible with the ecclesiology of Vatican II; this threatened to leave behind the juridical structure that appointed bishops to local dioceses without any consultation with, or participation of, the people of God in the process.[3] Rafael González Moralejo (then auxiliary bishop of Valencia, Spain) proposed that the schema also deal with the method of designating bishops and even the possibility that the bishops would take part, in some way, in the election of the pope.[4]

The conciliar commission *de episcopis* was already reluctant, in its majority, to accept the proposals of some fathers who asked for a definition of the procedures for choosing bishops and the qualities of candidates for the episcopate. On this point the commission did not take the opportunity to insert passages overcoming the status quo and subsequently proved compliant with, and defenseless against, the intervention of the Secretariat of State. The issue was not formally withdrawn from the agenda of Vatican II, but surely a decision coming from the Secretariat of State, acting on behalf of the "Superior Authority" (the pope) restricted the freedom of the conciliar commission, and hence of Vatican II, to discuss a key issue with vast ecclesiological, ecclesiastical, and ecclesial consequences.[5]

---

[3] See Hubert Müller, *Der Anteil der Laien an der Bischofswahl: Ein Beitrag zur Geschichte der Kanonistik von Gratian bis Gregor IX* (Amsterdam: Grüner, 1976), with an appendix on the failed discussion at Vatican II on the reform of the appointment of bishops.

[4] See *Acta Synodalia*, II/4 (Vatican City: Typis Polyglottis Vaticanis, 1972), 505–509.

[5] On the other issues withdrawn from the agenda of Vatican II and taken up by the pope (reform of the Roman Curia, bishops' synods, clerical celibacy, condemnation of the atomic bomb, condemnation of birth control, communism, and the rela-

In this case, the secretary of state sent a letter informing the president of the conciliar commission *de episcopis* that the issue of the appointment of bishops could not be discussed by the council given the sensitive political and diplomatic dimensions, but the conciliar decree could certainly express general principles in terms of the freedom of the church to appoint bishops, that is, vis-à-vis secular authorities. The letter of the secretary of state said nothing and assumed the decree said nothing about an ecclesiological or juridical change in the principle of papal appointment.[6] In some cases, the issue was at the center of ongoing bilateral negotiations between the Holy See and national governments at the same time Vatican II was in session.[7] This was, in short, the genesis of the text of Vatican II that was approved by the council fathers and which addresses the issue of the appointment of bishops in the decree *Christus Dominus*, paragraph 20:

> Since the apostolic office of bishops was instituted by Christ the Lord and pursues a spiritual and supernatural purpose, this sacred ecumenical synod declares that the right of nominating and appointing bishops belongs properly, peculiarly, and per se exclusively to the competent ecclesiastical authority.
>
> Therefore, for the purpose of duly protecting the freedom of the Church and of promoting more conveniently and efficiently the welfare of the faithful, this holy council desires that in future no more rights or privileges of election, nomination, presentation, or designation for the office of bishop be granted to civil authorities. The civil authorities, on the other hand, whose favorable attitude toward the Church this sacred synod [Vatican II] gratefully acknowledges and highly appreciates, are most kindly requested voluntarily to renounce the above-mentioned rights and privileges which they presently enjoy by

---

tionship between Judaism and the church), see Alberto Melloni, ed., *Vatican II: The Complete History* (Mahwah, NJ: Paulist Press, 2015), 232–235

[6] The letter of the secretary of state, Cardinal Amleto Giovanni Cicognani, to the commission *de episcopis* on the issue of the appointment of bishops, dated April 14, 1964, in *Acta Synodalia*, V/2 (Vatican City: Typis Polyglottis Vaticanis, 1990), 652. See also Faggioli, *Il vescovo e il concilio*, 300–301.

[7] Following the diktat of the Secretariat of State, within the commission *de episcopis* a special subcommission of experts was formed for the study of a formula on the freedom of the church in episcopal appointments. On June 26, 1964, the secretary of state approved the text proposed by the commission with some slight amendments.

reason of a treaty or custom, after discussing the matter with
the Apostolic See.[8]

If the conciliar commission chose a prudent solution on issue of
the resignation of bishops, leaving to subsequent legislation the
precise determination of the age limit, completely absent from the
conciliar debate on the decree was the question surrounding
procedures for the appointment of bishops. The decree *Christus
Dominus* preserved the role of the diplomacy of the Holy See, both
in its ecclesiastical dimension (such as for the appointment of
bishops) and in its political-diplomatic dimension (depending on
the social and political relevance of the Catholic Church in a particular country and the status and influence of the diplomatic
mission of the Holy See in that same country). *Christus Dominus* is
an ambivalent document with respect to the historical-theological
theme of overcoming the "Constantinian age" and medieval Christendom, and its repercussions on the close relationship between
church and state. On the one hand, the decree takes for granted
the spontaneous renunciation by civil governments of typical
privileges of the state concerning the appointment of bishops, and
a renewed freedom for the Catholic Church, but on the other hand,
it presupposes for the church an alliance between the bishops and
the civil authorities.

Vatican II was a turning point from the point of view of ecclesiology. But that turning point took place within a vision that,
despite the defeat of the texts of the 1960–1962 preparatory phase,
remained largely sociological and institutionally noncommittal
until the end. Above all, the institutional dimensions necessary
for a reform of the relationship between the bishops and the papacy on the one side, and the bishops and their local churches on
the other, remained dependent on the will of the papacy to implement the promises of a reform of the relations between papacy
and episcopate (reform of the Roman Curia, institution of the
Synod of Bishops, relationship with national episcopal conferences) and forced to coexist with the lack of any attempt within

---

[8] Second Vatican Council, decree *Christus Dominus*, October 28, 1965, 20, https://
www.vatican.va/archive/hist_councils/ii_vatican_council/documents/vat-ii
_decree_19651028_christus-dominus_en.html.

the document to discuss the modalities for the appointment of bishops (except for the request addressed to the constituted state powers to renounce the privileges obtained over the centuries). Moreover, in a debate focused on the balance of powers—between pope and bishops, between bishops and coadjutors and auxiliaries, between bishops and religious, between bishops and episcopal conferences, between bishops and nuncios—the relationship of bishops with priests and with lay people remained largely unaddressed in institutional terms.[9]

Vatican II was unable to fully settle the account of overcoming the Counter-Reformation: if it is true that after the Council of Trent, the Counter-Reformation, or Catholic Reform, had been almost synonymous with reform of bishops, a model of bishop of Vatican II emerges with difficulty in the course of the postconciliar period and is part of the difficulties surrounding the reception of Vatican II.

Recent Proposals during Pope Francis's Synodal Process

During the postconciliar period, proposals have emerged for a reform of the procedure for appointing bishops, especially in the context of the reception of the new Code of Canon Law of 1983, which better reflects the model expressed by its predecessor, the Code of 1917, than the ecclesiology of Vatican II: "The Supreme Pontiff freely appoints bishops or confirms those legitimately elected."[10]

---

[9] This is true for both the issue of the periodical celebration of diocesan synods and the existence of diocesan and parish pastoral councils, which were not thoroughly discussed at Vatican II.

[10] Canon 377 §1. See John M. Huels, OSM, and Richard R. Gaillardetz, "The Selection of Bishops: Recovering the Traditions," in *The Jurist* 59 (1999): 348–376; Joseph F. O'Callaghan, *Electing Our Bishops: How the Catholic Church Should Choose Its Leaders* (Lanham, MD: Rowman & Littlefield, 2007); Libero Gerosa, "Bischofsbestellung Und Mitverantwortung Aller Gläubigen," in *Kirchenrechtliche Bibliothek* 2001: 231–241; Norbert Greinacher, "Demokratisierung Der Kirche," in *Theologische Quartalschrift* 170, no. 4 (1990): 253–266; Matthäus Kaiser, "Die Bestellung der Bischöfe in Geschichte und Gegenwart. Wahl oder Ernennung?," in *Eine Kirche—Ein Recht?* 1990: 47–71; René Metz, "La libre nomination des évêques dans l'Église Catholique Romaine selon Vatican II et le Code de 1983: Souhaits exprimés et résultats obtenus," in *Zeitschrift Für Evangelisches Kirchenrecht* 32, no. 3 (1987): 451–466.

The situation has changed in the last few years, especially thanks to the decision of Pope Francis to open the synodal process in 2021 leading up to the assembly of the synod in October 2023, but with the expectation of effects enduring well after 2023: the project for a synodal reform of the Catholic Church.

In the synodal consultations and events in different churches around the world, the issue of the reform of the appointment of bishops has come up several times, particularly in two synodal processes, the two most structured of all: Australia and Germany.

In 2018 the Catholic Church in Australia began the listening phase for a plenary council, which, if carried forward to completion, would represent the first such council celebrated since 1937 in Australia. The impetus came not only from Pope Francis but also from the royal commission set up by the Australian federal government (2013–2017) to respond to the crisis of sexual violence against minors, which produced a thorough and comprehensive investigation of the entire society. As part of the process of the plenary council, the bishops and the heads of religious congregations of Australia appointed a task force, known as the Governance Review Project Team, that was asked to elaborate proposals in response to the Royal Commission.[11] In 2020 this task force submitted to the bishops' conference and the religious of Australia a study, titled *The Light from the Southern Cross*, which has one section on the reform of the appointment of bishops:

Section 6.3.1. The selection and appointment of diocesan bishops

1. That to increase trust in church governance and support for episcopal leadership among the People of God, the processes and procedures leading to the appointment of bishops by the Pope be explained to the public, for example by an entry on the ACBC website.

2. That the consultative processes within a local Church leading to a recommendation by the apostolic nuncio to the Apostolic

---

[11] Full disclosure: I was one of the four external experts called to work with the task force that wrote and submitted *The Light from the Southern Cross* to the bishops' conference and the conference of religious of Australia.

See concerning the appointment of bishops be structured so as to accommodate the following principles:

2.1 analysis of the needs of the diocese, and consequently a suitable episcopal appointment, must form part of the consultative process for episcopal appointments;

2.2 in the interests of transparency, efficiency and effectiveness, the consultation process leading to the creation of a terna should embrace genuine discernment that includes clergy and a larger number of lay people than is currently the case and that takes into consideration the potential bishop's experience in dealing with abuse; and

2.3 genuine discernment leading to the creation of a terna that includes clergy and a larger number of lay people than is currently the case and which takes into consideration the potential bishop's experience in dealing with abuse, be embraced in the interests of transparency, efficiency and effectiveness.[12]

In Germany, the Synodal Path that opened in 2019 is, together with the Australian Plenary Council, the most structured of all the synodal experiences in the Catholic Church. It has a focus on church reform, not only theological but also structural and institutional. An important part of it is the discussion on the appointment of bishops, thanks to the fact that the procedure for German-speaking dioceses has had, and often still has, rules that are, in part, different from the default case (at least in the last few centuries)—that the pope appoints freely but with a significant role

---

[12] *The Light from the Southern Cross: Promoting Co-Responsible Governance in the Catholic Church in Australia*, 16, https://drive.google.com/file/d/1TXZd4SP -EBk4VtH9JyB9PMSmjY9Mfj7E/view. (The document can be reached more easily by going to https://www.catholic.au/s/article/Church-Governance and clicking on "Click here to access The Light from the Southern Cross." It must be noted that proposals for a reform of the appointment of bishops was absent from the "Framework for Motions" for the second assembly of the plenary council, published on May 30, 2022, https://drive.google.com/file/d/1EiQBQV8U8-T5DemhN1TY-WSlT4uSzy-v /view.)

of the chapters of the canons of the cathedrals according to a tradition going back to the beginning of the second millennium.[13]

In the assembly of the German Synodal Path of February 2022, the delegates approved in second reading this text:

> According to Church law, the respective diocesan people of God only have very limited participation, insofar as the Nuncio can also 'seek individually and in secret the opinion of others from both the secular and non-secular clergy and from laity outstanding in wisdom' (can 377 §3). According to Concordat law, no rights of participation are provided for the faithful. Ecclesiologically, however, it would make sense to involve the entire people of God in the diocese—thus also priests outside the cathedral chapter, deacons, and above all the non-ordained faithful among the people of God—in the bishop's appointment.

Participation of the diocesan people of God

> Under the Church's current law and Concordats, the following forms of participation are open to the diocesan people of God: a right of co-decision in the preparation of the list of candidates, and a right to be heard prior to the selection being made from the list of candidates. These two rights can be realized through a voluntary undertaking on the part of the respective cathedral chapter.

Recommended resolution

> A model regulation for the voluntary self-commitment of the respective cathedral chapters in the appointment of bishops shall be drawn up and issued. Therein, the cathedral chapters are recommended to commit themselves to observe the following procedure in the case of a pending appointment of a bishop: The Synodal Council of the diocese elects a body that has as many members as the cathedral chapter and supports the chapter in exercising its rights in the process of appointing a bishop. The minimum criteria are:

[13] See Gerhard Hartmann, *Der Bischof: seine Wahl und Ernennung. Geschichte und Aktualität* (Graz: Styria, 1990); Klaus Ganzer, "Zur Beschränkung der Bischofswahl auf die Domkapitel in Theorie und Praxis des 12. und 13. Jahrhunderts," *Zeitschrift der Savigny-Stiftung für Rechtsgeschichte / Kanonistische Abteilung*, 57 (1971): 22–82; 58 (1972): 166–197. The bibliography is very abundant on this.

- The members of the body who are to be added are selected in a way that is as gender- and generation-appropriate as possible.[14]

Pope Francis has already given, in some sense, a response to these proposals; it's a cautious one, but not exactly a simple conservation of the status quo. In *Praedicate Evangelium*, Pope Francis's constitution of reform of the Roman Curia, article 105 on the appointment of bishops has an interesting addition compared to the text of its predecessor, *Pastor Bonus* (John Paul II, 1988), as it specifies the possibility of involving in this process, "in ways that are appropriate," the people of God in the dioceses that need a new bishop.[15]

This must be read in the context of the emphasis of Pope Francis's pontificate on the pastoral nature of the ministry of bishops but also in the context of the gap between the pope's visionary statements on reform and the pragmatism that is necessary to run the church. Discussing and legislating on the reform of the appointment of bishops in the Catholic Church today must take into account the significant changes both intra-ecclesial and in the relations between the ecclesiastical system and "the world" compared to the time of Vatican II.

The Reform of the Appointment of Bishops in Twenty-First-Century Global Catholicism

To understand the issue of the appointment of bishops for church reform in the global Catholic Church of the twenty-first century, there are three dimensions that call for special attention.

The first dimension is *theological and doctrinal development.* Ecclesial synodality is a very ancient practice and, at the same time, a

[14] *Presentation of Synodal Forum I, "Power and Separation of Powers in the Church: Joint Participation and Involvement in the Mission,"* https://www.synodalerweg.de/fileadmin/Synodalerweg/Dokumente_Reden_Beitraege/englisch-SVIII/SV-III-ENG_Synodal Forum-I-Implementation-text.AppointmentOfTheDiocesanBishop-Second-reading .pdf.

[15] Pope Francis, apostolic constitution *Praedicate Evangelium*, March 19, 2022, https://www.vatican.va/content/francesco/en/apost_constitutions/documents/20220319 -costituzione-ap-praedicate-evangelium.html.

recent theme. It is an integral part of the church's tradition, but the theology of synodality, which is now the basis of Pope Francis's push for a synodal reform of the church, is a post–Vatican II development: the approved conciliar documents never used the term *synodality*, even if the ecclesiology of Vatican II opens up to that perspective. At sixty years from Vatican II, the reception of the council is clearly not only about implementing the letter of the documents but also about enriching those documents with insights coming from the experience of the whole church. It suffices to look at postconciliar papal teaching on some key issues to see that there has been a growth in the understanding of ecclesiology. This has to have important institutional consequences; the post–Vatican II developments in ecclesiology must become institutional practice, including in the very delicate issue of the appointment of bishops— and in a way that goes beyond the long-standing goal in the last two centuries of protecting the freedom of the church by giving the pope absolute freedom in the appointment of bishops.

The second dimension, equally important and more complex than the first one, is *historical-political*. There is a long history of relations between the papacy and political authorities that goes back at least to the early fourth century, under the Roman Empire of Constantine, and later of Emperor Theodosius, when the church acquired public relevance. It was the beginning of a long history of bilateral relations between the church as a community of believers and the political community. It is a history that always had at the center the care of the bishop of Rome (the pope) for his brother bishops and the local churches, the good relations between the church hierarchy and the political authorities, and especially the appointment of bishops. These issues were crucial in the "investiture controversy" of the eleventh and twelfth century, in the tensions with emerging nation states in Europe in the early modern period, and in the struggle with nationalisms in the nineteenth and twentieth centuries. The issue of the appointment of bishops was important also in the relations between the Vatican and Soviet Russia and Eastern European countries under communist rule after World War II. It's not just in the past. There are new signs of friction and tension between what ecclesiology demands and what diplomatic relations concede, especially at a time of disruption of the international order.

The proper historical context for a correct understanding of the issue of the appointment of the bishops is the entire two-thousand-year long history of the church and of the papacy. In this long history, the procedures for the appointment of bishops have always been very complex; they were often, and in many cases still are (in various forms, always subject to change in the long run) a moment of collaboration between the papacy and secular political authorities. The negotiations between the Vatican and the government of the People's Republic of China, which include the agreement signed in September 2018, represent the most important diplomatic effort by the Holy See in decades, and it is no surprise they are encountering significant opposition in the Western hemisphere. There is an ideological issue of opposition to the Chinese regime, but there is also a problem of forgetting the complexity of the issue of the appointment of bishops.

The issue of the reform of the appointment of bishops must be seen from an ecclesiological point of view, that is, the need for the procedure to better reflect the idea of the church as the people of God, participating in the selection of their pastors in ways that foster the unity of the church but also accountability and responsibility. At the same time, this discussion must take into account the growing problem of religious freedom and its consequences on the sensitivity of the Holy See for the freedom of the church. During the last century, Roman Catholicism has become a more globalized church: Catholics and the papacy have come to terms with a wider variety of social and political contexts around the world. This means that the church does not look for the same kind of arrangement for all Catholics in all nations but strives for improving the relations of Catholics with the political authorities in order to maintain and foster the unity of the church. The goal of negotiations with political authorities is not ideological but pastoral, in the sense of helping the local churches live their faith in a given, concrete reality, without artificial divisions between factions in their midst.

This problem of the unity of the church at a time of growing pressures on the freedom of religion helps us understand a third dimension—new even since Vatican II—that complicates matters. The appointment of bishops has always been an extremely sensitive point of contact between the *ad intra* and the *ad extra* of the church. It is hard, not just from a theological point of view but also one of lived experience, to see the line dividing the *ad intra* from the *ad extra*. It is a line shaped by the shifting boundaries between religion and politics, and theological and partisan affiliations, at a time of (sometimes extreme) political polarization in our countries and in our churches; by a crisis of the democratic system; by the role of media and social media; and by the rise of postinstitutional religion even within Catholicism.[16]

What we have seen in the last two decades is a reversal of the Vatican II idea of a respectful coexistence, collaborative cooperation, and distinction of sphere between church and state, between religion and politics. In some sense, it's a return to a previous age, with some similarities with the Middle Ages: the struggle is not anymore between a church under the papacy and the empire, but between a church that is more "liquid" internally and new empires asserting their control on religion (more visibly when it's national governments and international organizations, more stealthily in the case of new multinational corporations and private and corporate donors).[17]

On the other hand, the present procedure for the appointment of bishops is the fruit of the "golden age of the concordats" which reflected a centralization of power in the state and in the papacy, typical of early modern and modern history.[18] But that model is over, as Italian historian Paolo Prodi convincingly stated in his last essay: politics is no longer about the state and in the state, religion is no longer about the church and in the church.[19] This breakdown of the division of labor between church and state provides the current debate on the reform of bishops' appointments in the global Catholic Church with some opportunities.

[16] See Massimo Faggioli, *Catholicism and Citizenship: Political Cultures of the Church in the Twenty-First Century* (Collegeville, MN: Liturgical Press, 2017).

[17] See Nick Couldry and Ulises A. Mejías, *The Costs of Connection: How Data Is Colonizing Human Life and Appropriating It for Capitalism* (Stanford: Stanford University Press, 2019); Massimo Cacciari, *Il lavoro dello spirito: Saggio su Max Weber* (Milano: Adelphi, 2020); Remo Bodei, *Dominio e sottomissione: schiavi, animali, macchine, Intelligenza Artificiale* (Bologna: Il Mulino, 2019).

[18] See *Il processo di designazione dei vescovi: Storia, legislazione, prassi*. Atti del X Simposium canonistico-romanistico (24–28 aprile 1995), ed. D. J. Andrés Gutierrez (Vatican City: Libreria Editrice Vaticana, 1996).

[19] See Paolo Prodi, "Europe in the Age of Reformations: The Modern State and Confessionalization," *Catholic Historical Review* 103, no. 1 (Winter 2017): 1–19.

Conclusions

The development of a more global, less Europe-centered Catholicism has to deal with the disruption of the international order, against the assumption—typical of Euro-Western Catholicism between Vatican II and the early 2000s—that the future would bring more freedom for the church and consequently also more participation for Catholics within the institutional procedures of the church. From the time of Vatican II to today, the framework of relationship both inside the Catholic Church, and between the church and the states, has not developed in a way that favors radical reforms in the way bishops are appointed.[20] On the other hand, it is hard to imagine that some kind of reform in the appointment of bishops can be denied or completely ignored in a church that has experienced such developments in ecclesiology, both *ad intra* and *ad extra*, at Vatican II and in the post–Vatican II period.

It is easier to imagine reform in the sense of greater consultation for local churches in need of a new bishop, rather than radical reforms in the sense of a return to the early church model of election of the bishop by the clergy and the people. But in light of the abuse crisis, it is urgent to imagine a better way for the church to appoint bishops, especially when it comes to the questionnaires used to inquire regarding the qualities that confirm any episcopal candidate to be considered worthy of the office as they are outlined in canon law. The recommendation processes at diocesan and archdiocesan levels can, and should, require formal consultation with groups of committed Catholic men and women.

But reform proposals will have to consider the wide variety of situations in which the local churches in the global Catholic Church find themselves today, from a theological, ecclesial, ecclesiastical, and political point of view.[21] This could lead to a variety of different procedures for different churches in different parts of the world—for the appointment of bishops, as for much else in the future of Catholicism.

---

[20] See *Gli accordi della Santa Sede con gli Stati (XIX–XXI secolo): Modelli e mutazioni: dallo Stato confessionale alla libertà religiosa*, ed. Roberto Regoli and Marie Levant (Annuarium Historiae Pontificiae 54, 2020).

[21] See Massimo Faggioli and Bryan Froehle, *Global Catholicism: Between Disruption and Encounter* (Leiden: Brill, 2023).

The reflections and proposals made during the synodal process that started in 2021 are the most relevant example of the centrality of a reform to the process of appointing bishops. Ultimately, the chances of reform will largely depend on the success of synodality, and the turn of the church to a less hierarchical and more synodal style of governance.

Toward an Effective Synodalization
of the Whole Church

Rafael Luciani

In 2013 the Catholic Church entered a new phase of conciliar reception that gave way to the recovery of the normative character of the category *people of God*.[1] At the beginning of his pontificate, Francis spoke of "the church as the people of God, pastors and people together. The church is the totality of God's people,"[2] and in *Evangelii Gaudium* he developed the fundamental aspects of "this way of understanding the Church": "The Church, as the agent of evangelization, is more than an organic and hierarchical institution; she is first and foremost a people advancing on its pilgrim way towards God . . . transcending any institutional expression, however necessary."[3] Thus, "Being Church means

[1] See Serena Noceti, "Popolo di Dio: un incompiuto riconoscimento di identità," *Concilium* 54 (2018): 397–412; Giovanni Mazzillo, "L'eclissi della categoria popolo di Dio," *Rassegna di Teologia* 36 (1995): 553–587; Dario Vitali, *Popolo di Dio* (Assisi: Cittadella, 2013); Rafael Luciani, "The Centrality of the People in Pope Francis Socio-cultural Theology," *Concilium* 3 (2018): 55–68.

[2] Antonio Spadaro, "A Big Heart Open to God: An Interview with Pope Francis," *America*, September 30, 2013, https://www.americamagazine.org/faith/2013/09/30/big-heart-open-god-interview-pope-francis.

[3] Pope Francis, apostolic exhortation *Evangelii Gaudium*, November 24, 2014, 111, https://www.vatican.va/content/francesco/en/apost_exhortations/documents/papa-francesco_esortazione-ap_20131124_evangelii-gaudium.html. Hereafter cited as EG.

being God's people" (EG 114). In fact, during the Second Vatican Council, Bishop Emiel-Jozef De Smedt said, "We must be careful when speaking about the Church not to fall into a certain hierarchicalism, clericalism, and obispolatry or papolatry. What comes first is the People of God."[4]

Therefore, when we speak of the church as the people of God, we understand it as the totality of the faithful, because this concept intrinsically includes all its members in their reciprocity of identities and the essential co-responsibility in pursuit of the fulfillment of the church's mission.[5] This concept opens an opportunity for the reconfiguration of identities and relationships among the different ecclesial subjects and, therefore, of the church as a collective and organic subject: the *ecclesial we*.

It is in this hermeneutical frame that synodality can be understood as the operative principle that sets in motion this *ecclesiogenesis*, the integral and organic transformation of the whole church. Hence, it is not only a constitutive dimension but also a constituent one, a whole process of ecclesial transfiguration that finds its foundation in the *essential*—and not auxiliary—commitment of *co-responsibility* proper to the model of the church as the people of God understood as the *totality of the faithful*,[6] according to which "pastors and the other faithful are bound to each other by a mutual need" (LG 32).

Consequently, this understanding of the church implies that "renewal in the ecclesial hierarchy by itself does not bring about the transformation to which the Holy Spirit impels us."[7] A conversion of the hierarchical ministry presupposes a hermeneutics that

---

[4] *Acta Synodalia Sacrosancti Concilii Oecumenici Vaticani II* (32 vols. Vatican City: Typis Polyglottis Vaticanis, 1970–1999), 1/4, 143.

[5] See Yves Congar, "The Church, the People of God," *Concilium* 1 (1965): 10.

[6] "If we were to be asked what we consider to be that seed of life deriving from the council which is most fruitful in pastoral consequences, we would answer without any hesitation: it is the rediscovery of the people of God as a *whole*, as a single reality; and then by way of consequence, the co-responsibility thus implied for every member of the church." Léon Joseph Cardinal Suenens, *Coresponsibility in the Church*, trans. Francis Martin (New York: Herder, 1968), 30.

[7] Pope Francis, "Carta del Santo Padre Francisco al pueblo de dios que peregrina en Chile," May 31, 2018, http://www.vatican.va/content/francesco/es/letters/2018/documents/papa-francesco_20180531_lettera-popolodidio-cile.html. My translation.

follow the structure of *Lumen Gentium*, that is, situating and reading chapter 3 (on the hierarchy) in the light of chapter 2 (on the people of God)[8] in order to form an ecclesial *us*. The reformulation of the theology of the ordained ministry entails a questioning of the exercise of power in the church, as well as the redesign of the primacy and episcopal collegiality. As Cardinal Suenens said after the council, "History teaches that, if the structure of the Church is hierarchical by the will of its Founder, the modalities of the exercise of this authority vary in the course of the centuries. One could trace a long series of these variations caused by a thousand historical and contingent factors, whether it is a question of the election of Popes, the appointment of bishops or so many other uses. All this has occurred throughout history according to the conditions of each epoch."[9] Moving forward in this ecclesiology implies overcoming two juxtapositions that remain unresolved in the postconciliar period, the first between collegiality and primacy and the second between collegiality and synodality.

The Unresolved Juxtaposition between Collegiality and Primacy

The postconciliar reception of the ecclesiology of the people of God encountered a first obstacle in the existing conceptual fabric around the relationship between collegiality and primacy. *Lumen Gentium* 22, later received in *Christus Dominus* 4, explains collegiality in the context of differences of power between the episcopal college and the primate. Therefore, the emerging institutions will be marked by the exercise of *potestas*. This is the case of the Synod of Bishops, created by Paul VI, which reinforces the idea of a

---

[8] "The sequence [of *LG*]—the Mystery of the Church (chapter 1), the People of God (chapter 2), the Hierarchical Constitution of the Church (chapter 3)—stresses that the ecclesiastical hierarchy is at the service of the People of God in order that the Church may carry out her mission in conformity with God's plan of salvation, in the logic of the priority of the whole over the parts." International Theological Commission, *Synodality in the Life and Mission of the Church*, March 2, 2018, 54, https://www.vatican.va/roman_curia/congregations/cfaith/cti_documents/rc_cti_20180302_sinodalita_en.html. Hereafter cited as SLMC.

[9] Suenens, *Coresponsibility in the Church*, 191.

hierarchical episcopal collegiality exercised strictly *with* and *among* some (bishops) and *for* one (Pope).[10] The problem arises when taking *Christus Dominus* 5 as a hermeneutical criterion to define the nature and operability of collegiality itself, without understanding the Synod of Bishops as a particular case of the exercise of power between the episcopate and the primacy. Juan Arrieta summarizes it as follows: "The debate on collegiality in *Lumen Gentium* and that of *Christus Dominus* 5 do not coincide and cannot be juxtaposed."[11] They cannot be juxtaposed because their result is a notion of collegiality interpreted in the light of a *hierarchica communio*, which does not take into account the normative character of the *communio ecclesiarum.*

By projecting the relationship between collegiality and primacy on the basis of subordination, a juxtaposed image appears of two entities that give the impression of being endowed with autonomy with respect to the rest of the people of God.[12] According to O'Malley, "The Synod would be subject . . . to the power of the Pope. . . . *Apostolica Sollicitudo* [the motu proprio with which Pope Paul VI instituted the Synod of Bishops] was, with all its merits, an expression of papal primacy, and not of collegiality, a word that was not even mentioned in the text."[13] Indelicato agrees that this is an unfinished debate on "the exercise of deliberative power exercised *ex sese* as a college, with and under the pope, but not delegated."[14] Anton confirms that in the drafting history of *Christus Dominus* 5 there appears the proposal to create "a council of bishops with full and effective stability, both in its configuration and in its activity, through which the episcopal college could act

---

[10] See Hervé Legrand, "Lo sviluppo di chiese-soggetto: un'istanza del Vaticano II," *Cristianesimo nella Storia* 2 (1981): 152–153.

[11] Antonino Indelicato, *Il Sinodo dei Vescovi: La collegialità sospesa 1965–1985* (Bologna: Il Mulino, 2008), 56.

[12] Rahner mentions "two different procedures of one and the same subject," "two aspects of one and the same power, or as two concepts that formally include each another." See Karl Rahner, "On the Divine Right of the Episcopate," in Karl Rahner and Joseph Ratzinger, *The Episcopacy and the Primacy*, trans. Kenneth Barker, Patrick Kerans, Robert Ochs, and Richard Strachan (Freiburg: Herder, 1962), 97, 100.

[13] John W. O'Malley, *What Happened at Vatican II* (Cambridge, MA: Harvard University Press, 2008), 252.

[14] Indelicato, *Il Sinodo dei Vescovi*, 365.

with the fullness of its collegial power."[15] It was a desire that went unanswered.

A further element that hindered a more organic reception of the model of the church as the people of God and strengthened the juxtaposition between collegiality and primacy was the so-called *Nota Explicativa Praevia* that was read "by order of the supreme authority" before the vote on chapter 3 of *Lumen Gentium*. This came as a result of pressure from the conservative minority that wanted to save the doctrine of the primacy promulgated at Vatican I. In the text, Paul VI points out that "the Supreme Pontiff can always exercise his power at will, as his very office demands. Though it is always in existence, the College is not as a result permanently engaged in strictly collegial activity; the Church's Tradition makes this clear. In other words, the College is not always 'fully active [*in actu pleno*]'; rather, it acts as a college in the strict sense only from time to time and only with the consent of its head."[16]

Since it was not voted on by the council fathers,[17] the note does not belong to the proper documents of the council and, therefore, cannot be taken as a normative hermeneutical criterion. Nevertheless, it has marked the postconciliar understanding of collegiality. It is an equivocity that has repercussions on an elusive reception of conciliar ecclesiology, suitable only for an auxiliary model of relations between the college and the papacy with service to the primacy under the "personal" authority of the pontiff. In the 1969 motu proprio *Sollicitudo Omnium Ecclesiarum*, Paul VI ratified that the bishop of Rome has *"full, supreme and universal power and can exercise it freely."*[18]

The lack of theological articulation caused the doctrine of episcopal collegiality to accentuate the difference between ecclesial

[15] Angel Anton, "Sinodo e collegialità extraconciliare dei vescovi," in Gino Concetti and Vincenzo Fagiolo, eds., *La collegialità episcopale per il futuro della Chiesa* (Firenze: Vallecchi, 1969), 74.

[16] *Lumen Gentium*, Nota Explicativa Praevia, 4.

[17] The *NEP* was signed by the secretary general of the council, Bishop Pericle Felici, and not by the president of the commission. It was read on November 16, before the last vote on the third chapter of *Lumen Gentium*, without discussion.

[18] Pope Paul VI, motu proprio *Sollicitudo Omnium Ecclesiarum*, June 24, 1969, https://www.vatican.va/content/paul-vi/it/motu_proprio/documents/hf_p-vi _motu-proprio_19690624_sollicitudo-omnium-ecclesiarum.html. My translation; emphasis in original.

subjects, leaving aside the necessary respectivity and reciprocity. Over time, the practice of an *affectus collegialis* within the hierarchical communion with the papacy was privileged, rather than an *effective*, horizontal, binding collegiality, with a view to achieving *consensus*. This vision was finally institutionalized in the Extraordinary Synod of 1985, from which a hermeneutic turn in the understanding of the notions of participation and co-responsibility in the church emerged once the *hierarchica communio*[19] was assumed as a principle of relationship among all ecclesial subjects. A necessary reform of the Synod of Bishops should be to rectify the exercise of collegiality starting from its link with the local churches and their realities, because, as O'Malley has written, "The creation of the Synod of Bishops limited collegiality, that doctrine that empowered the ecclesial periphery. . . . Collegiality was reduced to an abstract teaching without roots in social reality. . . . Collegiality, which was the axis promoted by the majority to think about the center-periphery relationship, ended up being an abstract teaching without connection with the social reality of the Church. It ended up being an ideal, without rivalry for the established system."[20]

In order to deepen this doctrine, it is necessary to situate it beyond the problem of the *potestas* between the bishops and the Pope and to grasp it in a pastoral and not a juridical perspective: in the framework of an ecclesiology of the people of God. This inconclusive juxtaposition is the basis of another, more recent, juxtaposition that has arisen between collegiality and synodality, since the very nature of the former continues to be considered on the basis of its exercise within the institution of the Synod of Bishops.

Toward an Open Juxtaposition of Collegiality and Synodality

The pontificate of Francis has made steps toward overcoming the above-mentioned juxtaposition by broadening the exercise of episcopal collegiality in the light of synodality, with a greater em-

---

[19] See Gianfranco Ghirlanda, *Hierarchica communio: Significato della formula nella LG* (Rome: Università Gregoriana Editrice, 1980).

[20] O'Malley, *What Happened at Vatican II*, 311.

phasis on the Synod of Bishops.[21] This synodality is "expressed on the level of the universal Church in the dynamic circularity of the *consensus fidelium*, episcopal collegiality and the primacy of the Bishop of Rome" (SLMC 94). It is what the pope understands as a "synodal collegiality"[22] that "manifests the *collegialitas affectiva*, which can become effective in some circumstances,"[23] but not in a permanent way.[24] It is a context in which, notwithstanding its insufficiency, synodality offers a greater integration and interaction between the hierarchy and the rest of the faithful through the synod as an institutional mediation that articulates "the ministry of the personal and collegial exercise of apostolic authority with the synodal exercise of discernment by the community" (SLMC 69).

Francis emphasizes in his 2018 apostolic constitution on the structure of the Synod of Bishops, *Episcopalis Communio*: "Although structurally it is essentially configured as an episcopal body, this does not mean that the Synod exists separately from the rest of the faithful. On the contrary, it is a suitable instrument to give voice to the entire People of God."[25] This is something that has been crystallizing, in part, in broad consultation processes no longer limited to the episcopal conferences, with a greater participation of the believing community in discernment and decision-making in the church, while always having as a reference point the better functioning of ecclesial structures.

---

[21] "In a synodal Church, the Synod of Bishops is only the most evident manifestation of a dynamism of communion which inspires all ecclesial decisions." Pope Francis, "Commemoration of the 50th Anniversary of the Institution of the Synod of Bishops," October 17, 2015, https://www.vatican.va/content/francesco/en/speeches/2015/october/documents/papa-francesco_20151017_50-anniversario-sinodo.html.

[22] Pope Francis, "Letter to Cardinal Lorenzo Baldisseri Secretary General of the Synod of Bishops on the Occasion of the Elevation of Msgr. Fabio Fabene Undersecretary of the Synod to the Dignity of Bishop," April 1, 2014, https://www.vatican.va/content/francesco/es/letters/2014/documents/papa-francesco_20140401_cardinale-baldisseri.html. See also SLMC 99.

[23] Pope Francis, "Commemoration of the 50th Anniversary."

[24] Paul VI also privileged the spiritual and affective dimension, before the legal and effective. See Edmond Farhat, "La collegialità episcopale nei discorsi di Paolo VI al Sinodo dei Vescovi," in *Paolo VI e la collegialità episcopale: International Study Colloquium, Brescia 25–27 September 1992* (Rome: Studium, 1995), 244.

[25] Pope Francis, apostolic constitution *Episcopalis Communio*, September 15, 2018, 6, https://www.vatican.va/content/francesco/en/apost_constitutions/documents/papa-francesco_costituzione-ap_20180915_episcopalis-communio.html. Hereafter cited as EC.

In the path of a reform of the constitution and meaning of the synod, it would be necessary to insert the exercise of episcopal collegiality in an ecclesiology of the local churches and to move from the model of *hierarchica communio* to that of *communio ecclesiarum*. In this perspective, the bishop should not attend a synodal assembly to give his individual opinion but would be called to gather and express the sentiments of the faithful or *sensus fidei* of his particular church, a practice that requires the preexistence of local ecclesial spaces and procedures, such as assemblies at various levels, prior to the realization of a universal synod—a whole ecclesial process from the bottom up.

The duty to build a synodal church for the third millennium obliges us to develop a more complete doctrine of collegiality that dispenses with *Christus Dominus* 5 as a hermeneutical criterion for interpreting *Lumen Gentium* 22. Otherwise, collegiality will end up relativizing the *sensus fidei* and the question of the binding character of the laity in the whole organization and operation of the church.[26] It may be appropriate to create procedures and structures that are ecclesial and not episcopal, binding and not merely consultative, inspired by the exercise of the *essential co-responsibility* of all the faithful by reason of baptism and of participation in the common priesthood. This is the great challenge of moving from a reform of the synod to the *synodalization* of the whole church for the third millennium.

Certainly, with Francis there has been an expansion of the exercise of episcopal collegiality under the auspices of a synodal modality in order "that the anointing of the people of God may find concrete means to manifest itself."[27] This synodal collegiality does not mean a reform of the ordained ministry or of episcopal structures as such, but it does mean the beginning of a recovery of the theology of the *sensus fidei*, which was largely ignored after the council. It is exercised "on the basis of the doctrine of the *sensus fidei* of the People of God and the sacramental collegiality of the

---

[26] "In the absence of this dimension, reflection on collegiality seems to be reduced to a functional dignity, with an almost corporate implication that completely neglects the other great question of the role of the laity." Indelicato, *Il Sinodo dei Vescovi*, 359.

[27] Francis, "Carta del Santo Padre Francisco al pueblo de dios que peregrina en Chile." My translation.

episcopate in hierarchical communion with the Bishop of Rome," which presupposes (1) creating the link between the communitarian aspect that includes the whole people of God, the collegial dimension that is part of the exercise of episcopal ministry, and the primatial ministry of the Bishop of Rome; (2) promoting the principle of co-responsibility that expresses the active character of all the baptized and the specific role of episcopal ministry in communion with the Bishop of Rome; and (3) fostering a collaborative dynamic at the level of local churches.[28]

In this model, synodality comprises two subjects, which are no longer the college and the pope but rather (1) a collective one that is concretized in "the exercise of the *sensus fidei* of the *universitas fidelium*" and is composed of all the faithful who are heard prior to the celebration of a synod, and (2) "the ministry of guidance of the college of Bishops, each one with his presbyterate (some)" and "the ministry of unity of the Bishop and the Pope (one)" (SLMC 64). This form of synodal collegiality continues to have as its fullest realization the Synod of Bishops, but, although it achieves a better articulation between the people of God (all) and the hierarchy (collegiality), it does not resolve the integration of the hierarchy as part of the people of God because it continues to serve a paradigm "of bishops" and of a "consultative" nature with respect to the primacy.

A suggestive aspect of this new form of collegiality is found in *Episcopalis Communio* 18, which allows the pontiff to ratify and promulgate, as part of his ordinary magisterium, the final document of a synod. Although it has not happened explicitly, in an emergent way it appears in the post-synodal apostolic exhortation *Querida Amazonia*, in which the pope says that it does not replace the final document of the synod but "assumes it" and invites us to read it and to apply it in the local churches.[29] This could be a first step toward an effective collegiality.

[28] SLMC 64. Here I have closely followed the Spanish original. https://www.vatican.va/roman_curia/congregations/cfaith/cti_documents/rc_cti_20180302_sinodalita_sp.html.

[29] Pope Francis, post-synodal apostolic exhortation *Querida Amazonia*, February 2, 2020, 2–4, https://www.vatican.va/content/francesco/en/apost_exhortations/documents/papa-francesco_esortazione-ap_20200202_querida-amazonia.html. See Rafael Luciani, "Reconfigurar la identidad y la estructura eclesial a la luz de las

What we have seen up to this point allows us to maintain that the request of Paul VI to find a new and more complete definition of the church[30] could take concrete shape in an effective *synodalization* of all its structures and mentalities, and not in a mere formal or isolated procedural modification, which continues to coexist with its current operativity, heir to the onslaught of a cultural-institutional theological clericalism.

The Challenge of an Effective Synodalization of the Whole Church

Cardinal Suenens wrote that "the episcopacy for its part is not a self-sufficient oligarchy, but reaches out in both directions in a twofold living relationship: one, with its leader the pope, and the other with the whole presbyterate and laity."[31] The canonist Eugenio Corecco expressed this same idea when he wrote, "The problem of power within the People of God . . . is ultimately none other than the nature of the operational-decisional relationship between the bishops and other Christians and, as a consequence, the mode of participation of the clergy and the laity."[32]

But it is not possible to outline a reform of the hierarchical ministry without a clear theology of the laity because, as Burkhard warns, an "adherence to the Church" that does not include a lively participation in the evolution of the church is not very solid: "Co-responsibility, based on a deep sense of the *sensus fidei*, could include appropriate ecclesial forms through which the laity can express their points of view on a wide range of issues."[33] Thus,

---

Iglesias locales: *Querida Amazonia* y el estatuto teológico de las realidades sociocul-turales," *Revista Medellín* 179 (2020): 487–515.

[30] See Pope Paul VI, "Solenne inizio della seconda sessione del concilio ecumenico vaticano ii," September 29, 1963, https://www.vatican.va/content/paul-vi/it/speeches/1963/documents/hf_p-vi_spe_19630929_concilio-vaticano-ii.html.

[31] Suenens, *Coresponsibility in the Church*, 190.

[32] Eugenio Corecco, "Struttura sinodale o democratica della Chiesa particolare," in Graziano Borgonovo and Arturo Cattaneo, eds., *Ius et Communio: Scritti di Diritto Canonico*, II (Casale Monferrato: Piemme, 1997), 18.

[33] John Burkhard, "*Sensus fidei*: Meaning, Role and Future of a Teaching of Vatican II," *Louvain Studies* 17 (1992): 33.

the final word is not left to a *few* (bishops) or *one* (pope) in isolation but must be the fruit of an exercise of power as a shared responsibility[34] for the sake of achieving the consensus of all the faithful, including the pope and the bishops. *Dei Verbum* teaches that the deposit of the word of God has been entrusted to "the whole People of God, united to their pastors," who must "constitute a singular consensus" (*fidelium conspiratio*).[35]

This scenario places us before a moment of *ecclesiogenesis* that stimulates us to take a new ecclesiological turn: to go from the *collegial we* of the episcopate gathered in unity *cum Petro et sub Petro* to the *"ecclesial we*, in which each 'I,' being clothed with Christ (cf. *Gal* 3:27), lives and walks with the brothers and sisters as a responsible and active subject in the one mission of the People of God" (SLMC 60, 107). Therefore, the revision of episcopal collegiality—a great novelty of the council—in the perspective of a synodal collegiality—a contribution of the pontificate of Francis—must still advance toward a *synodal ecclesiality*, which requires a prior process of *reconfiguration of ecclesial identities and vocations* under the imprint of relational modalities of a binding character between the common priesthood of the faithful and the ministerial priesthood.

Pending Challenge:
The Recognition of the Laity as a Subject

The council offers, as a hermeneutical framework for thinking about joint dynamics based on the essential co-responsibility that springs from baptism, the equal participation of all in the common priesthood. We are not talking about a collaborative relationship,

---

[34] See Robert T. Kennedy, "Shared Responsibility in Ecclesial Decision Making," *Studia Canonica* 14 (1980): 5–23; Eugene Duffy, "Processes for Communal Discernment," *Jurist* 71 (2011): 77–90; Judith Gruber, "Consensus or Dissensus?," *Louvain Studies* 43 (2020): 239–59; Bradford E. Hinze, *Prophetic Obedience: Ecclesiology for a Dialogical Church* (Maryknoll, NY: Orbis, 2016).

[35] Second Vatican Council, Dogmatic Constitution on Divine Revelation *Dei Verbum*, November 18, 1965, 10, https://www.vatican.va/archive/hist_councils/ii_vatican_council/documents/vat-ii_const_19651118_dei-verbum_en.html.

as was proposed in the Extraordinary Synod of 1985[36] nor of co-operation as established in canon 129 n. 2 of the current Code of Canon Law. These contributions have made it possible to advance in the recognition of the laity without achieving it fully. Making Christocentrism the foundation of the ordained ministry has devalued baptism, emphasizing the ministerial priest as an *alter Christus* who can live his identity without a permanent and living bond with the Christian community.

Current canon law defines participation in terms of cooperation,[37] but, although canon 129 represents an important step, the reception of the council on this question cannot end there, for even the council fathers were not always clear about the implications of all that they proposed. A new hermeneutical perspective could start from the principle of *identity complementarity* based on the exercise of the *essential co-responsibility* of all the faithful—the *christifideles*. This would generate a process of *effective synodalization* of the church in the light of an ecclesial reconfiguration resulting from a more complete normative reception of the model of the church as the people of God, because "all that has been said about the People of God is addressed equally to laity, religious and clergy" (LG 30).[38]

The theological basis for this was already present in the first drafts of *Apostolicam Actuositatem*, which asserted that the common priesthood grants to all equally "the right, the honor and the charge to exercise in a proper way the apostolate of the Church."[39] Lay discipleship is presented as a proper way of exercising the common priesthood and of participating in the priesthood of

[36] See *Vatican II, Gift of God: The Documents of the Extraordinary Synod of 1985* (Madrid: PPC, 1986), esp.section 6, entitled "The Church as Communion."

[37] "The current law, in particular the issues expressed in canon 129, deals with questions concerning cooperation or participation. However, understanding lay and ordained ministry as being complementary to each other might lead to a new and fresh approach of understanding the cooperation between them." Myriam Wijlens, "Ecclesial Lay Ministry, Clergy and Complementarity," *CLSA Proceedings* 64 (2002): 39–40.

[38] See Gaudenzio Zamnon, "Riconoscimento reciproco di soggettività tra laici e ministri ordinati in ordine ad una forma sinodale di chiesa," in Riccardo Battocchio and Serena Noceti, eds., *Chiesa e sinodalità* (Milano: Glossa, 2007), 194.

[39] Schemata Constitutionum et Decretorum de quibus disceptabitur in Concilii Sessionibus. Schema Decreti De Apostolatu Laicorum, Typ. Polyg. Vat. 1963, 5.

Christ. This occurs, as the *textus prior* says, in different ways and to different degrees.[40] It is not a delegated or deficient condition. The use of the word *diversitas* from the *textus emendatus* of the decree *De apostolato laicorum* emphasizes an "essential" distinction to highlight the specificity of each ecclesial identity[41]: "diversity of ministries and unity of mission."[42] The laity is recognized as a subject living on equal footing with the hierarchy (LG 31), with a co-responsible participation in the mission of the church (SC 14), *suo modo et pro sua parte* (AA 29), through charity (*diakonia*) and preaching (*martyria*).[43] *Apostolicam Actuositatem* connects us with the logic of *universitas fidelium* and encompasses all the faithful—bishops, clergy, religious, laity—in complementary identity relationships, and the apostolate of the laity and the pastoral ministry are mutually completed or realized (AA 6).

We can, then, ask ourselves if, instead of reforming structures that are episcopal and auxiliary in nature, what is needed is to create other ecclesial and synodal structures in which the exercise of co-responsibility is essential, binding, and works through consensus-building. It is worth remembering the golden rule of St. Cyprian: *"Nihil sine consilio vestro et sine consensu plebis mea privatim sententia gerere"*: What affects all must be treated and approved by all.[44] For this bishop, taking counsel from the presbyterate and building consensus with the people were fundamental experiences throughout his episcopal exercise to maintain communion in the church. To this end, he was able to devise methods based on constant dialogue and common discernment, which

[40] Schema Decreti De Apostolatu Laicorum, Typ. Polyg. Vat. 1964, 6.

[41] Schema Decreti De Apostolatu Laicorum. Textus recognitus et modi a Patribus Conciliaribus propositi a Commissione de fidelium apostolatu examinati, Typ. Polyg. Vat. 1965, 23.

[42] Second Vatican Council, decree *Apostolicam Actuositatem*, November 18, 1965, 2, https://www.vatican.va/archive/hist_councils/ii_vatican_council/documents/vat-ii_decree_19651118_apostolicam-actuositatem_en.html. Hereafter cited as AA.

[43] See Peter De Mey, "Sharing in the Threefold Office of Christ: A Different Matter for Laity and Priests? The *tria munera* in *Lumen gentium, Presbyterorum ordinis, Apostolicam actuositatem* and *Ad gentes*," in Anne M. Mayer, ed., *The Letter and the Spirit: On the Forgotten Documents of Vatican II* (Leuven: Peeters, 2018), 155–79.

[44] "Quando a primordio episcopatus mei statuerim, nihil sine consilio vestro, et sine consensu plebis, mea privatim, sententia gerere." Jacques Paul Migne, *Patrologiae Latina*, Tomus 4 (S. Cypriani), 234.

made possible the participation of all, and not only of the presbyters, in deliberation and decision-making.

One way could be the renewal of the meaning and functioning of the various existing councils—pastoral, presbyteral, economic. Another could be parish assemblies, meetings between various pastoral zones, and diocesan assemblies. There are proposals of the council that were not incorporated in the Code of Canon Law—for example, the council of the laity, as it appears in *Apostolicam Actuositatem* 26, in which clergy, religious, and laity are to work together at all levels—parish, diocesan, national, and international. There are also pastoral experiences such as the *collaborative ministry* in the Anglo-Saxon world and the *pastoral teams* in France and Italy. It would be necessary to rethink them starting from the theology of *sensus fidei* and *consensus omnium fidelium*. The problem may lie in the willingness to overcome "insufficient consideration of the *sensus fidelium*, the concentration of power and the isolated exercise of authority, a centralized and discretionary style of governance, and the opacity of regulatory procedures."[45]

In addition, it is essential to reflect on the actors that sustain ecclesial structures. The type of people—diversity of gender, experience, formation, origin, culture—is decisive because it shapes the practices of relationship and communication in which listening, discernment, and consensus-building take place.[46] It is time for women to participate more fully in the church, not only where decisions are made but also where they are implemented. Finally, the recognition of the laity as a subject is essential to build a synodal ecclesiality, and the hierarchy is called to create concrete mediations "by recourse to the participatory bodies provided for by the law, without excluding other methods that they deem appropriate" (EC, canonical disposition n. 6).

---

[45] Alphonse Borras, "Sinodalità ecclesiale, processi partecipati e modalità decisionali," in Carlos Maria Galli and Antonio Spadaro, eds., *La riforma e le riforme nella Chiesa* (Brescia: Queriniana, 2016), 208.

[46] "It does not depend simply and first of all on the good functioning of the various organisms or on simple criteria of democratic participation, such as the criterion of the majority, but requires from its members an ecclesial awareness, a style of fraternal communication, which translates communion and the common convergence on a project of the Church." Antonio Lanfranchi, "Prassi spirituale del discernimento comunitario," in Battocchio and Noceti, *Chiesa e sinodalità*, 194.

The Missing Link:
Sensus Fidei and *Consensus Omnium Fidelium*

To conclude this reflection, we should ask ourselves "whether the deepening of the collegiality of the bishops in the Synod of Bishops should be linked to the obligation to work collaboratively with theologians and in a consultative way with lay women and men, representing the whole People of God in the various phases of the synodal process,"[47] or whether an effective synodalization of the church must transcend this model. It will be necessary to develop *decision-making* and communicative modalities that are binding on the elaboration of the decisions of the pastors (*decision-taking*) and, in particular, new ecclesial ways of proceeding and structures of shared decision-making power in the church.[48] The Latin American bishops gathered at the Aparecida Conference in 2007 asked that "the laity participate in discernment, decision-making, planning and execution."[49] If they do not do so, how can we achieve "the unique consensus of all the faithful" (*Dei Verbum* 10)?

If synodality is a constitutive dimension of the church as the people of God (see SLMC 42), it is more than a method and a synod. It invites us to recognize that the binding character between the *sensus fidei* and the *consensus omnium fidelium* is transversal to the whole institution; it is not the people of God that must be integrated into the hierarchy by participating in episcopal structures—synod or episcopal conferences—but the hierarchy that must place itself among the faithful within the people of God, listening to the voice of all the faithful,[50] because the bishop must gather and express the *sensus ecclesiae totius populi* and not only

[47] Bradford Hinze, *Practices of Dialogue in the Roman Catholic Church: Aims and Obstacles, Lessons and Laments* (New York: Continuum, 2006), 177.

[48] See Rafael Luciani, "Lo que afecta a todos debe ser tratado y aprobado por todos: Hacia estructuras de participación y poder de decisión compartido," *CLAR Magazine* 63, no. 1 (2020): 59–66.

[49] Consejo Episcopal Latinoamericano (CELAM), *V General Conference of the Bishops of Latin America and the Caribbean, Concluding Document, Aparecida* (Bogotá: CELAM, 2007), 371.

[50] Émile-Joseph De Smedt, *The Priesthood of the Faithful* (New York: Paulist Press, 1962), 89–90.

that of his peers, as the one responsible for communion. An emerging model and unique experience in this regard is the new model of the Ecclesial Assembly for Latin America and the Caribbean created by CELAM (Latin American Episcopal Council).[51]

Francis has said that "a synodal Church is a Church of listening," so that the act of listening defines the process of ecclesial life. It is about "a reciprocal listening in which each one has something to learn," that is, "faithful people, episcopal college, Bishop of Rome: one in listening to the others; and all in listening to the Holy Spirit, the Spirit of truth (*Jn* 14:17), in order to know what he says to the Churches (*Rev* 2:7)."[52] Therefore, the recovery of the *sensus fidei*[53] plays a normative role. This is the novelty of *Lumen Gentium* 12 when it teaches that "the totality of the faithful, who have the anointing of the Holy One (cf. 1 *Jn* 2:20 and 27), cannot err when they believe, and this peculiar prerogative of theirs is manifested by the supernatural sense of the faith of the whole people when "from the Bishops down to the last of the lay faithful" they give their universal assent in things of faith and morals" (LG 12).

This assumption implies, therefore, the personal involvement of the bishop, because the *sensus fidei* proper to each baptized person empowered by the Spirit is discerned and realized within the framework of the *sensus fidelium*, that is, in the interaction of the baptized as a whole in pursuit of the *consensus fidelium*. And the faithful must participate in joint discernment, as the International Theological Commission warns: "The whole community, in the free and rich diversity of its members, is called together to pray, listen, analyze, dialogue and advise so that the pastoral decisions most in conformity with God's will may be made" (SLMC 68). This discernment as a whole is the act of the faithful most proper to the church, because discernment is not only done in the church, but it *makes the church*.[54]

---

[51] See https://asambleaeclesial.lat.

[52] Pope Francis, "Ceremony Commemorating the 50th Anniversary of the Institution of the Synod of Bishops," October 17, 2015, http://w2.vatican.va/content/francesco/en/speeches/2015/october/documents/papa-francesco_20151017_50-anniversario-sinodo.html.

[53] See Burkhard, "*Sensus fidei*," 18–34; Dario Vitali, *Lumen Gentium: Storia, Commento, Recezione* (Rome: Studium, 2012), 67.

[54] Alphonse Borras, "*Votum tantum consultivum*: Les limites ecclésiologiques d'une formule canonique," *Didaskalia* 45 (2015): 161.

We can conclude with the words of the International Theological Commission, which has clearly expressed that "the synodal dimension of the Church must be expressed through the realization and governance of processes of participation and discernment capable of manifesting the dynamism of communion that inspires all ecclesial decisions" (SLMC 76), because "what affects all must be dealt with and approved by all."[55] For all that has been said in this essay, the synodalization of the whole church is the great challenge of this third millennium.

---

[55] See Yves Congar, "Quod omnes tangit ab omnibus tractari et opprobari debet," *Revue historique de droit français et étranger* 36 (1958): 210–59.

Reforming the Church in the Era of Synodality

Bishop Vincent Long, OFMConv

The clerical sexual abuse crisis has devastated the church in Australia and many other countries around the globe, but it has also made sure that we cannot go on the way we have. We must humbly and boldly address the biggest challenge of our time and build a healthier church for future generations. This disruption calls for deep discernment and courageous action rather than fear, intransigence, and defense of status quo. Like the ancient disruption of the biblical exile, this unprecedented crisis can catalyse the church into a new era of hope and possibility. The matrix of brokenness can become the venue for a revitalised future.

> I am about to do a new thing;
>> now it springs forth, do you not perceive it?
> I will make a way in the wilderness
>> and rivers in the desert. (Isa 43:19)

These words of the prophet are an extraordinarily prophetic utterance in the midst of profound disruption in Israel's history. The capture of Jerusalem, the destruction of the temple, and the exile that followed constituted the worst crisis that the people of God had faced. But the astonishing reality of the ancient disruption was that the matrix of brokenness became the venue for new possibility. Against the background of loss and hopelessness, of utter humiliation and vulnerability, Isaiah speaks of the new things that summon the people to a life-transforming future.

Isaiah's prophecy enlightens and challenges us as we seek to understand and to live the meaning of our faith experience in the church and in the world. In so many ways, we feel like the Jewish exiles facing the monumental task of rebuilding from the ground up after the devastation of the clerical sexual abuse crisis, which was a symptom of deeper malaise of clericalism and the ecclesial culture in which it festered. We are witnessing the passing of the old and the emergence of the new in our own time.

Like Israel before the exile, the institutional church has failed to be a place of promise and freedom, of covenanted communion and solidarity. It has not fully lived out the radical vision of powerlessness of the Servant Lord. Its dysfunctional and destructive culture of clericalism has betrayed the Gospel. There is a sense in which the church must change into a more Christlike pattern of humility, simplicity, and powerlessness, as opposed to worldly triumphalism, splendour, dominance, and power which were often the manifestations of the preconciliar Catholicism.

In view of the devastating child sexual abuse crisis, we Catholics are adrift like the Jews in the great exile. The future of the church, like the new Jerusalem that Isaiah speaks of, will not be revitalized by way of simply repeating what was done in the past. It will not be simply a restoration project or doing the old things better. Rather, we must have the courage to do new things; we must be open to the Spirit leading us to new horizons even as we tend to revert to the old ways.

Discerning and Enacting God's New Direction

There is a need for deep discernment and courage to embrace God's new direction. The experience of darkness, fragility, and loss provides us with an opportunity for necessary change, conversion, and transformation. It is characteristic of true believers to embrace the newness that the Holy Spirit awakens in and through crisis.

In *The Wizard of Oz*, Dorothy wakes up to find that she is no longer in her safe, comfortable, and familiar Kansas hometown but in the topsy-turvy land of Oz. We Catholics need to wake up to the reality that the church is no longer in the safe harbor of Christendom or any semblance of it. Instead, we are in this uncharted territory of the new Babylon. The church is in this liminal space between the death of the old comfort zone and the emergence of the new reality, which we must come to terms with.

In fact, in the wake of the Royal Commission,[1] the church in Australia finds itself in a kind of a perfect storm: the sexual abuse crisis, the near total collapse of active participation of the laity in the life of the church, a loss of credibility of the church in public life, a shrinking pool of clerical leadership, and more. Yet, like Israel, we must seek fresh ways of embodying God's redeeming, forgiving, and empowering love. The church must not lose sight of the invitation to embark on a new adventure with God as he helps us to step out of the old and into the new. What is indisputable is the need for deep institutional change that will restore confidence and trust in the church. Nothing less than a root-and-branch reform that aligns our minds and hearts to the Gospel will do.

Despite our resistance to change, we will need to let go of the old paradigms in order to truly see the reality and hope that God is a work in the church today. This liminal space challenges our sense of security, continuity, and predictability. It is our openness and humility that allow us to recognize moments of divine rupture at the critical juncture in history.

We are called to be a blessing for the church and the world by the measure of our authentic witness. This authenticity lies in our courage to be the voice of the minority and the conscience of the outsiders to the totalizing system. We are called to be like the prophets of old who have the burning passion, urgency, discomfort, and the itch to speak God's alternate vision for humanity. Now we need to embody that vision in living as contrast communities, avoiding cultural accommodation and demonstrating a different way to be a society.

---

[1] See Royal Commission into Institutional Responses to Child Sexual Abuse, childabuseroyalcommission.gov.au.

Pope Francis has stated that the crisis caused by the COVID-19 pandemic is a propitious time to find the courage for *a new imagination of the possible*, with the realism that only the Gospel can offer us.[2] He has applied the art of prophetic reframing and challenged humanity to a new level of existential consciousness. For Pope Francis, understanding what God is saying to us at this time of pandemic also represents a challenge for the church's mission. It is also clear that we must first understand what we have done wrong.

And what we have done wrong in the sociopolitical sphere is to embrace the narrow paradigm of self-interest. The COVID-19 crisis, the Pope says, has exposed our vulnerability. It has revealed the fallacy of individualism as the organizing principle of our Western society.[3] It has given the lie to a myth of self-sufficiency that sanctions rampant inequalities and frays the ties that bind societies together. If we want a different world, we must become a different people.

In the light of this systemic flaw, we are not called simply "to restart" in order to return to the normality of a golden age that in reality never was golden. The narratives of the restart are harmful, because they naturally tend to restore balances and systemic injustices that must change. We cannot continue to maintain the status quo when it undermines the planet's sustainability. We need a new beginning.

The church, too, is at a point at which a courageous reframing in the way of the prophets must be articulated. What the church needs is not simply a renewal or an updating of methods of evangelizing. Rather we desperately need an inner conversion, a radical revolution in our mindsets and patterns of action.

The narrative of reevangelization, or new evangelization, is problematic when it glosses over the deficiencies of the old model of church and fails to acknowledge the fundamental structures

---

[2] See Antonio Spadaro, SJ, " 'A New Imagination of the Possible': Seven Images from Francis for Post-Covid-19," *La Civiltà Cattolica*, July 14, 2020, https://www.laciviltacattolica.com/a-new-imagination-of-the-possible-seven-images-from-francis-for-post-covid-19/.

[3] See especially Pope Francis, *Let Us Dream: The Path to a Better Future* (New York: Simon and Schuster, 2020).

and ecclesiological underpinnings that need to change. Until we have the courage to acknowledge the old ways of being church, which were steeped in a culture of clerical power, dominance, and privilege, we cannot rise to a Christlike way of humility, inclusivity, compassion, and powerlessness. As the prophets reimagined the faith tradition with fresh insights distilled from lived experience, we, too, need to put new flesh on the marrow of the Gospel for the people of our time.

The church in Australia is committed to charting a new way forward through the Plenary Council 2022. The time has come for us not only to admit the need for change but to discern together what the process and the agenda for change should look like. Pope Francis said poignantly that we are not living in an era of change but the change of an era. In other words, what we need is the cultural shift and the conversion of minds and hearts to be a truly humble, listening, inclusive, and synodal church. We don't just need to do the old things better. Carrying on former practices, agendas, and priorities, without acknowledging the need to change course, can be at best futile and at worst defiant against the movement of the Holy Spirit.

Some years ago, before the pontificate of Pope Francis, there was a phenomenon called restorationism. It was a movement toward a "reform of the reform" of Vatican II by bringing traditionalist approaches to liturgy and governance of parish life. Young clergy attempted to reintroduce clerical garb, vestments, music, and other elements that have their roots in practices preceding the Second Vatican Council.

I was in Rome for the Year for Priests in 2010, and I witnessed a manifestation of this restorationist movement. The streets of Rome were filled with young priests dressed up in every clerical attire and headwear that one could imagine. Do we need this type of renewal or something more substantive? I suspect Pope Francis has a different idea when he speaks of the need for the church to undergo a change of era. Perhaps it is more like a paschal process that involves dying and rising. Unless we genuinely repent of institutional failures and convert to the radical vision of Christ and let it imbue our attitudes, actions, and pastoral practices, we will not be able to restore confidence and trust in the church.

Furthermore, few Catholics have any appetite left for cosmetic changes, mediocrity, or worse, restorationism dressed up as renewal. We have struggled under the weight of the old ecclesial paradigm of clerical order, control, and hegemony with a penchant for triumphalism, self-referential pomp, and smugness. We yearn for a church that commits to a God-oriented future of equal discipleship, relational harmony, wholeness, and sustainability.

We must humbly and boldly address the biggest challenge of our time and build a healthier church for future generations. This disruption calls for deep discernment and courageous action rather than fear, intransigence, and defense of the status quo. Like the ancient disruption, this unprecedented crisis can catalyse the church into a new era of hope and possibility. Out of our "ground zero," like a phoenix the church can rise again with new life from the ashes.

Emerging Paradigms, New Wineskins

Many Catholics hope that the various synodal exercises around the world will bring changes in a number of issues, such as greater inclusion of the laity, the role of women, clerical celibacy, and more. While it is important that there is an openness and boldness to discuss these matters, what is more important is to envision a new way of being church in the world.

The model of the church based on clerical hegemony has run its course. Insofar as it is deeply embedded in patriarchal and monarchical structures, it is incapable of helping us to meet the needs of the world and the culture in which we live. We have long moved out of the *ancien régime* and the age of absolute monarchs. We are on this side of the secular state and the rise of democracy. Yet it seems that the deeply entrenched patriarchal and monarchical structures of the church have failed to correspond with our lived experience.

For the church to flourish, it is crucial that we come to terms with the flaws of clericalism and move beyond its patriarchal and monarchical matrix. What is urgent is that we need to find fresh ways of being church and fresh ways of ministry and service for both men and women disciples. New wine into new wineskins! The new wine of God's unconditional love, radical inclusivity, and equality needs to be poured into new wineskins of humility, mutuality, compassion, and powerlessness. The old wineskins of triumphalism, authoritarianism, and supremacy, abetted by clerical power, superiority, and rigidity are breaking.

The church cannot have a better future if it persists in the old paradigm of triumphalism, self-reference, and male dominance. So long as we continue to exclude women from the church's governance structures, decision-making processes, and institutional functions, we deprive ourselves of the richness of our full humanity. So long as we continue to make women invisible and inferior in the church's language, liturgy, theology, and law, we impoverish ourselves. Until we have truly incorporated the gift of women and the feminine dimension of our Christian faith, we will not be able to fully energize the life of the church.

The church cannot have a better future if it does not break with those old wineskins. In the world where the rules are made by the strong and the structures of power favor the privileged, the church must be true to its founding stories and responsive to the living presence of God. It must find ways to promote a community of equals and empower men and women disciples to share their gifts for human flourishing and the growth of the Kingdom.

Our founding stories are those of emancipation and liberation. It is the story of Moses and the movement of the new social order against the tyranny of empires that lies at the heart of the prophetic imagination. It inspires Mary who sings of the God who overthrows the powerful and lifts up the lowly. It is the story of Jesus who washes the feet of his followers and subverts the power structures that are tilted toward the strong. This narrative of the new reality that envisions radical reordering of human relationships was in fact the hallmark of the earliest Christian movement. When they understood themselves as constituting *ekklesia*, they perceived themselves as being equal in the household of God, regardless of their background in civil society.

The church must continue to embrace the alternative relational paradigm that Jesus exemplified and the early Christian community embodied as antidote to imperial domination. This alternative relational paradigm turns the world's system of power structures on its head because it is rooted in the biblical narrative of the new social order of radical inclusion, justice, and equality. The church cannot have a prophetic voice in society if we fail to be the model egalitarian community where those disadvantaged on account of their race, gender, social status, and disability find empowerment for a dignified life.

Toward the Church of Co-Responsibility and Synodality

Martin Luther King Jr. famously said that the arc of history bends toward justice. The parallel statement I want to make is that the arc of the church's history bends toward greater communion, participation, and mission through baptismal co-responsibility and synodality. Let me explain.

The best of the Judeo-Christian tradition has framed the church along the lines of a model egalitarian community, promoting the equal dignity and mission of its members over against the dehumanizing influence of the world's powers that be. As an alternative relational paradigm, it witnesses to the radical communion, inclusivity, and solidarity that have been the distinguishing features of both the Jewish covenant community and the early church.

The way of being church, however, has evolved over the centuries. When, after the early centuries of persecution, Christianity became the official religion of the Roman Empire, the early tradition of egalitarianism gave way to a more clerical and hierarchical governance system that took on many features of the empire. Throughout the long reign of Christendom and up to the Second Vatican Council, the church was often confronted by its human failings but yet still referred to itself as a perfect society. Its institutional functions and dynamics were steeped in clericalism.

The ecclesial internal ordering was largely dictated by ordination, with the laity often restricted to auxiliary roles. This model, which promotes the superiority of the ordained and an excessive emphasis on the role of the clergy at the expense of the nonordained, is at the very root of the culture of clericalism. The crisis we face is closely linked with a crisis of this particular paradigm of being church.

At the Second Vatican Council, there was a shift in the church's self-understanding. The dominant metaphor of a *societas perfecta* gave way to a more biblical image of a pilgrim people. The role of the lay faithful was highlighted along with the affirmation that the working of the Holy Spirit was granted not only to the ordained but to all baptized.

The council also spoke of episcopal collegiality in regard to the function and role of the bishops. Collegiality needed affirmation in the wake of the rather one-sided promulgation of papal primacy and infallibility a century earlier at Vatican I. Thus there was a new balance between papal power and the episcopacy.

How do we move from the highly centralized vision of the church as understood throughout much of the history of Christendom to an ecclesiology of the people of God as articulated by the Second Vatican Council? The shift from papal centralism to episcopal collegiality was significant enough. But what does a synodal church look like when, up to now, the ecclesial mechanisms for synodality have been largely cleric-centered and male-dominated?

The reforms since the council include the establishment of such bodies as national bishops' conferences and synods. The latter, even those convened by Pope Francis, largely enhance the function of collegiality. The Australian Plenary Council is no exception, and we now face the task of developing new forms of lay participation and engagement in collaboration with priests and bishops.

The idea of synodality and co-responsibility means that all members should be given equal voice and opportunity as we walk together. But modern synodality is grafted onto the old clerical and hierarchical church where power and authority are vested in the ordained. The process of "walking together" can be fraught with challenges when it comes to decision-making and good outcomes. Our Australian experience of the Plenary Council has illustrated these challenges. Many feel that at crucial points, the process is controlled by those with power.

Synodality is an ancient concept in the life of the church, which has been given new emphasis and vitality through the pontificate of Pope Francis. Though missing from the documents of Vatican II, it authentically translates and summarizes the ecclesiology of communion expressed by the council.

Thus a synodal church is one that engages the whole people of God in the process of discernment that guides its mission of proclaiming the Gospel. Never an elite process, it involves all the baptized, whatever their position in the church or their level of instruction in the faith. For the pope, it would be insufficient to envisage a plan of evangelization that would be carried out by professionals while the lay faithful were simply passive recipients.

Understood in a larger framework of what the church is and how it achieves its mission, synodality is much more than an expanded exercise of collegiality. It necessarily requires a whole-of-church approach. Synodality necessarily invites the participation of all the faithful in discernment and decision-making processes.

Hence, the pope often speaks of an inverted pyramid, which is a radical way of exercising power and authority. It is not a top-down and centralized approach, reminiscent of the monarchical model. Rather, it is a synodal church at every level, with everyone listening to each other, learning from each other, and taking responsibility for proclaiming the Gospel.

The synodal church, by its very nature, embraces participation by all the people of God. It invites believers to active engagement in the church and in the world. Whereas clericalism disempowers the faithful and distorts effective patterns of decision-making in ecclesial communities, a synodal process seeks to promote a church of co-responsibility and participation. This will not lessen but strengthen the role of the ordained for the good of the church.

With Pope Francis, synodality has evolved beyond collegiality to include the totality of the church. He has engaged an ecclesiological gear shift with regard to the understanding of revelation and the transmission of the faith. Since the Council of Trent, revelation was understood as a transmission of the faith in a hierarchically ordered way through the pope, bishops, and priests. The laity were recipients of the faith, often through a series of propositions, rather than active participants.

Vatican II, however, taught that revelation occurs within the whole people of God and that the working of the Holy Spirit is granted not only to the ordained but to all the faithful. *Dei Verbum*, for example, presents revelation in terms of God inviting men and women into fellowship with him. Instead of a package of set doctrines about God, it speaks of the Holy Spirit bringing believers into deeper understanding of revelation.

This rich trinitarian understanding of revelation implies that there is a need for mutual obedience and respect of laity and hierarchy and, even more importantly, that a participation of all the faithful is required for discerning the voice of the Holy Spirit. In other words, if revelation occurs within the whole church and not only through the ordained, then it requires the reconfiguration of the protagonists and the cooperation among all the people of God from the laity to the pope.

Pope Francis affirms the importance of the *sensus fidei* in *Evangelii Gaudium*: "All the baptized, whatever their position in the Church or their level of instruction in the faith, are agents of evangelization, and it would be insufficient to envisage a plan of evangelization to be carried out by professionals while the rest of the faithful would be simply passive recipient."[4] The *sensus fidei* renders the dichotomy of the teaching church and learning church inadequate. A synodal church is a church that listens, and the listening is not one-dimensional or linear, but mutual, because everyone (including bishops and the pope) has something to learn.

In fact, the traditional distinction between the hierarchy as teachers and the laity as believers can now be inverted. The teachers can learn as much as the learners can also teach. In his address to the 2015 synod on the family, Pope Francis stated, "The *sensus fidei* prevents a rigid separation between an *Ecclesia docens* and an *Ecclesia discens*, since the flock likewise has an instinctive ability to discern the new ways that the Lord is revealing to the Church."[5] Pope Francis went on to consider how this affects the understanding and practice of the Petrine ministry. The pope, he said, isn't above the church, but very much part of it. Therefore, as the church becomes more synodal, the papacy itself will change—not in essence but in the way it's exercised.

Sixty years after Vatican II, Pope Francis gave new expression of the church as the people of God by expanding the understanding of the relationship between the pope and bishops. Primacy and collegiality are now located within the people of God. Collegiality is located within the context of synodality. The hierarchy is understood as standing in service to God, to the church, and thus to the people of God. This leads him to say that synodality

---

[4] Pope Francis, apostolic exhortation *Evangelii Gaudium* (November 24, 2014), 120, https://www.vatican.va/content/francesco/en/apost_exhortations/documents/papa-francesco_esortazione-ap_20131124_evangelii-gaudium.html.
[5] Pope Francis, "Ceremony Commemorating the 50th Anniversary."

is an expression of the church understood as a journeying together of God's flock, each according to his or her task.

Conclusion

The church has entered a new era that is characterized by a crisis of a top-down centralized ecclesiology. With Vatican II, the *ressourcement* and *aggiornamento* led to a more biblical paradigm of a pilgrim people of God, called to be the sacrament of the Kingdom and the prophetic witness in the world. The emphasis on the superiority of the ordained gave way to an ecclesial communion based on common baptism.

Pope Francis took a step further with regard to the interpretation of the ecclesiology of the people of God. He expanded the notion of a collegial discernment to involve all of the baptized. Collegiality is at the service of synodality and therefore it must give voice to the entire people of God.

As the adage goes, the church is always in need of reform (*ecclesia semper reformanda*). What has transpired throughout history is the constant renewal and reimagination of the Gospel imperative through the signs of the times. Maybe we still have a long way to go in understanding this deep reform of our institutional existence as followers of Jesus gathered in the church. Synodality has emerged as a fresh way to reimagine the future of Christianity.

Synodality requires that all voices be heard. A view of synodality that fails the test of reforming the church in light of the abuse crisis is very problematic. This is why the future of ecclesial synodality is much more in the peripheries than in the synod hall at the Vatican. As the synodal church evolves, we need to address the issue of equity in ecclesial structures and frameworks in order to promote the culture of discernment, consensus, and decision making.

Pope Francis has applied a critical lens through which the church is renewed for the sake of its mission for the poor. The church is helped to decentralize and impelled toward the peripheries. The church, the people of God, should walk together, sharing the burdens of humanity, listening to the cry of the poor, reforming itself and its own action, first by listening to the voice of the humble, the *anawim* of the Hebrew Scriptures, who were at the heart of Jesus' public ministry.

Pope Francis's decisive embrace of the ecclesiology of the Second Vatican Council and particularly his resetting of the *sensus fidei* have given the new lease of life to the church and its mission. A synodal journey can be messy, painful, and uncertain. But it can lead to renewed and deepened commitment and even transformation. The various synodal exercises around the world, including our own Australian Plenary Council, were marked by disruption, chaos, and drama, but also by a deep sense of dialogue for the common good or *parrhesia*.

In the end, what was invigorating about them was not only the documents that they produced or the decisions that were made. Rather, it was the journey of synodality that energized the church. As far as I am concerned, it is the unleashing of the energy long locked up beneath the ice of institutional security that truly matters. The energy that had been trapped in a rigid control is being released by boldness, freedom, and frankness.

The Australian Plenary Council was an act of enormous trust, or perhaps in betting terms, a massive gamble. It was an Abrahamic journey from the start. We gambled on the invitation of Pope Francis to be the people of God, walking together, sharing the burdens of humanity, listening to the voice of the most marginalized, reforming its structures and ways of doing things. We did not set out to resolve every question of importance. For instance, on matters of sex and gender, there was very little on the agenda. The acceptance of LGBTQI+ as the reference to nonbinary brothers and sisters was perhaps not a small consensus among the members.

In the end, the significance of this synodal exercise was much more than what was decided. What was highly symbolic and paradigm-shifting was the fact that we met as a community of equals. The emphasis on the superiority of the ordained gave way to an ecclesial communion based on common baptism. Bishops, priests, religious, and laity were all addressed by our first names. No one's voice counted more than another's. There was a profound sense of being together and working together even if we have distinct roles in the church.

Ultimately, the plenary council was not merely an event but a process and a template for a new way of being church going forward. One hopes that embracing an ecclesiology of the people of God that nurtures a more dialogical, ecumenical, interfaith, ecological, and indeed cosmological reimagination, we can rise to become a more fit-for-purpose church and vehicle of the Gospel for humanity and all creation.

Problems and Prospects of Synodality and Church Reform in India

Francis Gonsalves, SJ

Introduction:
The Need for Listening and Journeying Together

Since its birth, the church has nurtured a spirit of genuine collegiality and synodality led by God's Spirit. The Council of Jerusalem (see Acts 15) is a prototype of a synodal way of functioning characterizing early Christianity.[1] There have sometimes been conflicts with popes, leading to the conciliarists, for example, contesting papal authority.[2] Yet, the word *synod* gained currency in the light of Vatican II's *aggiornamento* ("updating"), with Pope Paul VI outlining synodal principles in *Apostolica Sollicitudo*. Now, in convoking the XVI General Assembly of the Synod of Bishops in 2023, entitled "For a Synodal Church: Communion, Participation and Mission," Pope Francis calls and challenges Christians to proclaim more fully the joy of the Gospel of Jesus Christ.

---

[1] See John E. Lynch, "Co-Responsibility in the First Five Centuries: Presbyteral Colleges and the Election of Bishops," in *Who Decides for the Church? Studies in Co-Responsibility*, ed. J. A. Coriden (Hartford: The Canon Law Society of America, 1971), 14–53.

[2] See Brian Tierney, *Foundations of the Conciliar Theory: The Contribution of the Medieval Canonists from Gratian to the Great Schism* (Cambridge: Cambridge University Press, 1955), 179–98.

In his address at the ceremony commemorating the fiftieth anniversary of the institution of the Synod of Bishops, Pope Francis said, "From the beginning of my ministry as Bishop of Rome, I sought to enhance the Synod, which is one of the most precious legacies of the Second Vatican Council." He added, "It is precisely this path of synodality which God expects of the Church of the third millennium." Pope Francis stresses the importance of listening for a synodal church: "A synodal Church is a Church which *listens*, which realizes that *listening* is more than simply hearing. It is a mutual *listening* in which everyone has something to learn. The faithful people, the college of bishops, the Bishop of Rome: all *listening* to each other, and all *listening* to the Holy Spirit, the 'Spirit of truth' (Jn 14:17), in order to know what he 'says to the Churches' (Rev 2:7)."[3]

In this chapter, I will assess synodality and reform in the church in India. As a framework, I first map the religious landscape in India to see how religions function therein. Then I shall examine some of the problems and prospects of synodal functioning, which might help to achieve the "journeying together," the synodality, that Pope Francis envisages.

The "Little Flock" of Christians in the Religious Landscape of India

Let us look at the religious scenario of India, in general, to see how the ideals of dharma, religion, democracy, power-sharing, co-responsibility, and participation work in practice rather than in theory. By so doing, we will see how the macro, national, religio-socio-political setup influences the functioning of micro communities—one of which is the Catholic Church in India, comprising three *sui iuris* Churches: Latin, Syro-Malabar, and Syro-Malankara—of Indian Christians of diverse backgrounds, regions, classes, castes, and languages.

---

[3] Pope Francis, "Ceremony Commemorating the 50th Anniversary of the Institution of the Synod of Bishops," October 17, 2015, http://w2.vatican.va/content /francesco/en/speeches/2015/october/documents/papa-francesco_20151017_50 -anniversario-sinodo.html (my emphasis).

The inseparable marriage of the secular and the sacred

India is a democratic republic with a unique secular character. While many countries of the West maintain a strict separation between the secular (political) and sacred (religious) realms, this is not possible in India, since religion encompasses every sphere of life. Realizing this, freedom fighters like Gandhi, Ambedkar, and Nehru sought to harmonize religion and politics. Nehru strove to divorce religion from politics and keep the state neutral toward all forms of religion (*dharma nirpekshata*), while Gandhi intended that all religions be treated with equal respect (*sarva dharma samābhava*) within a traditional, caste-Hindu framework. Differing from Gandhi, Ambedkar critiqued Hinduism—especially the caste system[4]—and led many Hindus of the so-called "backward castes" to reject Hinduism and convert to Buddhism.

Today, Indian secularism is a hotly debated issue with some politicians and their political parties accusing others of pampering religious minorities—mainly Muslims and Christians—with allegations of appeasement of minorities, pseudosecularism, and so on. In sum, religion and politics are handy tools for those with vested interests to exploit others whenever needed.

The rise of conflicting nationalisms: Indian and Hindutva

Linked to the inseparability of politics and religion is the question of Indian nationalism. Today, those in power arbitrarily label some Indians as unpatriotic, aliens, antinational, and so on, and stake claims to own this multilingual, multicultural, multiethnic, and multireligious nation-state. We distinguish between "nation" (cultural entity) and "state" (political entity).[5] India is "nation" to 1.38 billion citizens of diverse cultures, creeds, classes, and castes; as a "state," India is governed by its constitution, which seeks to give all citizens certain rights based on principles of equity, fair-

[4] See, for instance, B. R. Ambedkar, *Annihilation of Caste: With a Reply to 'Mahatma' Gandhi* (Bangalore: Dalit Sahitya Akademi, 1987), for his scathing critique of caste and his debates with Gandhi.

[5] See T. K. Oommen, *State and Society in India: Studies in Nation-Building* (New Delhi: Sage Publications, 1990), 12, 31–42, for further clarifications with regard to nation, state, and ethnicity.

ness, and justice. Thus, the constitution guarantees Christians "minority rights" to help promote their religion and community interests.[6]

In India, especially over the past three decades or so, the borders of the state are being blurred with issues of nation and nationalism. This has created confrontations between those who endorse a particular brand of nationalism called *Hindutva* and those excluded from it.[7] The main aim of Hindutva is to establish a Hindu nation with caste-based structures. In striving to build a *Hindu Rashtra*, the ideologues of Hindutva brazenly defy constitutional guarantees by taking the law into their own hands on highly sensitive issues like *gau-rakshan* (cow protection), construction of the Ram Mandir temple, religious conversions, and *ghar-vapasi* (literally "homecoming," referring to forcible conversions of Muslims and Christians to Hinduism). In the face of such "Hinduization" of India, the Christian minority feels threatened and tends to withdraw into its own ghettos, thereby limiting its contribution to the cause of constructing a vibrant India.

The democratization of religion as defiance of caste hierarchism

The mixing of religion with politics and the rapid growth of Hindutva has given rise to new forms of religious practices. For example, first, attempts are being made to retain power among the so-called "upper castes" by enforcing elite practices like revival of the study of Sanskrit and astrology, recital of Gayatri mantra, and installation of Hindu idols in schools, making yoga compulsory, propagating cow-protection, and so on. Second, on the one hand, there is a devious attempt at "assimilation" of some members of the so-called "lower castes" into the majority religion to

---

[6] In terms of numbers, Hindus account for 79.8 percent, Muslims for 14.23 percent, and Christians for 2.3 percent of the total population. The number of Christians in India is approximately 27 million, with Catholics accounting for over 20 million. Apart from the major religions, there are many other smaller religious traditions: popular, folk, and bhakti traditions with many followers.

[7] *Hindutva* is not synonymous with Hinduism. The former refers to a militant brand of Hinduism aggressively propagated by the Hindu right, the latter to the normal practice of Hinduism. See V. D. Savarkar, *Hindutva* (Bombay: Veer Savarkar Prakashan, 1969).

peddle the lie that everyone is equal in society, while, on the other hand, aggressive alienation and violence is unleashed on the religious minorities and those who resist assimilation.[8] Third, having suffered violence for centuries, the Dalits, Adivasis, and women are now asserting themselves,[9] organizing themselves into movements, demanding their rights, converting to other religions, and even taking up arms to defend themselves.

As an outcome of the avatars that religion is assuming, we have today what can be called a "democratization of religion." Formerly, most religions were practiced within a hierarchical, pyramidal structure with a small clerical-priestly class in the upper strata enjoying maximum powers, since they officiated in "sacred services," while those at the bottom were passive "recipients" of these. Now, through the democratization of religion, power is more widely enjoyed among believers. This implies that many more common people assume leadership, wield authority, interpret scriptures, mediate cultic practices, assume prophetic-priestly roles, and determine religious policies.

The democratization of religion has been catalyzed by globalization, the infotech revolution, and processes of the Indian state, for example, by institutions like the Supreme Court and Parliament reforming unjust socioreligious practices like untouchability, the dowry system, triple talaq (instant divorce), exploitation of women, and so on.[10] Consequently, more commoners wield great power in the religiopolitical realm. For instance, the chief minister of the Indian state of Uttar Pradesh, Yogi Adityanand, and yogi-entrepreneur Baba Ramdev are immensely influential, as is the semiliterate Dalit Mata Amritanandamayi, the "Hugging Amma" who has a large global following.

[8] See John Dayal and Shabnam Hashmi, eds., *365 Days: Democracy & Secularism under the Modi Regime* (Delhi: Anhad, 2015), for details of many cases of violence and for understanding the causes.

[9] Dalits—literally meaning "broken ones"—refers to the former untouchables, and Adivasis—literally meaning "original inhabitants"—refers to the tribal or indigenous peoples of India.

[10] Pratap Bhanu Mehta, "Hinduism and Self-Rule," in *World Religions and Democracy*, ed. Larry Diamond, Marc F. Plattner, and Philip J. Costopoulos (Baltimore: Johns Hopkins University Press, 2005), 56–69, argues that Hinduism has been adapting to changing eco-socio-political processes.

The democratization of religion is seen in Christianity, too, as many believers accept leaders not on account of priestly ordination but by virtue of their personal charism and competence to preach effectively. Thousands have left the Catholic Church to join evangelical groups, and many lapsed Catholics have become pastors. So also, since conversion is a controversial issue in India, many of those who love Jesus and are unable to be baptized often assemble to pray, sing *bhajans*, and reflect upon Scripture. For example, the *Khrist-bhaktas* of Varanasi are Hindus who consider Jesus as their *ishtadeva* (personal deity). Many of the leaders are simple, unlettered believers. This shows that common people are no longer passive consumers of religion but seek the agency and power that religion offers to them.

Problems That the Church in India Faces in Synodality

Having seen the Indian religious scene and how religions are assuming new avatars in society, let us discuss some challenges that the Indian Church faces—especially with regard to synodality, sharing of power, decision-making, and participatory processes. Some of these problems were mentioned by those who participated in the synodal consultations in the diocesan phase of the 2023 synod on synodality, from October 2021 to July 2022.

Lack of apostolic and pastoral planning in most dioceses and parishes

Many lay faithful feel that proper planning is not taking place in the church in India. The Code of Canon Law stipulates very clear rules and guidelines for the establishment of the council of priests and the college of consultors.[11] However, in many dioceses and parishes such councils are nonexistent or exist merely on paper. Given this lack of consultative councils and synodal structures, bishops and parish priests make decisions without consulting others. Consequently, since many priests and lay coworkers feel that they are not trusted and their opinions not valued, they

[11] See the Code of Canon Law, nn. 495–502.

fail to cooperate with diocesan and parish projects. Hence, many go their own way without much concern for the common good.

Another lacuna in our apostolic planning is its myopic outreach. Many bishops and priests view church involvement merely as "religious activity," forgetting that in India one can never categorize any issue as "only secular" or "purely sacred." Lack of a broad, integral vision in planning adversely affects our Dalit and Adivasi communities, which are most disadvantaged.[12] Their needs, problems, and integral welfare are rarely discussed. Moreover, even when such issues are discussed, the stakeholders are rarely consulted. However, it is heartening to note that after much deliberation and consultation, the Catholic Bishops' Conference of India (CBCI) drew up a "Policy of Dalit Empowerment" in December 2016.[13]

Burdens of an overly institutionalized church

A glaring incongruity that people of other faiths see with Indian Christianity is that, on the one hand, it claims minority rights from the state while, on the other, it resembles an empire with large institutions: colleges, schools, hospitals, and social centers. While granting that some good is done by these institutions, questions also arise: Do these institutions truly serve the neediest? Who decides to build these institutions, and for whose benefit? Don't these institutions depend on foreign funds, thereby making us dependent on the West?[14] Who are these institutions accountable to? Experience indicates that such institutions give little room for corporate planning, co-responsibility in management, auditing, and transparency. Many institutions are run by a few religious or diocesan clergy with hardly any participation from anyone else—at least not in the planning, decision-making, budget allocation, and accounting.

[12] See Nandi Joseph, *Dalit Reality of the Indian Catholic Church* (Chennai: Foundation for Dalit Literature, 2001).

[13] See Catholic Bishops' Conference of India, *Policy of Dalit Empowerment in the Catholic Church in India: An Ethical Imperative to Build Inclusive Communities*, December 13, 2016, http://www.cbci.in/DownloadMat/dalit-policy.pdf.

[14] See Philip Muthukulam, "A Church of Interdependence," in *Church in the Third Millennium: Challenges and Prospects*, ed. J. Eruppakkatt (Mumbai: St Pauls, 2000), 90.

Institutionalization eclipses the human "faces" of Christianity and replaces them with buildings and finances. Those who manage institutions often lose touch with the harsh realities that people face: poverty, hunger, disease, corruption, exploitation, and ecological calamities. Moreover, institutional modes of functioning expose the gross mismatch between what the church professes to be and preaches, that is, a poor, servant church as envisaged by Pope Francis, and what it actually often is in practice: a wealthy, comfort-seeking, elitist community serving the rich and the powerful and not really those most in need.

Inadequate training and opportunities for the lay faithful

In the consultations that have been conducted at the diocesan phase from October 2021 to July 2022, participants have expressed a feeling that genuine power-sharing is not happening in the church in India. While there is a sharing of responsibilities, when it comes to decision-making there is reluctance on the part of the clergy. The "pray, pay, obey" axiom for the laity seems apt to a fairly large extent even today. An excuse often given to keep the lay faithful out of decision-making is that they do not have sufficient training. If this is true, then, while so much time and money is spent on training candidates for priesthood, why is there such hesitancy to train promising lay faithful to be leaders in the church? The lay faithful occupy some of the highest positions in public life. Surely, they can be entrusted with more opportunities for the sharing of power in the church, as well.

The role of women, women religious, and youth, and the space given to them in church life also requires attention. There is a tendency to sideline women and consider them less competent than men. Their opinions are rarely valued, and they are often assigned subordinate tasks in keeping with hackneyed stereotypes that women cannot lead but must be led, should not speak too much, but must submit humbly, and so on.

Failure to read the "signs of the times" and the "signs of place"

When the Second Vatican Council exhorted Christians to read the "signs of the times," nobody imagined that our world would change so drastically. Today, the progress of science and the info-tech revolution make us all neighbors in a "global village" with an overload of information available at our fingertips. Besides reading the "signs of the times," there is need to decipher the "signs of place"; in other words, with the explosion of possibilities of communication and global contraction, we do not need to do everything by ourselves. Networking, outsourcing, and collaboration are crucial to function effectively in today's world.

Religion, like other subsystems in society today, has numerous resources at its command. There are many possibilities for networking, collaboration with others, and outsourcing of work to others who are better equipped than us. Why, then, should anyone struggle to be a know-all, do-all, and be-all? The skills and competences of the church hierarchy are limited. Hence, there is need to seek advice and help from others who are more trained and competent to respond to the crying needs of the "least" of Jesus' sisters and brothers.

Prospects for Promoting Greater Synodality in the Church in India

Given the abovementioned challenges and problems facing a synodal way of functioning in the church in India, we briefly note some prospects and possibilities to increase participation of all the members of Christ's flock.

Call for conversion, renewal, and change of heart

Our church is truly an *ecclesia semper reformanda*: "She has to keep adopting new forms, new embodiments. She has to keep giving herself a new form, a new shape in history; she is never simply finished and complete."[15] As the church's mission unfolds in time, a change of heart and mindset must renew the whole ecclesial body and permeate all the domains of church life. Pope Francis humbly speaks of the need for "a conversion of the

---

[15] Hans Küng, *The Council, Reform and Reunion* (New York: Sheed & Ward, 1961; repr. 2015), 36.

papacy."[16] If more bishops strove for a "conversion of the episco-pacy," things would change and more people would be active in church life and mission. It would help to remember Pope Francis's advice to priests and pastors: "Shepherds walk with their people: we shepherds walk with our people, at times in front, at times in the middle, at times behind. A good shepherd should move that way: in front to lead, in the middle to encourage and preserve the smell of the flock, and behind, since the people too have their own 'sense of smell.' They have a nose for finding new paths for the journey, or for finding the road when the way is lost."[17]

While bishops and priests ought to realize their call to love and serve God's people, journeying along with them, the lay faithful too must hold their pastors accountable for *who* they are and *what* they do. Even at the risk of being sidelined, the laity must point out to the clergy their shortcomings and failings in a spirit of genuine concern and charity. This calls for conversion in the laity, too. Pope Francis's caution that ensuring the synodality of the whole church will be impossible if people misunderstand the church's hierarchy and see it as a structure in which some people are placed above others[18] is for every Christian. Nobody is exempt from constantly seeking conversion, renewal, and change of heart.

Warding off the dangers of clericalism, Hindutva, and Romanization

Those who wield power and feel superior to others tend to dominate others and impose their restricted views upon them. This is seen when one group dominates others within a religious tradition (clericalism), one fanatical religious ideology steamrolls over other religions (Hindutva), or a specific religiocultural expres-sion lords over others (Romanization). Such ideologies draw strength by exhibiting their superiority through subtly using

---

[16] Pope Francis, "Ceremony Commemorating the 50th Anniversary."

[17] Pope Francis, "Address of His Holiness Pope Francis to the Faithful of the Diocese of Rome," September 18, 2021, https://www.vatican.va/content/francesco/en/speeches/2021/september/documents/20210918-fedeli-diocesiroma.html.

[18] See Cindy Wooden, "Pope Calls for 'Synodal' Church that Listens, Learns, Shares Mission," *National Catholic Reporter*, October 17, 2015, https://www.ncronline.org/pope-calls-synodal-church-listens-learns-shares-mission.

sacred texts and symbols to establish their antiquity, vigor, and imagined timeless value. Such ideologies must be critiqued and the threats they pose to society exposed.

Pope Francis stoutly stands against all forms of clericalism. To the president of the Pontifical Commission for Latin America, he wrote,

> We cannot reflect on the theme of the laity while ignoring one of the greatest distortions that Latin America has to confront—and to which I ask you to devote special attention—clericalism. This approach not only nullifies the character of Christians, but also tends to diminish and undervalue the baptismal grace that the Holy Spirit has placed in the heart of our people. Clericalism leads to homologization of the laity; treating the laity as "representative" limits the diverse initiatives and efforts and, dare I say, the necessary boldness to enable the Good News of the Gospel to be brought to all areas of the social and above all political sphere. Clericalism, far from giving impetus to various contributions and proposals, gradually extinguishes the prophetic flame to which the entire Church is called to bear witness in the heart of her peoples.[19]

Similarly, resistance and protest against Hindutva must be carried out in collaboration with all people of goodwill irrespective of their religious or other affiliations. Hindutva's promotion of "unity in uniformity" and its subtle strategies of either "assimilation" (of certain groups) or "annihilation" (of religious minorities) can be countered by propagating discourses of "unity in diversity" and striving to build what can be seen as *"perichoretic communion"*[20] with all people of goodwill modelled upon the communion symbolized by the Trinity.

Likewise, in the Catholic Church, there are traces of *Romanization* and *Latinization* with Vatican dicasteries that sometimes foster distrust and suppression of attempts at inculturation, indigeniza-

[19] Pope Francis, "Letter of His Holiness Pope Francis to Cardinal Marc Ouellet, President of the Pontifical Commission for Latin America," March 19, 2016, https://www.vatican.va/content/francesco/en/letters/2016/documents/papa-francesco_20160319_pont-comm-america-latina.html.

[20] See R. Sahayadhas, *Hindu Nationalism and the Indian Church: Towards an Ecclesiology in Conversation with Martin Luther* (New Delhi: Christian World Imprints, 2013), 391–94.

tion, and interculturation while foisting a uniform agenda in matters of church life and liturgical and sacramental practice. Without granting legitimate autonomy to local churches, the catholicity of the church is compromised by Roman centralization.[21] Pope Francis's efforts to move toward decentralization by the promulgation of his motu proprio *Traditionis Custodes* (July 16, 2021) is a step in the right direction.

Accompaniment, encouragement, and empowerment of the lay faithful

In discussions on the new evangelization, new ways of being church, the church of the future, and a synodal church, the role of the laity always arises, since without the lay faithful there is no church at all. There is great need to accompany, encourage, and empower the laity.

First, we should foster "communion models" of church rather than "hierarchical models," and if we refer to Vatican II's "hierarchical communion," then we must view the presbyteral council and the college of consultors as Pope Francis does, namely, as "organs of communion" through which, "only to the extent that these organizations keep connected to the 'base' and start from people and their daily problems, can a synodal Church begin to take shape."[22] This requires listening to people and accompanying them in the ups and downs of their lives.

Second, accompaniment entails encouragement and empowerment of the laity. Delinking the ministerial functions of the clergy from the administrative tasks of the church will help in creating participative structures. Diocesan pastoral and parish councils should be entrusted with decision-making in specific areas and financial administration could be given to respective financial councils.[23] The clergy ought to spend more time in pastoral ministry rather than in mere administration.

[21] See Kurien Kunnumpuram, *The Indian Church of the Future* (Mumbai: St Pauls, 2007), 33–43.

[22] Pope Francis, "Ceremony Commemorating the 50th Anniversary."

[23] See "Laity in the Church: Identity and Mission in India Today," The Indian Theologians Association (ITA) 2006 Statement, nn. 55–56, in *Theologizing in the Indian Context: Statements of the Indian Theological Association*, ed. J. Parappally (Bengaluru: Asian Trading Corporation, 2017), 129–30.

Third, church movements where the laity are actively involved—like the Basic Ecclesial Communities (BECs) and the
Khrist-Bhaktas—should be fostered. The BECs, wherein organization, Scripture reading, prayer, and outreach are carried out
exclusively by the laity, have met with much success.[24] Finally,
the empowerment of women and women religious must be
fostered.[25]

Toward co-responsible, participatory, and prophetic communion

Pope Benedict XVI desired that the laity be given more responsibility in the church. Addressing the opening of a 2009 pastoral
convention of the Diocese of Rome on "Church Membership and
Pastoral Co-responsibility," he said that the church requires "a
change in mindset, particularly concerning lay people. They must
no longer be viewed as 'collaborators' of the clergy but truly recognized as '*co-responsible*,' for the Church's being and action,
thereby fostering the consolidation of a mature and committed
laity."[26] This will demand transparency, accountability, and lay
people who are well informed on what is going on in the church
and in the world.

Due to the democratization of religion seen nationwide, when
people are trusted and feel co-responsible for everyone and everything else, their participation is promoted. Moreover, they also
feel committed to the common good. Here the clergy could ensure
that papal directives are followed up. A good example of this is
the "synodal consultations" that were carried out from October
2021 to July 2022 as the diocesan phase of the 2023 synod. Many
lay faithful who partook of the consultations felt that they were

[24] See Thomas Vijay, ed., *Findings of a Survey of SCCs in India* (Nagpur: Pallottine
Animation Centre, 2010), for useful data in this regard.

[25] Lilly Francis and Loy George, *Empowerment of Women and Church in India* (Delhi:
CBCI Commission for Women, 2009) provides an overview of the situation of women
and suggests measures for empowerment.

[26] Pope Benedict XVI, "Opening of the Pastoral Convention of the Diocese of Rome
on the Theme: 'Church Membership and Pastoral Co-responsibility,'" May 26, 2009,
https://w2.vatican.va/content/benedict-xvi/en/speeches/2009/may/documents
/hf_ben-xvi_spe_20090526_convegno-diocesi-rm.html.

voicing their opinions freely and were consulted about church life for the first time. The synodal processes which have been initiated ought to continue even beyond the 2023 synod.

In India, where religion and politics are inseparable, the church must engage itself effectively in civil society.[27] This will demand bold initiatives in many ways. First, the church's institutionalized way of functioning must be evaluated at all levels, and, if need be, there should be a moratorium on building new institutions unless they are absolutely essential for evangelization. Second, in the face of burning intra-ecclesial and national problems, there is need to analyze the root causes of crises, fix policies, develop structures, and devise strategies for action. Third, with limited economic resources and personnel, there is also need to prioritize issues. This requires collaboration and networking with others, even beyond the confines of church.

As a church of "prophetic participation"[28] in favor of the "least" in society, we must not lose our faith perspective or our commitment to love and to serve. Pope Francis writes: "We need to keep hope and faith alive in a world full of contradictions, especially for the poorest, and especially with the poorest. It means, as pastors, working in the midst of our people and, with our people, supporting faith and its hope. We need to look at our cities–and therefore all the spaces where our people live their lives–with a contemplative gaze, a gaze of faith which sees God dwelling in their homes, in their streets and squares."[29]

Conclusion: Come, Holy Spirit, Lead Us Onward!

Quoting Saint John Chrysostom, Pope Francis reminds us that "Church and Synod are synonymous." No synod, no church! He says: "Inasmuch as the Church is nothing other than the 'journeying together' of God's flock along the paths of history towards the

---

[27] See Antony Kalliath and Francis Gonsalves, eds., *Church's Engagement in Civil Society* (Bengaluru: Asian Trading Corporation & Indian Theological Association, 2009).

[28] See Viju Wilson, *Ecclesiology of Prophetic Participation* (Delhi: ISPCK, 2012), 83–94.

[29] Pope Francis, "Letter of His Holiness Pope Francis to Cardinal Marc Ouellet."

encounter with Christ the Lord, then we understand too that, within the Church, no one can be 'raised up' higher than others. On the contrary, in the Church, it is necessary that each person 'lower' himself or herself, so as to serve our brothers and sisters along the way."[30]

All Christians are called to inculcate a spirit of self-emptying, service, and sacrifice. Synodality begins from the grassroots, first and foremost, by listening to the varied voices of Christ's faithful. These voices must be listened to with respect and then discussed in presbyteral councils and conferences of bishops in various regions. The current synodal processes and consultations that have been initiated at the diocesan and continental levels in the universal church will go a long way toward ensuring that the church in India becomes truly synodal.

Finally, at the universal level, collegiality gets consolidated with the pope. It is providential that Pope Francis has appointed cardinal consultors from every part of the world. He says, "It is not advisable for the Pope to take the place of local Bishops in the discernment of every issue which arises in their territory. . . . I am conscious of the need to promote a sound 'decentralization.'"[31] These are not only words but concretized in his works and witness.

Mindful of being a minuscule "minority" among a billion-plus Indians, Christians in India sense a "holy restlessness" in their journeying together with the whole church: "If Christians do not feel a deep inner restlessness, then something is missing. That inner restlessness is born of faith; it impels us to consider what it is best to do, what needs to be preserved or changed. History teaches us that it is not good for the Church to stand still (cf. *Evangelii Gaudium*, 23). Movement is the fruit of docility to the Holy Spirit, who directs this history, in which all have a part to play, in which all are restless, never standing still."[32]

May God's Spirit continue to guide and strengthen us on our pilgrim path!

[30] Pope Francis, "Ceremony Commemorating the 50th Anniversary."

[31] Pope Francis, "Ceremony Commemorating the 50th Anniversary."

[32] Pope Francis, "Address of His Holiness Pope Francis to the Faithful of the Diocese of Rome."

Synodality with the People:
A Latin American Perspective

Pedro Trigo, SJ

This essay does not intend to discuss the synodality of the people of God, which, as Vatican II teaches, encompasses all Christians and therefore includes the three vocations of hierarchy, religious life, and laity.[1] Rather, it considers the synodality of the whole people of God with the poor of the earth and also, more specifically, with poor Christians, understood in the deeper sense as those who follow Jesus of Nazareth and effectively allow themselves to be led by his Spirit.

In addition to its intrinsic significance, the special importance of this topic is that there will never be synodality *within* the people

---

[1] I want to insist from the beginning that "walking together" assumes that all members of the people of God fully recognize that this shared belonging takes priority over their specific vocations, which must be seen in function of that walking together. *Lumen Gentium*, a key document of Vatican II, describes the church in the following sequence: the mystery of the church (chapter 1), the people of God (chapter 2), the hierarchical constitution of the church (chapter 3). This sequence "emphasizes that the ecclesiastical hierarchy is placed at the service of the people of God so that the Church's mission can be updated in conformity with the divine plan of salvation, following the logic of the priority of the whole over the parts and of the end over the means" (International Theological Commission, *Synodality in the Life and Mission of the Church*, March 2, 2018, 54, https://www.vatican.va/roman_curia/congregations/cfaith/cti_documents/rc_cti_20180302_sinodalita_en.html; hereafter cited as SLMC).

of God as long as there is no synodality of the people of God with the poor of the earth. In places where Christians are a disrespected minority, for example, they may have strong cohesion among themselves without feeling solidarity with the poor, but such strong cohesion would not be synodality. The Latin American experience corroborates this clearly: solidarity between pastors and the rest of the people of God has existed in those dioceses where the bishop has walked in solidarity with the poor, following the example of Jesus of Nazareth. We might cite the examples of bishops like Hélder Câmara, Angeleli, Alvear, Proaño, Romero, and many others.

Walking Together toward the Community of the Children of God along the Path of Jesus of Nazareth

Synodality means understanding life as a walking together. Understanding life this way assumes that life is a path and that it requires us to keep moving beyond ourselves and our loved ones, beyond our desires and our longings, beyond established orders and sacralized institutions.

Life is a path in many ways. First of all, because we are not finished products. We are humanly open and incomplete. Our actions constantly construct us and therefore define us. But there is no act, no decision, that totally defines us. We can always backtrack or change course. Our nature is to *be being*.[2]

By our actions we can either humanize or dehumanize ourselves. The problem is that human acts are ambivalent and that human "qualities" do not neatly coincide with human worth. Often our actions are aimed at "qualifying" ourselves according to the goals of the established order, but the more we strive on that path, ignoring what leads to true human worth, the more we will be sacrificing that worth. This truth has been concealed in the West's dominant way of thinking, because human goals have been subordinated to the goal of acquiring qualities that are useful to the system while ignoring any other considerations. These utilitarian qualities are promulgated and promoted everywhere; they

[2] Ignacio Ellacuría, *Filosofía de la realidad histórica* (San Salvador: UMA, 1999), 345.

constitute the express goal of formal education.[3] Many people are therefore engaged in acquiring excellence in some field or other, and they strive to maintain and, if possible, to improve whatever position they manage to achieve, a difficult task given the intense competition.

Those living in this manner are not so much developing their human qualities as becoming distinguished members of their culture. The truth is that no culture has much room for genuinely human beings because all cultures, at least since the neolithic period, are ruled by principles of hierarchy and exclusion: there is an above and a below, an inside and an outside. Because we are cultural beings, our path to humanization necessarily takes place within a particular culture. We may try to transform whatever in the culture prevents humanization, but such a stance comes with great costs. To persist on that path requires a profound resolve, a real hunger for humanity.

We Christians, however, have a clearer vision of the path ahead: we desire to advance toward a true family of peoples in which we are all true brothers and sisters and, as such, strive to help one another in a constant synergy of mutual emulation. Synodality, then, presumes synergy, a confluence of efforts. This synergy is seeking a goal that does not exist but is not something capricious; it involves doing justice to reality, helping reality to go beyond itself. Synergy builds a shared path on which everyone constructively and creatively puts forth the best that they can. The problem is that the path must be built within a specific institutional setting that absolutely denies fraternity; it is a society made up of individuals who relate only to those they want to relate to and who relate only for the reasons they want and for as long as they want. To build this path, therefore, we must overcome formidable obstacles.[4]

---

[3] This is what is called educational quality, sometimes even in Catholic education.

[4] According to the International Theological Commission, it requires "the paschal transition from 'I' understood in a self-centered way to the ecclesial 'we,' where every 'I,' clothed in Christ (cf. Galatians 3:27), lives and journeys with his or her brothers and sisters as a responsible and active agent of the one mission of the People of God. . . . Without conversion of heart and mind and without disciplined training for welcoming and listening to one another the external instruments of communion would hardly be of any use; on the contrary, they could be transformed into mere heartless, faceless masks" (SLMC 107).

Now, since the mode of production determines the product, we cannot advance toward fraternity by somehow overpowering those who deny it or know nothing of it. We can defeat evil only by dint of good. Even if there were democratically promulgated and enforced laws by which individualists were obliged to contribute to the common good, those laws and the consequent practice would need to communicate a true fraternal solicitude that would make the individualists see that what is proposed is good for them and that all they have to do is accept it. This cannot be taken for granted; it requires a path, a process among us.

But following this path has still another connotation for us Christians: we walk on it to meet Jesus of Nazareth, the one who makes us brothers and sisters, children of God. He lives in the bosom of the Father, in the divine community, not only as the unique and eternal Son of the Father, but as our Brother, the one who truly carries us in his heart and destines us to participate, through him, in the divine community. For us, therefore, the path ends not in death, but in divine community.

What is more, for us Christians, Jesus is not only our destiny, but the path on which we travel (see John 14:4-6). That is why we follow him and define ourselves as his followers. We do not claim to be imitators, because in imitation there is no room for authenticity or human fullness. Imitation does not humanize us. Furthermore, since our situations are different from his, imitation would falsify what he intended to do in his life. Rather than trying to do the very same things that Jesus did, we try to do what would be the equivalent in our own situation. Thus, it is a matter of following him with creative fidelity. We seek to do in our own situation the equivalent of what he did in his.

United by the Heart of Jesus into the Singular Family of God's Children

Why do we seek to walk together on this path? The reasons are multiple and convergent. First, we seek it because positive reciprocity is anchored in our constitution as persons. I do not affirm myself as a person if in that act of affirming myself I do not also affirm others.

But we walk together also because our goal—and therefore our horizon and our program—is to make this contrary world the singular family of God's children in Jesus of Nazareth, the only Son and the universal Brother. This goal cannot be reduced to a proclamation, even if it is completely convincing. If the mode of production determines the product, then only those who walk together in solidarity can propose to shape humanity into a family of peoples.[5] Walking together is thus the embryo of that comradely people.

Walking together must not consist in a closed, institutional way of life; it must not absolutize our condition as the people of God. Rather, that condition should be experienced as service to the mission[6] and specifically as a sacrament of the union of all humankind.[7] This will be possible only if synodality occurs in the church primarily at the basic level of our common condition as Christians, a condition that is absolute, sacred, and eternal. All the different vocations and charisms are at the service of this condition. They are what God wants only if they are indeed rooted in this primordial ecclesial communion, which consists in walking together as Christians. It must be said that this communion does not now exist, except in the minorities that have accepted the council. This synodality is what Pope Francis so consistently practices and what he proposes in a thousand concrete ways to the institutional church, and that is why he encounters such tenacious opposition from much of the hierarchy.

Walking with the Poor in Order to Walk Together

What role do the poor play in our walking together? We have to say that the poor are generally the only place where we find real universality: only when things go well for the poor will things

[5] The first thing Jesus did when he began his earthly ministry was gather a group of disciples, because only a truly fraternal group can convoke the family of God's daughters and sons. That is also why he asked them to go in pairs when they went forth in mission.

[6] "Synodality is lived out in the Church in the service of mission" (SLMC 53).

[7] "The Church is in Christ as a sacrament or sign and as an instrument of the intimate union with God and of the unity of all humankind" (Second Vatican Council, Dogmatic Constitution on the Church *Lumen Gentium*, 1).

go well for all of us. But things will not go well for the poor as long as humanity's established game plan is the war of all against all. This is a war in which the most gifted, the best positioned, and the least scrupulous will always prevail. With such a game plan there will always be poor people, and they will even make up the majority.

If, as Spinoza proclaimed, the only principle of virtue is preserving oneself in existence by looking out solely for oneself, then an absolute competition is established, because resources are scarce and nobody will feel safe. In such a situation, you cannot lower your guard. Those who can afford to do so will stockpile and hoard. As a result, more and more people will be excluded, because those already advantaged will keep accumulating and the gap will keep growing between those who can insure their continued existence and those who cannot. In such a situation, where there is no room for walking together or mutual emulation or seeking the common good, there will always be poor people, and as technology progresses, more and more of them will be considered "disposable."

Not only does this system produce poor people, it also dehumanizes all those who benefit from it. It is simply not true that striving to preserve oneself in existence at any price is a principle of virtue, much less the only one. It cannot be such because it denies our condition as persons and the positive reciprocity among us, and it dissolves the ties that bind us together in mutual, horizontal commitment. In Christian terms, it negates our destiny as the communion of God's daughters and sons.

In the way things are now, the poor are those at the bottom of the system or completely outside it. They are the ones cast aside, rejected as walking companions because they have nothing to offer. They find no way to amass wealth in a system where accumulation of wealth is the activity most esteemed and pursued. If you cannot do any business with them and they have no attractive qualities, what reason can there be to seek them out and walk with them?

Moreover, from the establishment's point of view, the poor do not walk; they are immobile, lacking any dynamic qualities. For the ambitious, life means never stopping except to take a breath and savor your achievements, but only so long as the savoring does not numb your ambitious goals but spurs you on to achieve more. If you are constantly preoccupied with such matters, it does not occur to you to be concerned with the poor, because that would distract you from your endless endeavors. The most you might do is donate some money to an institution that will help the poor not to feel so helpless or, better still, that will assist the more capable ones to enter the ceaseless circuit of production and consumption. In the best of cases, then, you can do something for them, but what you cannot do is walk with them.

Those who live this way, I insist, are not living as full human beings. They engage with others in business or consumption, but they walk with no one. They do not coexist in the true sense of the word, and much less do they stand together (*con-sisten*). They do not form a body with other human beings except when it comes to business. They create corporations, which, as the name suggests, are solidly constructed economic bodies whose every activity—hiring labor, buying materials, and selling finished products or services—is geared to making a handsome profit.

As long as people lack awareness of their human fragility, they will think that true humanity can be achieved without a personal commitment that is horizontal, free, and open to the world. It is only when individuals, whatever their life circumstance, strive to give themselves to others, beyond all personal interest or indulgence, that they achieve a truly human level. Such persons can no longer see the poor as unfortunate individuals lacking in goods or incapable of making their way in the world. They can no longer ignore the fact that they are human beings who are in no way alien to them. They comprehend that the poor silently make claims on them with their naked humanity.[8] They realize that they must do

---

[8] In Touraine's words: "This irruption of the individual toward himself as a subject can be affected only through the recognition of the *other* as a subject: by accepting the other as a subject, I can recognize myself as a subject. Recognizing the other as a subject means recognizing the universal ability of everyone to recreate themselves as subjects" (Alain Touraine, *La mirada social* [Barcelona: Paidós, 2009], 202). Lévinas is more specific: "The infinite appears as a face in the ethical resistance that paralyzes my powers and rises up hard and absolute from the depths of defenseless eyes, and from this hunger it establishes the very proximity of the Other. . . . The being that expresses itself imposes itself, but precisely because it calls me from its misery and its nakedness—from its hunger—I cannot turn a deaf ear to its call. Thus, in express-

something for them, something that cannot be done from outside or from above.

Now, if people really make a commitment, they will come to realize, sooner rather than later, that the commitment is not just one activity added onto the other activities that have occupied them up to now. They will come to understand that this personal dedication to the poor as human beings belongs to a galaxy completely different from the one that contains the endless circuit of production and consumption in which they are living. They will also become aware that it is not easy to combine these two very diverse worlds, because in one of them the subject is the independent individual with no strong ties to anyone, and in the other the subject is the person, who is defined by humanizing relationships of commitment.

We can also walk together at the level of ethnic groups or business firms or religious confessions or interest groups, but that is not walking together at the basically human level. Giving oneself to others in a horizontal and gratuitous way, coming out of oneself with the best that one has—that is what walking together through life is all about. When we reach that level of humanity, all human beings are in some way present to us. We live in a universe in which no human being can be alien to us.[9]

Having attained that level, we grasp the humanity of the poor, and we grieve that it is unrecognized, rejected, and despised because they lack the means to live decently. And at a deeper level we understand that they lack the means because in the war of all against all, the obstacles they experience are almost insurmountable. The prevailing system has impoverished them. It is not as though they were of a different, inferior species. They are products of the same system that impoverishes them, a system that is inhumane because it will always produce poor people. It makes no sense to leave the system as it is and to implement compensatory

---

ing itself, the being that imposes itself does not limit but rather promotes my freedom, by eliciting my goodness" (Emmanuel Lévinas, *Totalidad e infinito* [Salamanca: Sígueme, 1987], 213–14).

[9] This is what we mean when we quote that phrase of Terence that is emblematic of Western humanism: "I am a human being, and therefore nothing human is alien to me" (Terence, *Heauton Timorumenos*, 77). For us, because we are human, no human being is alien to us.

measures, because these will treat the poor not as subjects but only as recipients. When viewed as recipients, as so many outstretched hands, they are not considered as human beings. Considering them as human beings requires us to include them in the horizons of our own lives, taking them fully into account as worthy sisters and brothers, and to walk side by side with them.

Walking with the Poor

What does it mean to walk with the poor? In what does synodality with them consist? At the very least, there must be a relationship that is horizontal and open. For most people, this can happen only when they are in their own environment. For example, at our 32nd General Congregation (1974–75), we Jesuits established that our identity was to be found in understanding faith and justice as a single reality with two facets.[10] After the congregation, the French Jesuits got together to see how to put that identity into practice. They decided that the preferential option for the poor should characterize all their works and that all works should give clear evidence that they were concretely in favor of the poor. To help make that a reality, all Jesuits were asked to spend at least a half-day every week in open and horizontal contact with poor people in their vicinity. A basic reason for this request was that "the heart does not feel what the eyes do not see." Without such close contact, our personal option for the poor deteriorates to the status of a cause or, worse still, of an ideology. The justice that springs forth from faith is not satisfied with working (or even working hard) to make sure that justice is done to the poor in our society. Faith-born justice comes about primarily by my doing them justice in my own life. That means making space for them, and since our life is so full of things, we must shrink some of these things so that there is room for the poor, not just as casual acquaintances but as beloved friends.

That fight for justice cannot somehow be just one of our many activities; it must color them all. To continue with the example,

---

[10] "What is it to be a companion of Jesus today? It is to engage, under the standard of the Cross, in the crucial struggle of our time: the struggle for faith and the struggle for justice that faith itself demands" (Decree 2, no. 2; see also Decree 4, no. 2).

the option for the poor requires that all our labors—social, educational, and pastoral—seek not only to have justice done for the poor but to help the poor themselves to become agents of their own liberation.

All we have said makes it clear that political and economic struggles are needed to change the structures of power; indeed, such struggles are vital and unavoidable.[11] Otherwise we will just be fighting for a cause, and our efforts will be fruitless.

Faith is believing, not in truths, but in the unique relationship that is possible between persons. We have faith in relationships that are personalizing and that do not objectify others. Children begin to have such a relationship with their mother in response to her constant love. The justice that springs forth from faith always includes such a personalizing relationship, which cannot happen unless we somehow are walking together with others in a real and palpable way.

Militancy Excludes Synodality with the People

We have stated that when the political struggle is reduced to a cause, it is dehumanizing for both the leaders and for the people

---

[11] This is how the International Theological Commission explains it in its document on synodality in the church:

> The Church's synodal life presents itself, in particular, as *diakonia* in the promotion of a social, economic, and political life of all peoples under the banner of justice, solidarity and peace. "God, in Christ, redeems not only the individual person, but also the social relations existing between them." The practice of dialogue and the search for effective joint solutions by which we commit ourselves to peace and justice are an absolute priority in a situation where there is a structural crisis in the process of democratic participation and a loss of confidence in its principles and inspirational values, with the threat of authoritarian and technocratic aberrations. In this context, it is an important obligation and a criterion of all social action of the People of God to "hear the cry of the poor and the cry of the earth," and to draw attention urgently, in determining society's choices and plans, to the place and the privileged role of the poor, the universal destination of goods, the primacy of solidarity, and care for our common home. (SLMC 119)

See also Pedro Trigo, "Asumir que la opción por los pobres es también, ineludiblemente, opción contra la pobreza" and "Hacerse cargo y repudiar el totalitarismo fetichista de mercado y luchar para que sea superado," in Pedro Trigo, SJ, *Echar la suerte con los pobres de la tierra* (Caracas: Centro Gumilla, 2015), 48–65.

whom the struggle favors. When people are dedicated to a cause, they see their dedication as an altruistic profession that gives them a sense of self-worth. Their day-to-day existence may not seem especially significant, but their tenacious and generous dedication to a cause within an organization gives meaning to their lives. Such is the situation of "militants," some of whom spend their entire lives "militating," so that everyday life no longer exists for them.[12] They live in and for the organization. Their lives, in the best of cases, are completely focused on liberating the people. In extreme cases, they want to do everything for the people—but not with the people. This is true of both the enlightened liberal and the socialist, and it is equally true of enlightened clerics.

Let us take the paradigmatic case of Che Guevara's programmatic essay, *Socialism and the New Man in Cuba*.[13] In this work, the Argentine revolutionary describes the ideal human type as the militant. Quite solemnly and sincerely he asserts that "the true revolutionary is guided by great feelings of love." No one can doubt that a life motivated by love is inspiring, but simply being motivated by love is not enough; love must also give shape to that life. Guevara seems not to understand this, because he goes on to state that revolutionaries "cannot descend with their small dose of ordinary affection to the places where the common folk show it. The leaders of the revolution have children who in their first babbling do not learn to say papa." True militants, and especially the leaders among them, are freed from other work so that they can dedicate themselves to making revolution through the organization; they live in and for the organization to the point that they believe that "there is no life apart from it."[14] If that is the case, then how will they ever know that what they are deciding to do is for the good of the people? If they live apart from the daily lives of the people and do not walk by their side, how will they ever know?

Che speaks of permanent self-vigilance and the importance of encouraging the masses, but ultimately everything depends solely

---

[12] Here "militants" is used to refer to persons who live their Christianity as an empty rite without relating the faith to the concrete problems and realities of people.

[13] Che Guevara, *Obras 1957–1967*, vol. II (Havana: Casa de las Américas, 1977), 367–84.

[14] Che Guevara, *Obras 1957–1967*, vol. II, 382.

on the revolutionary subject; there is no free, horizontal interaction with the people in the flow of their lives. Such commitment may seem very generous, but it suffers from being detached from everyday life, divorced from walking alongside the poor of the earth. Such commitment is dedicated to the liberation of the poor, but instead of an alternative life, it produces an alienated life. And for that reason, it causes disasters, even though we recognize in it the great generosity that can go as far as giving one's life for the people. The problem is that the people are only the recipients of the revolutionaries' ideologies but they are not their traveling companions in the daily rounds of life.

We must also recognize that pastoral care can be offered to the poor through an elaborate apparatus that requires such all-consuming dedication that it precludes walking with the poor. Just like leftist intellectuals, dedicated theologians can devote their whole lives to militancy in favor of the oppressed, but their militancy leaves them no time or energy for real contact with the poor. And sadly, they do not consider such contact important, because they believe that their real job is that specific militancy to which they consecrate the best of themselves.

The Poor Were His Companions on the Road

If we Christians truly believe that Jesus is the way, both in his life and in his message, then we must admit, first of all, that the poor were his vital milieu, his travel companions, the ones to whom he gave the first claim to his space and time. Twice the gospels tell us that so many people were crowding around Jesus and his companions that they were not even able to eat (see Mark 3:20; 6:31). The people's eagerness to have physical contact with Jesus was such that on one occasion they pressed hard around him, trying to touch him. When he felt that they were going to crush him, he got into a boat to gain some distance from the crowd and to make his relationship with them more personal (see Mark 3:8-9).

By being so close to them, Jesus showed the oppressed and the hopeless that they were not abandoned by God. When Jesus befriended them, they felt befriended by God and possessed of a new dignity. They began to stand up straight and think on their own; they met together with one another and mobilized around Jesus.

Poor people were the vital milieu in which Jesus lived and moved and had his being. They belonged to him, and they reciprocated by committing themselves to him. Thus, if we want to follow Jesus, we have to do in our own situation the equivalent of what he did in his. We cannot live outside the world of the poor. In one way or another, we have to walk with the poor, as Jesus walked with them and they with him.

The Poor Were at the Center of His Mission

According to Jesus, moreover, the poor are God's chosen ones. Jesus came to proclaim and make present God's reign in the world, and he made clear that God's Kingdom is first and foremost for the poor (see Luke 6:20). God becomes their Father in Jesus, the only-begotten Son who has joined them as a companion on their journey. With his encouraging presence, they stand up straight and walk in confidence, knowing that they are God's sons and daughters. For this reason, the poor who believe in the message of Jesus are already blessed, despite their neediness and weakness. Indeed, when they truly believe, they no longer feel helpless because, with Jesus as their faithful companion, they know they can count on God himself as their champion.

They are God's favorites, not only because he has given them, through Jesus, the Kingdom. (Of course, they must still accept this gift, because salvation takes the form of a covenant and a covenant requires a "yes" on both parts.) They are also God's favorites because they are the sacramental presence of Jesus himself: whatever is done or not done to them is done or not done to Jesus himself (see Matt 25:40, 45—a paradigmatic text for Pope Francis). That is why our eternal destiny depends on our relationship to the poor. And that is so not because of some whim of Jesus, but because serving them horizontally is a primary exercise of obedience to the Spirit of Jesus that moves us from deeper within ourselves than we can even imagine. Not serving the poor means resisting the impulse of the Spirit; it means refusing to live as sons and daughters in the Son.

This service to the poor is so decisive that Paul warned the Corinthians that they were not truly celebrating the Lord's Supper because, while they performed all the rites, they discriminated against the poor. The servants in the Corinthian community were kept working late in the homes of the affluent, and when they arrived for the service, they found that the others had already feasted (see 1 Cor 11:20-22). Only through the door of the poor does Jesus make himself present in the community (see Matt 18:20), and only then will the community's relations express the solidarity that Jesus has brought us.

Walking in the Discipleship of the Poor in Spirit[15]

Those who count for little can believe in this proclamation of Jesus, because, as we learn from his own prayer (see Luke 10:21), the Father has revealed to them the secret of the Kingdom, a secret hidden from the wise and learned.[16] This revelation happens through Jesus and much to his delight; he gives thanks and praise to his Father, who is pleased to act in this way.

This is the supreme paradox: if we take seriously the content of this prayer of Jesus, which is the only one that the gospels make explicit during his ministry, we not only have to be his companions on the journey of the poor, but we have to become also the disciples of those poor persons who have received and accepted this definitive revelation from God.[17] Thus, it is not just a matter of extending our positive reciprocity so that it reaches the poor. We must also learn from them; that is, we have to let them introduce us into the secret of the Kingdom, for only that will make us worthy.

Two statements of Pope Francis cited by the International Theological Commission express this point with great insight. "Listen

[15] Trigo, *Echar la suerte con los pobres de la tierra*, 139–46 (with bibliography).

[16] Pedro Trigo, "Dios revela el Reino a los pobres," *Revista Latinoamericana de Teología* 83 (2011): 145–83.

[17] As far as I know, Dussel was the first to use this expression, which may sound absurd but which, if taken seriously, is highly provocative: Enrique Dussel, *Método para una filosofía de la liberación* (Salamanca: Sígueme, 1974), 181–97.

to God until you hear with him the cry of the people; listen to the people until you hear in them the will to which God calls us," he said to a meeting of families in 2014.[18] Most ecclesiastical officials and most theologians are not going to hear the people if they are not listening to the God who hears the cry of the people. But it is also true that it is only by listening to the people that Christians can hear, in the people, what God demands of them. This means that for the pope, "the disciples of Christ must be 'contemplatives of the Word and also contemplators of the people.'"[19]

In the present order of things, this is so paradoxical as to seem almost ridiculous, but it was what Jesus felt in the depths of his heart, and it was what he confessed with gratitude to his Father. In this perspective, the poor are not just grateful recipients of the refined cultural goods we so generously offer them. They are the recipients of the greatest treasure, and it is to them that we must have recourse if we are not to remain in the outer darkness. That is why, to our surprise, walking with the poor is of vital interest to us.[20] We are the ones graced by their gift.

Of course, the poor don't give classes, so we cannot technically become their disciples. But neither can we technically become disciples of Jesus, who was not a trained teacher of the law. People became his disciples by following him, and not just by walking after him physically but by accepting him as the definitive revelation of God's will for his people and for all humankind. In a sense, they truly became his disciples only after the resurrection. Before that, they followed him because they found in him a fullness that they could not do without, but they still were not willing to serve, as he did, from below. They did not realize that he would

---

[18] Pope Francis, "Discourse during the Encounter for the Family," October 4, 2014, *AAS* 106 (2014), 831.

[19] Pope Francis, apostolic exhortation *Evangelii Gaudium* (November 24, 2014), 154, https://www.vatican.va/content/francesco/en/apost_exhortations/documents /papa-francesco_esortazione-ap_20131124_evangelii-gaudium.html. See Dussel, *Método*, 114.

[20] That is why I tell the sisters and brothers of the communities with whom I pray that I do not attend their prayer services for their sake but because I, like them, need to attend. Naturally, they know that I love them and give them my best, but they are very happy to hear that I am not there just to give; more than that, I am there to receive their gift.

never impose himself on those who rejected him because, like his Father, he was utterly love: he was God's "yes" to his people and to humanity, an unconditional and irrevocable "yes."

Obviously, the poor are not teachers like Jesus. The poor are teachers insofar as they accept God's revealing to them the mystery of the Kingdom, which comes as the reign of Jesus the Messiah. The poor have difficulty accepting revelation because they feel needy, helpless, and tremendously disadvantaged; they have to make a mighty effort just to survive. Living in such adverse conditions, how can they believe that they are favored with God's definitive blessing? The poor with whom Jesus lived saw him as the sacrament of what he proclaimed, and they could accept it because they felt blessed by being in his company even if they continued to be poor. Today the poor will not easily accept this very gracious revelation unless they are closely accompanied by faithful followers of Jesus. We can testify, nonetheless, that there are many poor people who receive this revelation in one way or another, and they feel blessed by it. Even persons without a penny to their name trust that God is on their side and will always take care of them. And that is why, miraculously, they do not lose their humanity.

How do the poor show that they accept revelation? They do so by living lovingly and humanly, which means living in obedience to the Spirit of God, who is, as we confess in the Creed, the "Lord and Giver of life." They accept revelation when they live, not with anguish, but in peace with and in openness to others. They accept it by not surrendering to their base passions and not seeking to advance themselves while turning their back on their own. They accept it when they live together as brothers and sisters and not as fierce competitors for scarce goods. They accept it when they are fellow travelers, giving from their poverty and gratefully receiving from others. They can live in peace because they are in the hands of the God who in Jesus gives himself to them as the life of their life. By accepting God as their traveling companion, they realize that human beings live not only by bread but by the Father's life-giving nearness. And they do all this fully aware of their feebleness and fragility, while also striving mightily to better themselves and to take advantage of the opportunities life offers them.

If this is the magisterium of the poor in spirit, then it is only by drawing close to their lives and walking with them, in one way or another, that we can grasp and accept all this. We can accept it because drawing close to them and their world allows for a new openness, both of the poor themselves and of those who draw close to them humanly.

But if we do not normally live in their world, how can we walk with them? We can do so by belonging to the same Christian community, if it is a true community, because we are all hearers of the Word, and our respective roles are strictly secondary. Or we can do so by being in regular contact with their world through some service institution, when the service provided is truly horizontal and fraternal, and when the needy are not merely recipients of charity, however humbly and respectfully it is dispensed. The relationship must be open so that mutuality flourishes at the level of persons and not merely at the level of predetermined roles.

The Discipleship of the Poor

In the prayer of Jesus that we mentioned above, God's revelation of the mystery of the Kingdom to the insignificant is contrasted with God's hiding it from the wise and the learned. Jesus was referring not to scientists and philosophers but to those who had studied the sacred Scriptures, especially the Torah. The equivalent in Christianity would be those who have doctorates in canon law, moral theology, or Scripture; more generally, it would include theologians and ranking members of the institutional church. "The wise and the learned" of Jesus' day were not expecting the mystery of the Kingdom to arrive as a "reign" in the way that it did. They could not conceive that God would seal his covenant by having his only Son become an ordinary human being, a man who would save us by embracing us in solidarity and joining us with the poor so that, through the poor, we might become brothers and sisters to one another in Jesus, the universal Brother. They could not imagine that he would save us the way he did, independently of the law and the temple. Having no such expectation, they had a hard time accepting the message of Jesus. Some teachers of the law were able to see something of God in Jesus, and so they allowed him to speak in their synagogues, but they were definitely not open to his message.

The problem today is that Christian theologians tend to be equated with with specialists and experts. Or, more exactly, they are satisfied with being specialists while failing to understand that conceptual knowledge of realities has nothing to do with experiencing them in life and living by them. Until they grasp that difference and realize that knowledge is an invitation to live, they will hardly be Christian. Moreover, mere conceptual knowledge of Christianity does not allow us to discern concrete situations and decide what is relevant here and now from a Christian perspective. Such discernment becomes possible only by following Jesus.

The same can be said of Christian pastors. The charism they have been given makes sense only when they are following Jesus together with their fellow disciples. It cannot be exercised outside of joint discipleship, which is what opens the door to the real content of Christianity. The only true teachers of the following of Jesus are the poor in spirit, because they in fact have received that gift from God in a special way and their lives are guided by it. That is why theologians and pastors are asked especially, more than other people, to walk side by side with the poor.[21] They have to take the following of Jesus very seriously, not embedding themselves in their "specialties" but seeking wholeheartedly to become genuine experts. Only then will this countercurrent discipleship make sense, not only for the pyramidal society in which they live but more directly for the aspirations they may have of being recognized by colleagues at the heights of that pyramidal world. This is what Pope Francis stated expressly, using a somewhat shocking metaphor, as Jesus did:

> If we understand, as Saint John Chrysostom says, that "Church and Synod are synonymous," inasmuch as the Church is nothing other than the "journeying together" of God's flock along the paths of history towards the encounter with Christ the Lord, then we understand too that, within the Church, no one can be "raised up" higher than others. On the contrary, in the Church, it is necessary that each person "lower" himself or herself, so as to serve our brothers and sisters along the way.

---

[21] It is not, then, a question of doing field work by using the method of participatory observation, but rather of being companions with the poor in following Jesus—and in the best of cases, being their companions in community.

Jesus founded the Church by setting at her head the Apostolic College, in which the Apostle Peter is the "rock" (cf. *Mt* 16:18), the one who must confirm his brethren in the faith (cf. *Lk* 22:32). But in this Church, as in an inverted pyramid, the top is located beneath the base. Consequently, those who exercise authority are called "ministers," because, in the original meaning of the word, they are the least of all. It is in serving the people of God that each bishop becomes, for that portion of the flock entrusted to him, *vicarius Christi*, the vicar of that Jesus who at the Last Supper bent down to wash the feet of the Apostles (cf. *Jn* 13:1-15). And in a similar perspective, the Successor of Peter is nothing else if not the *servus servorum Dei*.

Let us never forget this! For the disciples of Jesus, yesterday, today and always, the only authority is the authority of service, the only power is the power of the cross. As the Master tells us: "You know that the rulers of the Gentiles lord it over them, and their great men exercise authority over them. It shall not be so among you; but whoever would be great among you must be your servant, and whoever would be first among you must be your slave" (*Mt* 20:25-27). *It shall not be so among you*: in this expression we touch the heart of the mystery of the Church, and we receive the enlightenment necessary to understand our hierarchical service.[22]

In the neolithic age, the development of agriculture and animal husbandry allowed a few people to feed many. As a result, there could be a division of labor: people could specialize in pottery, stonework, carpentry, metallurgy, administration, public services, security, religious worship, and so on. Those directing each occupation and those coordinating everything were given special authority, and so there developed an increasingly accentuated social hierarchy.

Today we live in the steepest pyramidal society in modern history. The most scandalous development is the growing number of unemployed *surplus workers*, especially young people. Being young in the first world today means being a candidate for poverty. Not

[22] Pope Francis, "Ceremony Commemorating the 50th Anniversary of the Institution of the Synod of Bishops," October 17, 2015, http://w2.vatican.va/content/francesco/en/speeches/2015/october/documents/papa-francesco_20151017_50-anniversario-sinodo.html.

only is this the reality but those on top have convinced a great number of those on the bottom that such a situation is inevitable. So overwhelming is the power of those on top that the people on the bottom submit to this system that impoverishes them, meekly acquiescing to this obscene spectacle that is their only means of survival. Those in the middle are, on the one hand, seduced by the attractiveness of all kinds of merchandise and, on the other, paralyzed by fear of the crises caused by unrestrained capital.

It is precisely in this situation that the pope conceives of the church as an inverted pyramid: on top are the people of God, especially the poor; the hierarchy, which literally means "sacred power," is located below; and the pope is lowest of all (and so is called "the servant of the servants of God"). This is so because power in the church is service—service from below, not from on high. That is how Jesus explained it to those apostles who were striving to reach the pinnacle of the pyramid. The pope reminds us that Jesus made a sharp distinction between power in the church and the power exercised in the established order by rulers who tyrannize and by rich people who oppress. Those who want to be the first must become servants to all. The example was set by Jesus himself, who served all who came to him. And he served them from below, as one who waits on table and washes feet.

Moreover, this is a reality that cannot be otherwise, because the true God differs from idols, which are an unbearable burden on their worshipers. In contrast, the true God shoulders his worshipers; he has done so always and will forever do so. We see this expressed in the words of the prophet Isaiah:

> [You] have been borne by me from your birth,
>   carried from the womb;
> even to your old age I am he,
>   even when you turn gray I will carry you.
> I have made, and I will bear;
>   I will carry and will save. (Isa 46:3-4)

No one can serve God because God needs nothing, and even if he needed something, he would not ask us, because everything is already his (see Psalm 50:7-13). God, who created us out of love, is always our servant. That is why Jesus does what he sees his Father doing, and that is why we who are followers of Jesus must do what he does. We cannot wash the feet of everyone, but it is enough that we wash the feet of one another (see John 13:12-17).

I want to insist that this way of proceeding is not only contrary to that of the established order; it is quite contradictory. It is not the opposite pole on the same horizon; it is a radical alternative. It would be the polar opposite only if it were conceived as self-sacrifice, as earning merit by doing something humiliating and difficult in order to obtain an eternal reward. This notion of service, which has been held and is still held by part of the ecclesiastical institution and by clericalized Christians, continues to esteem the established order. For them, to serve is to do something degrading; it involves "lowering oneself" below one's state. One puts up with acting as a servant because the reward is worth it. This is not the life-giving stance of Jesus, nor is it what he proposed for others. As one who had no place to lay his head, Jesus walked with those who had nothing, and he did so out of love and filial devotion: "The Son can do nothing on his own, but only what he sees the Father doing; for whatever the Father does, the Son does likewise" (John 5:19).

As long as we feel that serving from below—serving the poor by walking with them—is something humiliating, we will continue to esteem the established order and not allow ourselves to be swept up by the Spirit of Jesus. We walk with the poor only by serving them with the Spirit of Jesus. When we experience that as a graced relationship, it is something good not just for those being served but even more for those who serve. So if we are really following Jesus, we will serve the poor with gratitude.

Only in this way will the vital practice of synodality with the whole people of God, and especially with the poor, become an alternative that can overcome the present pyramidal society. Understanding, proclaiming, and practicing synodality, as Pope Francis undoubtedly does, is a great grace, and that is precisely why he meets such great resistance.

For all these reasons, in this pyramidal society in which all aspire to climb as high as possible, synodality with the poor, especially with the poor in spirit, marks the measure of our fidelity to the path of Jesus, to Jesus the Way.

I want to emphasize that this image of the pyramid, although odious, is essential, because it is the real starting point and cannot be ignored. The alternative that overcomes it can be created only by taking what already exists and transforming it. Attempting a fresh start that ignores the current situation would be ahistorical and therefore illusory. In liberated environments, it makes sense to cultivate polyhedral relationships, that is, horizontal relationships in which all of us are necessary because all of us contribute our riches and receive the treasures of others. It makes sense to propose this mutuality as the true alternative, as Pope Francis has been doing, but we must remember that, unless the present situation is transformed, our other efforts will fall short. The transformation that Jesus proposes in the gospels is to go from dominating to serving. This is a shift that has nothing to do with turning the tables of power. Rather, it involves the progressive elimination of servitude. Or rather, it means refusing to serve those who set the rules of the game for their own convenience and instead placing ourselves at the service of everyone, especially the oppressed and excluded, until we are all finally able to see one another as sisters and brothers. We may never achieve this goal in history, but we will still be obliged to serve those forced into servitude and those excluded from the system—and even the excluders themselves, so that they will experience another way of relating in our mutual service to one another.

Translated by Rafael Luciani

Between Crisis and Renewal: The Synodal Path of the Catholic Church in Germany

Julia Knop

On December 1, 2019, the first Sunday of Advent, the Synodal Path of the Catholic Church in Germany began. It is a process of consultation and reform that the German Bishops' Conference together with the Central Committee of Catholics have initiated and taken responsibility for. This double responsibility of the two representative institutions of Catholicism in Germany, the organizations of the bishops and of the lay people, is one of the most notable characteristics of this reform process for the universal church.

Another specific characteristic is its limited selection of topics: the reason for this synodal format of ecclesial conversion (*metanoia*) is the systemic failure of the church, which has become evident in the scandal of sexualized violence and its cover-up by church leaders. This systemic failure also determines the huge but clearly defined task of this process. It is about identifying and correcting the crucial theological, spiritual, and institutional factors that have facilitated such violence and cover-up, failed to prevent them, and worked to prevent their punishment.

Both specific characteristics—the common responsibility of bishops and lay people, and the focus on ecclesiastical catharsis in light of the abuse crisis—distinguish the Synodal Path of the Catholic Church in Germany, which began in 2019, from the worldwide Synodal Path, which Pope Francis initiated two years later. But the experiences and results of the process in Germany so far will certainly contribute to the synodal reflections being undertaken at a global level.[1]

The Synodal Path in Germany has attracted close attention in neighboring countries and worldwide for many reasons,[2] especially because the problems of abuse and cover-up have come to light everywhere in the world church.

Formerly taboo issues now receive significant attention at the level of the universal church: ecclesiastical power structures, priestly life, the role of women in the church, and the church's teaching on sexuality. To reflect on and correct these is certainly a task that extends beyond Germany or Western Europe. In Germany, though, important resources exist that can facilitate discussion of them in a competent way: renowned institutions of academic theology, an organization of Catholic laity, and a democratic culture of consultation and decision-making that has been developed over many decades. Out of these resources at a local church level arises a particular responsibility to support this reform process at the global level.

The format chosen by organizers of the Synodal Path in Germany opens to German Catholics synodal experiences that go further than canon law and church practice had permitted up to now. Not only does the Synodal Path allow the experiences and expectations of the faithful to be heard but bishops and the faithful, experts and lay people, discuss and decide important matters together. As a result, responsibility is shared. Interdisciplinary expertise is called for. Binding decisions are generated in the syn-

[1] See German Bishops' Conference, "For a Synodal Church—Community, Participation and Mission: The Report of the German Bishops' Conference to the World Synod of Bishops 2023," May 8, 2022, https://www.dbk.de/fileadmin/redaktion /diverse_downloads/presse_2022/2022-114eng-Report-of-the-German-Bishops -Conference-to-the-World-Synod-of-Bishops-2023.pdf.

[2] See the thematic issue "Universal Church in Motion: Synodal Path," of the magazine *Herder Korrespondenz*, September 2022, https://www.synodalerweg.de /fileadmin/Synodalerweg/Materialien/HerderThema-SW-ENG_UniversalChurch inMotion-SynodalPaths.pdf. Also available in German and Italian editions.

odal assembly by persuasion and consent rather than solely in terms of authority and doctrine. The decision to implement the changes voted for by a majority, however, still remains wholly in the bishops' hands: "Decisions of the synodal assembly take no legal effect by themselves. The authority of the bishops' conference and of the individual diocesan bishops to enact legal norms in the context of their respective jurisdiction and to exert their teaching office remains undisturbed by the decisions."[3]

It is, therefore, simply wrong to state that the common discussion and decision-making in the synodal assembly would undermine the authority of the bishops or tie their hands, or that the episcopal office would be "hollowed out" (as Cardinal Walter Kasper has put it). The chosen format has the potential, though, to change Roman Catholic self-understanding and church structures from within—with the bishops, not against them—and, further, to highlight the need for a deeper reflection on, and reimagining of, the episcopacy for the twenty-first century. That is urgently necessary.

Occasion and Aim of the Synodal Path—Why?

The reason for the Synodal Path reform process is the contemporary crisis of the church in general and the ecclesial teaching office in particular. In autumn of 2018, the results of an extensive investigation (the MHG-Studie) on the sexual abuse of minors by Catholic clergy in Germany were released by the German Bishops' Conference.[4] In this survey, statistics regarding acts of sexual

---

[3] Statutes of the Synodal Way, Article 11 (5): https://www.synodalerweg.de /fileadmin/Synodalerweg/Dokumente_Reden_Beitraege/Satzung-des-Synodalen -Weges.pdf.

[4] The MHG Survey (MHG-Studie) is named after the locations of the research institutions involved. Scholars of the Central Institute for Mental Health in Mannheim, the Institute of Criminology and Institute for Gerontology of the University of Heidelberg, and the Chair of Criminology, Youth Law and Penal System of the University of Gießen. The complete study is available in German at https://www.dbk.de /fileadmin/redaktion/diverse_downloads/dossiers_2018/MHG-Studie-gesamt.pdf. A summary in English is available at https://www.dbk.de/fileadmin/redaktion /diverse_downloads/dossiers_2018/MHG-eng-Endbericht-Zusammenfassung-14-08 -2018.pdf.

violence against vulnerable persons by Catholic clergy were uncovered and analyzed. The German Bishops' Conference commissioned this survey of its own accord. The results were shocking. Church personnel records spanning the period from 1946 to 2014 revealed that around 5 percent of diocesan priests—that is, one in every twenty priests—was accused of sexual abuse of minors. But that is likely to be an underestimate, given that there were significant deficiencies in episcopal file management, including deliberate file manipulation. Unrecorded cases, as well as the abuse of power and the sexual abuse of adults, especially of women and female members of religious orders, as well as seminarians, were not considered in the study.

Since then, many other reports have been published, and more are still to appear. All confirm what we already know of the numbers of perpetrators and those affected. They provide details of the perpetrators and the circumstances of the crimes. They expose the mechanisms of cover-up and the downplaying and denial of clerical violence in the church. Some reports focus on individual dioceses, congregations, or institutions, such as the Schönstatt Movement, the Catholic Integrated Community (Katholische Integrierte Gemeinde), and the Regensburg Cathedral Boys' Choir (Domspatzen). The reports cover various time periods. Research by journalists focused on individual (and multiple) perpetrators (e.g., the priest Peter H. in the dioceses of Essen and Munich-Freising), criminal trials (e.g., against the priest Ue. of the diocese of Cologne before the county court of Cologne), or dioceses (e.g., the Diocese of Trier). They show the human beings behind the structures and proceedings: the perpetrators, the people behind the cover-ups, and the many forgotten and disregarded victims of sexual violence by clergy. Some reports (e.g., those prepared by the Dioceses of Cologne, Aachen, and Munich-Freising) work simply on the basis of files; they take a purely juridical approach, collating litigable facts and listing objectifiable "breaches of duty" by the leading people in charge. Others (e.g., in the Dioceses of Münster and Paderborn) approach the issue from a historical and anthropological angle, highlighting problematic institutional, environmental, and ideological interconnections.

Not a single study has been proved wrong or undermined the statistics already available and mentioned above. On the contrary, there can no longer be any doubt that there are specifically Roman

Catholic factors that threaten the physical, mental, psychological, and spiritual integrity of children and adolescents, as well as of women and female members of Catholic religious orders. These include a self-enclosed clerical power structure; fraternal-like structures and customs; the sacralization of the institution; a gay clerical subculture alongside a homophobic orientation in doctrine and practice; sexual ethics predominantly shaped by taboos, restrictions, and fear; and a religious exaltation of the sacred office in particular and the institutional church in general, whose reputation must be preserved at all costs. Taken together, these factors have a toxic impact. They give rise to sexually immature, regressive, and narcissistic men and protect them even when they become perpetrators—all at the expense of those who have fallen, and continue to fall, victim to their physical, sexual, psychological, and spiritual abuse.[5]

The Synodal Path, therefore, has addressed four topics—power, priesthood, the role of women, and sexual ethics—primarily in view of the above-mentioned problematic consequences and their link to clerical violence, but also because of the need for a more general reflection on these questions, which many laity have sought for decades. Their wish has not instigated any serious ecclesial reform process up to now, however. To the contrary, during the pontificates of John Paul II and Benedict XVI, theological debate about power and gender questions had become downright taboo. But now, in this particular interweaving of power and gender, a particularly dangerous potential for sexual violence and spiritual abuse has been identified. Catholics in Germany have now made it clear that in following the Synodal Path, we cannot avoid these questions anymore. The power structure of the Roman Catholic Church, its understanding of priesthood, its understanding of women,[6] and its sexual ethics—and in particular the condemnation and tabooing of homosexuality—and the way these have supported a system that has massively damaged, still damages,

---

[5] See Doris Wagner, *Spiritueller Missbrauch in der katholischen Kirche* (Freiburg: Herder, 2019).

[6] This field has only recently been explored. See Doris Wagner [Reisinger], *Nicht mehr Ich: Die wahre Geschichte einer jungen Ordensfrau* (Wien: edition a, 2014); Barbara Haslbeck, Regina Heyder, Ute Leimgruber, and Dorothee Sandherr-Klemp, eds., *Erzählen als Widerstand: Berichte über spirituellen und sexuellen Missbrauch an erwachsenen Frauen in der katholischen Kirche* (Münster: Aschendorff, 2020).

and can further damage the physical and psychological integrity of boys, girls, women, and female members of religious orders must all be examined anew.

The Synodal Path faces up to this challenge. Four working groups within the synodal forum addressed the four key topics:

1. "Power and Separation of Powers in the Church: Joint Participation and Involvement in the Mission,"

2. "Priestly Life Today,"

3. "Women in Ministries and Offices in the Church,"

4. "Life in Successful Relationships—Living Love in Sexuality and Partnership."[7]

This work has been accompanied by academic conferences and networks, academic publications,[8] and the genre of "narrated life," which includes witness statements of people affected by abuse, queer Catholics, and church employees, and autobiographical reports of women who, as far as official Catholic theology is concerned, are not allowed to live their vocation.[9]

The Synodal Path: Structure, Format, and Process

Synodality, it's often said, is above all a style and the promotion of a culture of listening. That is true. Without a cultivated synodal style, any ecclesial discussion becomes a farce. But synodality is

[7] Three of the four topics—power, priests, sexuality—had already been named in the MHG survey. The fourth topic—women in the church—had been proposed by the Central Committee of Catholics, which made its discussion a condition of a synodal process for which all are responsible together.

[8] See, e.g., Birgit Aschmann, ed., *Katholische Dunkelräume: Die Kirche und der sexuelle Missbrauch* (Paderborn: Schöningh, 2022); Thomas Bahne, ed., *Verletzbarkeit des Humanen: Sexualisierte Gewalt an Minderjährigen im interdisziplinären Diskurs* (Regensburg: Pustet, 2021); Thomas Großbölting, *Die schuldigen Hirten: Geschichte des sexuellen Missbrauchs in der Kirche* (Freiburg: Herder, 2022); Doris Reisinger, ed., *Gefährliche Theologien: Wenn theologische Ansätze Machtmissbrauch legitimieren* (Regensburg: Pustet, 2021); Matthias Remenyi and Thomas Schärtl, eds., *Nicht ausweichen: Theologie angesichts der Missbrauchskrise* (Regensburg: Pustet, 2019).

[9] See Philippa Rath, ed., ". . . weil Gott es so will": Frauen erzählen von ihrer Berufung zur Diakonin und Priesterin* (Freiburg: Herder, 2021).

not limited to questions of style. Synods are institutions of church governance. Therefore, synodality also always implies a responsibility for the governance and shaping of the church. In the official structures of the Roman Catholic Church, this ultimate responsibility is assigned to the bishops. Whether they exert this responsibility in a synodal manner, whether they cultivate a synodal style in their office of leadership, depends on their goodwill. Some have been operating in a synodal manner for some time, out of conviction, but without the necessary structural support. A lack of synodal structures allows others, however, the opportunity to "reign" in an authoritative style, intolerant of objections and accountable to no one but the pope. Without doubt, then, synodality needs a synodal culture and a synodal mindset, but it also needs synodal structures. Otherwise, arbitrariness will ultimately win out. Structures can relieve the pressure since they delineate procedures and responsibilities. They can be reviewed and shaped.

New synodal formats are being tried out at the Synodal Path of the Catholic Church in Germany.[10] The shared discussion and decision-making by bishops and lay people, and their institutional representation on all levels, are crucial in this process. Organs of the Synodal Path include the synodal steering committee, the extended synodal steering committee, the synodal forums, and especially the synodal assembly.

The *synodal steering committee* consists of the chairman (until March 2020, Cardinal Reinhard Marx, archbishop of Munich and Freising; at this time of writing Georg Bätzing, bishop of Limburg) and vice chairman of the German Bishops' conference (Franz-Josef Bode, bishop of Osnabrück) and the president (until November 2021, Thomas Sternberg; currently Irme Stetter-Karp) and a vice president of the Central Committee of Catholics (until November 2021, Karin Kortmann; at present Thomas Söding).

The *extended steering committee* consists, alongside these four, of the chairpersons of the synodal forums as well as the two "spiritual accompaniers" of the process.

[10] Information on the participants, procedures, polling votes, documents, explanatory notes, and discussion statements related to the Synodal Path of the Catholic Church in Germany can be found in German and (partly) in English, Italian, and Spanish at https://www.synodalerweg.de.

The *four synodal forums* each consist of about thirty members—bishops, laity, and experts—and are each led by a member of the German Bishops' Conference and a member of the Central Committee of Catholics. They work on the four central topics of the Synodal Path:

1. "Power and Separation of Powers in the Church: Joint Participation and Involvement in the Mission," led by Claudia Lücking-Michel (Central Committee of Catholics) and Bishop Franz-Josef Overbeck (German Bishops' conference, Diocese of Essen);

2. "Priestly Life Today," led by Stephan Buttgereit (Central Committee of Catholics) and Bishop Felix Genn (German Bishops' Conference, Diocese of Münster);

3. "Women in Ministries and Offices in the Church," led by Dorothea Sattler (Central Committee of Catholics) and Bishop Franz-Josef Bode (German Bishops' Conference, Diocese of Osnabrück);

4. "Life in Successful Relationships—Living Love in Sexuality and Partnership," led by Birgit Mock (Central Committee of Catholics) and Bishop Helmut Dieser (German Bishops' conference, Diocese of Aachen; Bishop Georg Bätzing was the episcopal chairman of this forum before he became chairman of the German Bishops' conference in March 2020).

The crucial organ of the Synodal Path is the *synodal assembly*, to which 230 people belong. These members pass the resolutions of the Synodal Path. The synodal assembly consists of all (69) members of the German Bishops' Conference, the same number of representatives from the Central Committee of Catholics, and 92 representatives of various professional and interest groups in the church, including priests, parish workers, catechists, teachers, members of religious orders, young people, and theologians. This allocation means that almost half of the synod members are clergy. The bishops comprise around one-third of the assembly; another third (63) are women. The recommendation of the statutes to seek an even balance of gender and generations in team composition is rendered impossible by the high number of clergy. The inclusion of bishops in an organization where they are not the majority, as well as the current gender allocation where one-third of the board are women, are innovations for a Roman Catholic setting and overall has been a positive experience.

All texts go through two readings. In the first reading, those involved decide on the direction of the discussion: Is it possible to reach a consensus on the objective and the approach to the topic? What is missing and what should be changed? The second reading is about fine-tuning and the general approval or rejection of the motion. It is here that things get serious. While in the first reading, a simple majority of the plenary is enough to continue working, in the second reading a "double" two-thirds majority is required to approve a text: the majority of the plenary (including the bishops) and the majority of the bishops. Furthermore, a two-thirds majority of the non-male members of the synodal assembly may be requested. This must be requested in advance. It is also possible to make a motion for a vote by roll call in both polling rounds. A text that doesn't receive the required majority in the second reading is rejected. When it appears that further discussions are necessary beyond the second reading, a motion for a third reading can be made before the second vote.

For a resolution to pass, a minimum of 154 affirmative votes from the plenary, 46 from the group of bishops, and 42 from the female synod members are required, with the voting taking place at the same time and in full assembly. To block a resolution, 24 episcopal votes—10 percent of the assembly—is sufficient, due to the "double" two-thirds majority required for a resolution to be approved. Thus the bishops can form a kind of "blocking minority." They are accorded a privileged position because they are members of the synod by virtue of their office rather than by delegation or election and, canonically, too, they enjoy a higher rank.

Resolutions, which require approval by the Vatican, are relayed via the German Bishops' Conference to the Holy See; no one is planning a solo run at the level of the national church. The Synodal Assembly shall adopt resolutions. The bishop must ensure their legal enactment at the diocesan level. If an individual diocesan bishop does not agree with a resolution that has been voted for by a majority, he is free not to implement it in his diocese. This is a paradox and maybe also an opportunity for this reform process. On the one hand, it is the explicit task of the Synodal Path to critically reflect on and to reform the power structures of the Catholic Church, developing new ways of sharing, limiting, and controlling clerical power. But in the decision-making of the Synodal Path itself, this intention has not yet found expression. The previous rules are still operative: the bishops' majority still decides, and even at local level things will depend again on the "goodwill" of each individual bishop. So the discussions and decisions of the synodal assembly are a work of persuasion. It will only be successful if the individual bishops themselves are convinced by the project of reform, participate actively in the debates, work together on the texts, and are ready and capable of implementing the resolutions. Thus, progress on a range of synodal resolutions will only come about if the bishops are committed to the process and, without prejudice to their episcopal authority, are willing to limit and share their episcopal power; bind their power to group decisions, procedures, checks; and be held to account for their decisions.

Successes

The four synodal forums have worked intensively. Each forum submits a "base text" of around thirty to forty pages. In these base texts, the theological principles of renewal, corresponding to the respective topic (power, office, women, sexuality), are grounded and developed. Further, "action texts" of two to four pages are compiled. From these, the forums develop concrete recommendations for church teaching and practice, and they formulate, according to each topic, recommendations for the bishops, the pope, or the universal church. A preamble as well as an "orientation text" form a preface, which is introduced by the steering committee.[11]

In the third and fourth general assembly, groundbreaking, significant texts were passed with large majorities (in the plenary, over 80 percent approval; among the women, over 90 percent; among the bishops, over 70 percent). At the third general assembly

[11] All texts together with the voting results can be viewed at https://www .synodalerweg.de/dokumente-reden-und-beitraege#c4376.

in February 2022, a theologically nuanced orientation text was passed. In this text, the "signs of the times" (*Gaudium et Spes* 4) and the *"sensus fidelium"* (*Lumen Gentium* 12) are given particular importance. While they were emphasized at the Second Vatican Council, they were not effectively put into practice afterwards. Moreover, the episcopal teaching office is taken out of its isolated special position and placed into a network of testimonial authorities: Scripture and tradition, teaching office and theology, *sensus fidelium* and signs of the times are all to be taken seriously as qualified *loci theologici*.

The base text of forum 1, "Power and the Separation of Powers in the Church," describes the church, along the lines of Vatican II, as "sacrament of salvation" (*Lumen Gentium* 1, 48), that is, as sign (*signum*) and instrument (*instrumentum*) of God's love. In its nature as a sign, the church is intelligible, plausible, and persuasive. As instrument, it effectively fosters its salvific aspect. A church that claims to be a sign and instrument of salvation must, therefore, prove this claim in its life; its way of acting must be convincingly salvific. By the same token, "unsalvific" ways of church behavior must be excluded. Otherwise, the church's self-understanding is contradicted. This can be put into practice with standards such as checks and balances, including checks on how power is exercised, quality control at management level, transparent and gender-equal access to positions of importance in the church, and the incorporation of accountability and conflict management into the church. The episcopal office is not thereby rendered superfluous, but professionalized and placed in an appropriate context. Thus, if a bishop's responsibility is shared, this doesn't mean less responsibility; rather, it offers episcopal leadership the opportunity to profit from the support of the faithful while meeting all the requirements of quality control.

At the fourth general assembly in September 2022, the base text of forum 3, "Women in Ministries and Offices in the Church," was passed with all the required majorities. With this text, for the first time worldwide, a local church with an episcopal majority has spoken out, affirming, "The goal of becoming a gender-equitable Church requires the presence of more women in leadership positions"—thus begins the first sentence of the paper. The dogmatic obstacle of the Roman Catholic Church, established by John Paul II with *Ordinatio Sacerdotalis* in 1994 regarding women's ordination, should be reexamined. The text reviews the biblical, historical, ecumenical, and anthropological arguments that could make possible women's ordination in the Roman Catholic Church. It examines the problematic history of the church, which for centuries marginalised women and failed to appreciate their gifts. This doesn't mean that women will be ordained priests and bishops tomorrow. But reopening this question for debate at the global level is a crucial step in the right direction.

Alongside these comprehensive and theologically substantial texts were ones of a more concrete character that were also passed in a second reading with all the required majorities. Bishops can directly implement these suggestions, which apply at the level of the local church. Votes that have consequences at the level of the universal church—for example, those that concern church doctrine—will be forwarded to the pope or brought to the world Synodal Path.

Forum 1 (Power and the Separation of Powers in the Church) approved declarations concerning the participation of the faithful when a new bishop is chosen (at the level of the local church) and on the establishment of a synodal council, which consolidates in a representative way the leadership responsibility of the bishops and the faithful (at the level of the local church).

Forum 3 (Priestly Life Today) approved a text on increasing the liturgical presence of women, including by delivering homilies, baptizing, and assisting at weddings (at the level of the local church).

Forum 4 (Sexuality and Partnership) passed a vote in favor of correcting the church's doctrine on homosexuality (at the level of the universal church) and a text on the reform of church workplace law, according to which, up to now, church employees may be fired for homosexuality or divorce, among other factors (at the level of the local church).

At a *first* reading, some texts (as of September 2022) were discussed and accepted for further editing. These included, from forum 1 (Power and the Separation of Powers in the Church), texts on the accountability of the bishop (at the level of the local church) and on the consolidation of synodal structures in dioceses and parishes (at the level of the local church); from forum 2 (Priestly Life Today), texts on the prevention of abuse and dealing with perpetrators of abuse (at the level of the local church), the professionalisation and personal development of priests (at the level of the local church), the reconsideration of mandatory celibacy (at local and universal church level), and the difficult (because taboo) situation of homosexual priests (at local and universal church level); from forum 3 (Women in Ministries and Offices in the Church), texts on the opening of all sacramental offices (universal church level) and specifically on women's diaconate (universal church level), and on women's pastoral ministry of leadership (at the level of the local church) and their promotion in the theological academy (at the level of the local church); from forum 4 (Sexuality and Partnership), texts on blessing ceremonies for (homosexual) couples (at the level of the local church), the reform of church teaching on marital love (universal church level), and on the acknowledgment of gender diversity (LGBTQI+) (local church level).

Texts that are, at the time of writing, prepared but still to be discussed include, from forum 1, on the implementation of fundamental rights in the church (universal church level), on a framework for diocesan finances (at the level of the local church), on the setting up of offices of ombudsman for the prevention and reprocessing of abuse (at the level of the local church), and on the guarantee to the rights of legal process (at the level of the local church); and from forum 3, a text that deals with the abuse of adult women and female members of religious orders by clergy.

Crises: Black Thursday

Of course, the reform process of the Catholic Church in Germany is not immune from crises. Just as the Second Vatican Council had in its day, the Synodal Path in Germany also had its own "Black Thursday" on September 8, 2022. This was a moment in which the whole synodal process was in danger of collapsing. What happened?

Like each synodal forum, forum 4, "Sexuality and Partnership," submitted a base text. It recommended the initiation of a renewal of Catholic sexual teaching. The text was passed in the first reading by a large majority in the second general assembly a year before. Further, in a second reading, it was approved by over 82 percent of all synod members during the fourth general assembly. But it failed, nevertheless, because it did not receive the backing of a two-thirds majority of the bishops (required by the statutes), with 21 bishops (39 percent) voting against the text and only 33 (61 percent) voting for it. What was behind this, and what was the dissent about?

The text raises many old issues that have been discussed since the 1960s: sex before and outside of marriage, family planning, sexual self-determination, and the moral evaluation of homosexuality. In contrast to traditional doctrine, the text put love rather than procreation at its center. It insisted that committed relationships between two adults are good. They are blessed by God, even when they are same-sex relationships.

Moreover, the text introduced new topics: about women and men and those born between the poles of female and male, about the distinctions between sex from a biological perspective and from a gender (social) perspective. With these topics, the text tries to bring the Catholic Church up to date (still very cautiously—for many of those involved, too cautiously). But it finds itself in opposition to the Congregation for the Doctrine of the Faith and the Congregation for Catholic Education and the Vatican's polemics against so-called "gender ideology" and sexual diversity, while claiming to fully understand womanhood and what women are capable of doing or not doing.

The text thus suggests important adjustments for a renewed and more up-to-date approach to sexuality, family, and partnership. Church teaching should no longer focus on prohibitions nor provoke feelings of guilt but rather promote an appreciation of human sexuality as a positive power and respect the right of human self-determination. Further, it calls for a more self-critical view of the church's teaching and acting. At the very beginning, the text states: "Because of the [church's] doctrine on sexuality and church practice the members of our church and the church as an institution and community of the faithful, are guilty."[12]

[12] This guilt consists of a merciless pastoral and rigorous penitential practice in the field of sexuality, marriage, and family, which has troubled people's consciences for decades, and by the tabooing and condemnation of queer sexuality, which has pushed those affected, lay people and clergy, into a duplicity of life.

Forty percent of the bishops present rejected this desire for a paradigm shift in the church's sexual doctrine. Hardly any had taken the opportunity in the previous months to obtain information about the text or actively participate in its development. Hardly any had integrated the insights of theology and the human sciences reflected in the text. Hardly any had expressed an informed opinion in the debate or expressed misgivings. Subsequently, only arguments from authority were put forward; they had sworn, after all, to keep the deposit of the faith "unharmed," and as they see it, this oath forbids any effort to reform the church's sexual doctrine.

In this way, a text that could have finally reconciled Catholic sexual teaching with real life failed because of the resistance of 21 bishops who are clearly still not ready to allow people to shape their partnerships and sexuality in an autonomous and personally responsible way—something they have been doing now for decades anyway. Their vote was a discouraging signal to anyone who lives their sexuality and partnership responsibly, even though the way they choose to do it doesn't fit into the church's framework. It was a decisive signal to those who are excluded and discriminated against by the church's teaching and practice, a signal that protecting church doctrine from "harm" is more important than the faithful who are harmed by the church.

Faced with this, some in the assembly hall were visibly upset. Many cried. Some left the room and the assembly because they simply couldn't bear this vote. Once again, they felt betrayed by their church. Once again, they experienced that "Catholic and queer" still don't belong together. The Catholic Church is still not a "safe space" for them. Nonetheless, in the meantime, some bishops have taken public positions of support, sought to implement the text's recommendations in practice in their dioceses, and introduced its ideas into the world synodal process. The Central Committee of Catholics has asked the German Bishops' Conference for "public clarification and verifiable actions . . . so that every form of (church) discrimination [of queer people] will be overcome."[13]

---

[13] https://www.zdk.de/veroeffentlichungen/erklaerungen/detail/Erklaerung-des-ZdK-Praesidiums-nach-der-vierten-Synodalversammlung-297M/.

Regarding this crisis of September 8, 2022, three things may be noted. First, in view of the text's *contents*, disillusionment was expressed that at a church governance level, when it comes to questions of sexuality and partnership, there is still no willingness to respect the reality, the experience, and the faithful's assessment of their own conscience. Second, in view of the *process*, there was anger that 40 percent of the bishops, without any recognizable participation in the process of opinion-forming, chose simply to anonymously use their instrument of power, the blocking minority, that the Synodal Path's statutes grants them. Third, in so doing, a blatant *leadership failure* finally became visible: poor communication and profound conflicts within the bishops' conference, as well as between diocesan and auxiliary bishops; a failure in the episcopal ministry to preserve unity; perception of the bishops as no longer representatives of the faithful; and abdication of the specific responsibility attached to the privileged position of the bishops: the one who leads "must work more, reflect more, listen more, and say more than the others. For his voice has more weight than that of the others,"[14] as the professor for pastoral theology from the University of Bochum, Matthias Sellmann, aptly commented.

After this "Black Thursday," votes by roll call were called for on a regular basis, so that the votes of all—the bishops as well as the nonepiscopal male and female members of the synod—would be publicly visible and thus scrutinized. Moreover, the bishops retreated for private discussion among themselves before every subsequent vote. All the following resolutions, including the action texts emerging out of the dismissed implementation text of forum 4 (on the reassessment of homosexuality as well as on the acknowledgment of gender diversity and the overcoming of the church's homophobia and transphobia), resulted in the required two-thirds majority of the synodal assembly and the bishops.

Learning Synodality

The Synodal Path of the Catholic Church in Germany is a way of learning. Its male and female members—the bishops and the

[14] "Synodaler Weg: Sellmann fordert mehr Professionalität der Bischöfe," September 13, 2022, https://www.katholisch.de/artikel/40974-synodaler-weg-sellmann-fordert-mehr-professionalitaet-der-bischoefe.

faithful alike—are learning in a practical way what will also be the case in the future on an institutional level in the church, namely, that bishops and the faithful discuss together and decide together, that all shape the church and together take responsibility for the life of the church.

This process is anything but a revolution. It is developing, even though its concrete format isn't fully incorporated in canon law, within a valid ecclesial framework that attributes a special authority to the bishops and acknowledges their final say in decision making. Within this framework and these conditions, it simultaneously expects from them a commitment not to make decisions on their own and not to exercise their pastoral office in an absolutist manner. It expects that they engage in conversation with the faithful, take their experiences seriously, and face their questions. It implies they should take advice from experts and engage in ongoing formation so as to exercise their teaching office in a well-informed and competent way. It requires them to cede their authority to the better argument, doctrine to real life, and tradition to "the joys and the hopes, the griefs and the anxieties of the men of this age" (*Gaudium et Spes* 1). And because the church system is as it is—clerical and hierarchical—all this ultimately depends on the goodwill of clergy and the hierarchy, and whether they accept these challenges. Indeed, it asks whether their concern for, their sympathy with, and their connection to the faithful, who have been entrusted to them, has more weight than their interest in supporting the ecclesiastical system and protecting their own positions of power. This reform process demands quite a lot from the faithful, too. It challenges them, despite the horrendous history of guilt of the church, despite the systemic abuse and cover-ups, despite the structural and doctrinal discrimination toward women, homosexuals, and trans people, to nevertheless have confidence in the bishops.

The world church's broad interest in the Synodal Path of the Catholic Church in Germany also mirrors these reciprocal challenges. This applies especially to the voices of those who wish to protect the authority of the episcopal office, stress the continuity of doctrine without dissent, and, even today, deny the systemic, doctrinal, and spiritual backgrounds of clerical abuse. The reservations that, for example, the Polish and the Scandinavian bishops' conferences, as well as a dozen or so bishops from the United States and Africa, have articulated in open letters are diametrically opposed, however, to the perceptions of official international male and female observers. These are a testimony to the wide interest of their countries and dioceses in the German synodal texts and process. It was the male and female observers from Switzerland, Luxembourg, and Belgium, who, on the day after "Black Thursday" in Frankfurt, passed a vote of confidence in the synodal assembly and encouraged its members to keep going.[15] Their support was much appreciated.

The Synodal Path of the Catholic Church in Germany will test whether the call for ecclesiastical reform and renewal will be taken seriously and whether the bishops and the faithful have sufficient strength and will for such genuine conversion.

Translated by Astrid Schilling and Declan Marmion

---

[15] See the statements of the male and female observers of the fourth general assembly: https://www.synodalerweg.de/dokumente-reden-und-beitraege#c4596. All observers are listed here: https://www.synodalerweg.de/fileadmin/Synodalerweg /Dokumente_Reden_Beitraege/Synodalversammlung-Beobachter.pdf. Three of them speak at every general assembly.

A Conversion to Dialogue: The Church's Dialogical Reform in the Light of *Gaudium et Spes*

Agnès Desmazières

Since the beginning of the 1990s, Jorge Mario Bergoglio, the future Pope Francis, has promoted a "culture of dialogue," or "culture of encounter," in the context of a postdictatorial Argentina that was socially and politically divided.[1] At the beginning of his pontificate, he enlarged his call to a "culture of dialogue" within the church itself.[2] If this invitation to dialogue responds to the current situation of the church, increasingly polarized and suffering from clericalism, it also corresponds to the "relational nature of the Church," its relationality being "dialogical."[3]

The affirmation of the dialogical character of the church is associated with a new awareness of its missionary character, which led Pope Paul VI to state, "Evangelizing is in fact the grace and

---

[1] See Agnès Desmazières, *Le dialogue pour surmonter la crise: Le pari réformateur du pape François* (Paris: Salvator, 2019).

[2] See, for instance, Pope Francis, "Meeting with the Academic and Cultural World," September 22, 2013, https://www.vatican.va/content/francesco/en/speeches/2013/september/documents/papa-francesco_20130922_cultura-cagliari.html.

[3] Walter Kasper, *L'Église catholique: Son être, sa réalisation, sa mission*, Cogitatio fidei 293 (Paris: Cerf, 2014), 212, 421.

vocation proper to the Church, her deepest identity. She exists in order to evangelize."[4] In this perspective, the dialogical nature of the church cannot be authentically understood without reference to its mission to dialogue with the world. Such a dialogue is particularly necessary in a world that values authentic, respectful, and equalitarian relationships.

This chapter highlights how the church's dialogue with the world, as it is envisaged in Vatican II's *Gaudium et Spes*, impacts dialogue within the church and thus can help present dialogue within the church in a more horizontal and transparent way, grounded in a reevaluation of the notion of *competence* and of the contribution of the lay faithful to the life of the church. It will especially examine part one of *Gaudium et Spes*, on "The Church and Man's Calling," in relation to several accounts from one of the key theologians of that council, Yves Congar, including some unpublished papers found in his archives and his *Journal of the Council*.

It will first show how *Gaudium et Spes* is crucial for an understanding of the relationship between dialogue with the world and dialogue within the church. It will then move to a study of the first chapter of the document, which offers a renewed anthropology centered on the dignity of the human person and her social identity, opening out to a consideration of the necessity of conversion, both personal and communal; the increased sensitivity to the church's historicity facilitates a true dialogue where the church recognizes her faults. Finally, following *Gaudium et Spes*, dialogue with the world requires a dialogue of the various vocations within the church, giving primacy to the lay faithful, with their competence and freedom.

Dialogue within the Church, Dialogue with the World

The pastoral constitution *Gaudium et Spes*'s late appearance in the Second Vatican Council agenda is representative of a shift of understanding of the church. It concretized the conciliar fathers'

---

[4] Pope Paul VI, apostolic exhortation *Evangelii Nuntiandi*, December 8, 1975, 14, https://www.vatican.va/content/paul-vi/en/apost_exhortations/documents/hf
_p-vi_exh_19751208_evangelii-nuntiandi.html.

decision to abandon an essential conception of the church as *"societas perfecta"* (a "perfect society") and to adopt a more existential and historical one: a church that is on pilgrimage on earth, journeying toward eternal glory.

Gaudium et Spes, the only schema, or draft document, not to have been prepared before the first session of the council, was the result of extensive work by Cardinal Suenens. With Pope John XXIII's support, the Belgian Archbishop of Malines-Brussels had proposed a work plan for the council, orientated in two directions: the church *ad intra* (in itself) and the church *ad extra* (outwards). *Gaudium et Spes* was designed to form the backbone of the *ad extra* perspective. Moreover, though written toward the end of the council, *Gaudium et Spes* was also considered by its writers as a complement to the dogmatic constitution *Lumen Gentium*, on the church *ad intra*, which did not reflect later developments of the conciliar ecclesiological debates because it had been promulgated a year before.

In this perspective, this conciliar document overcame the dialectical tension between *ad intra* and *ad extra*, notably pointed out by Karl Rahner, and constituted a "synthesis of all the schemas."[5] In *Dialogue in the Church* (1967), the German theologian had criticized Suenens's dual perspective and stressed that the "'world' is not simply 'outside,' but [is] rather present in the Church herself," in such a way that "the decisive dialogue with the world [was] that which [took] place precisely within the Church."[6] The world was no longer estranged from the church.

Interestingly, *Gaudium et Spes* marks the emergence of the theological category of dialogue in the context of Vatican II.[7] The appearance of the term highlights how dialogue with the world induced a progressive change of theological vocabulary. This evolution can be explained by the loss of influence of scholastic philosophies and the concomitant increased importance of the

---

[5] Roger Etchegaray, "Autour du schéme XIII," October 13, 1964 (Archivio Vaticano [AV], Fondo Concilio Vaticano II, f. 14, b. 1190, 306).

[6] Karl Rahner, "Dialogue in the Church," in *Theological Investigations*, vol. 10 (New York: Crossroad, 1977), 106.

[7] See Ann Michele Nolan, *A Privileged Moment: Dialogue in the Language of the Second Vatican Council, 1962–1965* (Bern: Peter Lang, 2006).

philosophies of dialogue, born in the interwar period in the Germanophone context. Martin Buber, for instance, had a deep impact on the thought of both Yves Congar and the future Pope Paul VI. It is no wonder, then, that Paul VI's first encyclical letter, *Ecclesiam Suam* (1964), defined the church's mission in terms of dialogue. Dialogue was intimately related to church reform and crucial for the church's renewal.

This shift toward dialogue did not come easily, however, especially because the term evoked a more horizontal understanding of the church. Remarkably, while Paul VI used the Italian word *dialogo* in the original version of *Ecclesiam Suam*, in the official document, in Latin, the word became *colloquium* ("conversation").[8] If *dialogue* had penetrated the common language, it was not yet domesticated by the church. The first drafts of *Gaudium et Spes* and *Unitatis Redintegratio*, the decree on ecumenism, also spoke of dialogue in terms of "conversation." It was only in February 1965, a few months before the promulgation of *Gaudium et Spes* and the closure of the council, that the word *dialogue* appeared in the pastoral constitution, replacing *conversation*.

A careful study of the various versions of *Gaudium et Spes* shows that *conversation* was not replaced in every case by *dialogue*, highlighting a differentiated use of the two words. *Dialogue* was adopted to characterize the church's engagement with the world: "By virtue of her mission to shed on the whole world the radiance of the Gospel message, and to unify under one Spirit all men of whatever nation, race or culture, the Church stands forth as a sign of that brotherhood which allows honest dialogue (*dialogum*) and gives it vigor."[9] Dealing with relationships within the church, the pastoral constitution retained *conversation* in order not to downplay her hierarchical character. However, translations of the document into the various languages preferred to use *dialogue*, giving more weight to the fundamental equality of all the baptized, also emphasized by the council.

[8] See Thierry-Marie Courau, *Le salut comme dialogue de saint Paul VI à François* (Paris: Cerf, 2018), 97.

[9] Second Vatican Council, Pastoral Constitution on the Church in the Modern World *Gaudium et Spes*, December 7, 1965, 92, https://www.vatican.va/archive/hist_councils/ii_vatican_council/documents/vat-ii_const_19651207_gaudium-et-spes_en.html. Hereafter cited as GS.

This vocabulary analysis highlights how the church's horizontality is directly connected with its mission of dialoguing with the world. It depends also on a new awareness of human dignity and of the correlative and fundamental equality of all the baptized. Rosemary Goldie, a prominent lay auditor at the council, rightly recalled that dialogue "takes on a *plenary meaning* only if the interlocutors are *more or less on a plan of parity*."[10]

Toward an Anthropology of Dialogue: Human Dignity and Social Responsibility

In its introduction and part one, *Gaudium et Spes* offers a renewed anthropology, centered on the dialogical identity of the human person in the image of God. Starting with an introductory statement on "the situation of men in the modern world," the pastoral constitution embraces the dialogical approach of Jesus himself, who entered "in dialogue with his interlocutors from their experience of life."[11] It is remarkable that the conciliar fathers felt compelled to continue with a key chapter on the dignity of the human person.

Distancing itself from the antimodernist rejection of conscience as the root of secularism, the council emphasized that human dignity is founded on the dignity of the conscience, for conscience is the place of a personal encounter with God: "Conscience is the most secret core and sanctuary of a man. There he is alone with God, whose voice echoes in his depths" (GS 16). From this affirmation of the dignity of conscience, *Gaudium et Spes* concludes that the human person accomplishes herself when she acts freely, that is, in "fidelity to her conscience" (GS 16). The recognition of religious freedom by Vatican II is to be understood in this light, as suggested by the title of the decree on the topic: *Dignitatis Humanae*.

---

[10] Rosemary Goldie, *Da una finestra romana: Il mondo, la Chiesa e il laicato cattolico* (Rome: AVE, 2000), 202.

[11] Philippe Bordeyne, "Pour une herméneutique contemporaine de l'anthropologie morale de *Gaudium et spes*," *Studia moralia* 50 (2012): 316.

Consequently, the traditional understanding of the common good needs to be rethought through this new lens of the dignity of the human person. To support its relational anthropology, *Gaudium et Spes* stresses, in the first chapter, that the human person is a "social being" (GS 12), prolonging this line of reflection in chapter 2 on "The Community of Mankind." Interrelationships are the path for an increasing dignity of the person who, "unless he relates himself to others" can "neither live nor develop his potential" (GS 12). Rafael Tello, an Argentine theologian, has deduced from that statement that "the human person is of supreme worth, but her plenitude can only be realized in community."[12]

Interestingly, the Code of Canon Law, inspired by *Dignitatis Humanae* 7, applied this notion to the common good of the church in its section on "The Christian Faithful": "In exercising their rights, the Christian faithful, both as individuals and gathered together in associations, must take into account the common good of the Church, the rights of others, and their own duties toward others."[13] Following Tello, the common good of the church takes on a deeper meaning, for it is no longer absolutized but considered in relation to the "supreme worth" of the human person, whoever she is.

This fruitful tension between the "supreme worth" of the person and the common good of the church helps to understand the church as a "privileged place of ethics."[14] While applied ethics concentrated on social and family ethics, the reality of a moral person acting inside the church has been notably overshadowed. The crisis of sexual violence, which impacts the church worldwide, invites us to give more attention to this forgotten theological field and especially to the respect for the conscience and freedom of all the baptized, recalling that an act can only be considered moral if it is conscious and free.

---

[12] Rafael Tello, *Pueblo y cultura I* (Buenos Aires: Patria grande, 2011), 26.

[13] Code of Canon Law, 223.1, https://www.vatican.va/archive/cod-iuris-canonici/cic_index_en.html.

[14] Jean-Noël Aletti, *Essai sur l'ecclésiologie des lettres de saint Paul*, Etudes bibliques 60, (Pendé: Gabalda, 2009), 190. See Agnès Desmazières, "Dialogue, coresponsabilité et conversion de l'Eglise: Jalons pour une morale ecclésiale à partir de Bernard Häring," *Nouvelle revue théologique* 144 (2022): 216–31.

The Church's Past and Penance:
A Conversion to Sincere Dialogue

At the council, some steps toward a moralization of the church had already been taken, if insufficiently, according to Yves Congar, one of the influential writers of *Gaudium et Spes*. The French Dominican was at that time more concerned by the inadequacy of the church's discourse and practice in relation to the contemporary world. He criticized especially its "seigneurial," that is, clerical, posture and encouraged her to take on the mantle of "service."[15] For him, the conversion of the church required not only changes in spirit and acts but also requests for forgiveness for the sins committed by members of the church.

This new emphasis on forgiveness and penance coincided with the rediscovery of the dialogical identity of the church. In line with his conception of a "servant Church," Congar maintained that "the first service that the Church gives to the world is to tell the truth."[16] The conversion to the service of the truth assumed a particular relevance in the contemporary world, because of its growing expectations of "sincerity."[17] To dialogue with the world, the church needs to speak the language of authenticity and honesty, not of power and self-importance.

Additionally, the shift from an essentialist conception of the church, as perfect and thus pure, to a more historical one led to a greater focus on its institutional dynamics that are tainted by human sinfulness. Consequently, the church's service is a service to the historical truth.[18] In *True and False Reform of the Church* (1950), Congar had already acknowledged the weight of the church's "historical faults," an expression that anticipated the later one of "sinful structures."[19] This acknowledgement of the church's

---

[15] Yves Congar, *Pour une Eglise servante et pauvre* (Paris: Cerf, 2014), 11.

[16] Yves Congar, "Propositions en vue de la révision demandée du schéma XVII [*Gaudium et spes*]," September 1963, 2 (YC 1564 pro 1716, Yves Congar papers, Saulchoir library, Paris).

[17] Congar, "Propositions en vue de la revisión," 2.

[18] For Congar's discussion of the "historical faults" of the churches, see his *True and False Reform in the Church*, trans. Paul Philibert (Collegeville, MN: Liturgical Press, 2010), 61–62.

[19] Congar, *True and False Reform in the Church*, 61–62.

"historical faults" was, however, slowed down by a certain pusil-
lanimity of the writers of *Gaudium et Spes*, caused, according to
the Dominican, by a lack of distinction between nature and grace,
which encouraged them to maintain a proselytical discourse on
the blameless church tainted by "clerical domination."[20]

In this respect, the necessity to confess the church's "historical
faults" and to do penance responded to a "new attitude of the
Church towards its past."[21] Despite its limits, *Gaudium et Spes*
recognized that the church "is very well aware that among her
members, both clerical and lay, some have been unfaithful to the
Spirit of God during the course of many centuries; in the present
age, too, it does not escape the Church how great a distance lies
between the message she offers and the human failings of those
to whom the Gospel is entrusted. Whatever be the judgement of
history on these defects, we ought to be conscious of them, and
struggle against them energetically, lest they inflict harm on the
spread of the Gospel" (GS 43).

This passage, from the fourth chapter on "The Role of the
Church in the Modern World," shows that the council took a significant step in confessing the faults of the past and in admitting
their negative impact on the Gospel's preaching. Moreover, it
stressed the necessity of being conscious of them: conscience examines not only personal deeds but also collective actions and the
mentalities of persons who are meant to "develop their potential"
in community.

It seems, however, in the light of the sex abuse crisis, that this
discourse lacked performativity, for it was not followed by effective action, especially regarding the struggle against the "human
failings of those to whom the Gospel is entrusted." This partly
came from a misleading understanding of "pastorality," another
main line of the council, wrongly opposed to the juridical perspectives of canon law. In fact, the pastoral and juridical approaches
were supposed to operate jointly for the common good of the
church. Moreover, the neglect of Vatican II's teaching on the
various vocations, the lay vocation especially, favored an asym-

[20] Congar, "Propositions en vue de la revisión," 3.
[21] Congar, "Propositions en vue de la revisión," 3.

metrical comprehension of "pastorality," primarily defined as the bishops' concern for their priests.

The Dialogue of Various Vocations

The dialogical anthropology of *Gaudium et Spes* intersects with a theology of vocation that is developed through the first part of the document, entitled "The Church and Man's Calling," with *calling* here a translation of the Latin *vocatione*. Vocation embraces all humanity and is the expression of human dignity. Community is grounded in a common human vocation to grow communally in humanity. *Gaudium et Spes* also considers Christian vocation from the perspective of the universal call to holiness, based on chapter 4 of *Lumen Gentium*, accentuating its various realizations regarding dialogue with the world, depending on the different states of life. Finally, it draws attention to the unicity of the vocation of each person called to a dialogue in conscience with God.

In chapter 4 on "The Role of the Church in the Modern World," the document details the missions of the diverse vocations in relation to the church's dialogue with the world. Interestingly, the order of exposition of the different states of life is distinct from the one chosen for *Lumen Gentium*.[22] While clerics were treated first in the dogmatic constitution, the lay faithful came before them in the last and official version of *Gaudium et Spes*.[23] The lay faithful are, in fact, at the outpost of the church's dialogue with the world. The pastoral document thus mirrors a more horizontal ecclesiology, favorable to dialogue. In this line, the new consideration of the church's dialogue with the world affects the church's internal dialogue, generating more requests for reciprocal relations.

This is also an invitation to think of the different vocations in terms of reciprocity and to define their respective identities

---

[22] See Agnès Desmazières, *L'heure des laïcs: Proximité et coresponsabilité* (Paris: Salvator, 2021), 34–35.

[23] A preliminary version had reproduced the order of *Lumen Gentium*. See Yves Congar, "Le rôle de l'Eglise dans le monde de ce temps (1re partie, chapitre IV)," in *L'Eglise dans le monde de ce temps: Constitution pastorale "Gaudium et spes,"* vol. 2, *Commentaires,* ed. Yves Congar and Michel Peuchmaurd (Paris: Cerf, 1967), 317.

relationally.[24] The vocation of priesthood cannot be fully understood without reference to the lay faithful. By the same token, the lay vocation requires the presence of clerics. Moreover, the current identity crisis of the church is in a great part caused by the crisis of consecrated life, forgetful of its vocation to be a sign of gratitude for God's gift. The infidelity and loss of identity of consecrated persons accentuates the confrontational dialectic between clerics and lay faithful, preventing a recognition that all the baptized are destined to experience and witness to God's gracious love.

When Discourse Encounters Experience: The Dialogue with the Lay Auditors on *Gaudium et Spes*

In this logic of reciprocity, the clerical and the lay vocations illustrate two aspects of Christian vocation: the first one expresses more the service of the church while the second manifests a commitment to the world. As *Gaudium et Spes* pointed out, the commitment to the world belonged "properly," but not "exclusively," to the lay faithful (GS 43). This does not mean that the lay faithful were excluded from church's affairs; they were called, rather, to participate in the church's governance in accordance with their own professional competence. The decree on the lay apostolate, *Apostolicam Actuositatem*, made this explicit: "Deserving of special honor and commendation in the Church are those lay people, single or married, who devote themselves with professional experience, either permanently or temporarily, to the service of associations and their activities."[25]

Significantly, when Pope Paul VI decided to appoint some lay faithful as auditors at the council, he chose international expertise as the main criterion of their selection—choosing the international

---

[24] This approach is not in opposition to a more "ontological" one, the relational also having ontological roots. See Paul Bernier, *Ministry in the Church: A Historical and Pastoral Approach*, 2nd ed. (Maryknoll: Orbis, 2015).

[25] Second Vatican Council, decree *Apostolicam Actuositatem*, November 18, 1965, 22, https://www.vatican.va/archive/hist_councils/ii_vatican_council/documents/vat-ii_decree_19651118_apostolicam-actuositatem_en.html.

leaders of Catholic Action.[26] It had been even thought at one point that these lay faithful would be called "experts." If the term *auditors* was ultimately chosen to distinguish them from the theological and canonical "experts," the lay persons participating in the writing of *Gaudium et Spes* were, however, signing on the same attendance sheets, together with the theological and canonical experts.

This highlights how the preparation of the pastoral constitution became an occasion to experience authentic dialogue between different vocations, including religious life, represented by some nun auditors. *Gaudium et Spes* was a pioneer project in this respect, and its late writing favored a lay contribution that began even before the nomination of thirteen lay male auditors in September 1963. Anticipating Paul VI's decision, the commission in charge of the schema organized a meeting in Rome in April 1963, where sixteen lay men were invited to discuss the text.

This early participation of lay faithful in Vatican II intensified with the invitation of women at the third session of the council in September 1964. The role of women in the church was abundantly discussed during the writing of *Gaudium et Spes*, prolonging the reflection initiated with *Apostolicam Actuositatem*.[27] Women, together with lay men, encouraged the jettisoning of the discourse of complementarity between men and women, which they considered tainted with gender prejudices, and they campaigned for gender equality. In several instances, women auditors nevertheless experienced discrimination, being, for example, forbidden to deliver a speech to the plenary assembly at St. Peter's Basilica, while six lay men were allowed to do so.

Lay participation in *Gaudium et Spes* intensified as the commission became more convinced that the style of the document should fit its purpose—dialoguing with the world—and thus be comprehensible to everyone. First written by clerics, the schema was soon

---

[26] See Agnès Desmazières, "L'affermazione del laicato e le trasformazioni dell'expertise al Vaticano II: La genesi dello statuto di uditore al Concilio (1959–1963)," *Quaderni storici*, no. 1 (2019): 101–32.

[27] See Agnès Desmazières, "Généalogie d'un 'silence' conciliaire: Le débat sur les femmes dans l'élaboration du décret sur l'apostolat des laïcs," *Archives de sciences sociales des religions* 61, no. 175 (2016): 297–317.

deemed too clerical, too scholastic, and too moralizing, to the extent that Congar even suggested it should be rewritten by the lay auditors and "only helped by clerics as technicians."[28] Though the Dominican's proposal did not prevail, the lay contribution reached a peak at the Ariccia meeting, in February 1965, where fifteen lay auditors, among them Rosemary Goldie, discussed the revisions of the schema. At the end of the meeting, Michel de Habicht, one of the lay auditors, testified that "for the first time . . . a collaboration with lay people, men and women, on an equal footing" occurred in the work of the council.[29] This exemplary experience was not continued in the following decades, however, primarily due to a clerical backlash.

Dialoguing with the World Requires Competence and Freedom

Despite this regression, *Gaudium et Spes* offers a basis for a more inclusive participation of the lay faithful. In line with the experience of Vatican II, the pastoral constitution intimately connects the vocation of the lay faithful to the acquisition and the implementation of expertise through their studies and professional activities (GS 43). This approach was developed in the fourth chapter, where, by acknowledging the value of human activity, the council encouraged the development of a competence that was at the service of church's dialogue with the world. If this competence was first destined to flourish in society, it was also crucial for the church in order to accomplish its mission. Synthesizing the experience of the writing of *Gaudium et Spes*, the conciliar fathers indicated that "the Church requires the special help of those who live in the world, are versed in different institutions and specialties, and grasp their innermost significance in the eyes of both believers and unbelievers" (GS 44).

---

[28] Yves Congar, "Remarques du Père Yves Congar sur le projet de schéma XVII proposé en mars 1964," April 14, 1964 (AV, Fondo Concilio Vaticano II, b. 1193, f. XVIII, 266).

[29] Mentioned in Congar, *My Journal of the Council*, trans. Mary John Ronayne and Mary Cecily Boulding, ed. Denis Minns (Collegeville, MN: Liturgical Press, 2012), 719.

Correlatively, the possession of a competence endorses a just freedom for the lay faithful: "Let the layman not imagine that his pastors are always such experts, that to every problem which arises, however complicated, they can readily give him a concrete solution, or even that such is their mission. Rather, enlightened by Christian wisdom and giving close attention to the teaching authority of the Church, let the layman take on his own distinctive role" (GS 43).

Congar proposed, in fact, that "competence" and the freedom, expressed in terms of "loyalty to things," be considered the main characteristics of the lay vocation.[30] The freedom of the lay faithful was to be understood in relation to their responsibility, grounded in their competence, which allowed them to speak up. For the Dominican, being responsible meant "taking sides."[31] This is well expressed in *Lumen Gentium*: "They [the lay faithful] are, by reason of the knowledge, competence or outstanding ability which they may enjoy, permitted and sometimes even obliged to express their opinion on those things which concern the good of the Church."[32] Congar's "loyalty to things" can be connected to *parrhesia*—the courage to speak—that Pope Francis regularly encourages, associating it with a "listen[ing] with humility."[33]

Finally, if competence is proper to the lay faithful, it is not exclusive to their vocation. The council also referred—if less frequently—to the competence of clerics, inviting them to a greater consideration of competence in the discernment of clerical and consecrated vocations, as well as in the appointment to offices. Competence should be considered as part of the economy of grace and from the perspective of the parable of the talents: the talents are given by grace to persons who are responsible for their growth. This would help underscore the theology of the "call" in such a

[30] Yves Congar, *Jalons pour une théologie du laïcat*, 2nd ed. (Paris: Cerf, 1954), 608.

[31] Congar, *Jalons pour une théologie du laïcat*, 613.

[32] Second Vatican Council, Dogmatic Constitution on the Church *Lumen Gentium*, November 21, 1964, 37, https://www.vatican.va/archive/hist_councils/ii_vatican_council/documents/vat-ii_const_19641121_lumen-gentium_en.html.

[33] Pope Francis, "Greeting of Pope Francis to the Synod Fathers during the First General Congregation of the Third Extraordinary General Assembly of the Synod of Bishops," October 6, 2014, https://www.vatican.va/content/francesco/en/speeches/2014/october/documents/papa-francesco_20141006_padri-sinodali.html.

way that the faithful could be more proactive in proposing their talents to the church, instead of waiting passively for the pastor's call.

A deeper attention to competence would also favor the emergence of a new ecclesial culture, emphasizing co-responsibility and transparency. Similarly, Vatican II's concern for the lay faithful's freedom should resonate more strongly in the context of the abuse crisis. In fact, lay ministers are more often subject to requests of blind obedience than are clerics. The reference to competence helps move away from an arbitrary conception of obedience and an individualistic understanding of freedom. Finally, it contributes to a reevaluation of human work as a locus for sanctification and growth in human dignity.

Synodality will only be effective if it allows an authentic dialogue within the church, based on the recognition of human dignity and of every person's unique talents. It supposes a conversion to a culture of competence and responsibility. The participation of the lay faithful in the governance of the church is therefore grounded in the equal dignity and reciprocity of the various vocations, the participation of all the baptized in Christ's royal function, and the specific competence of some of its members.

Toward Ecclesial Ethics:
A Reforming God, a Just Church,
and Reformed Subjectivity

Ethna Regan

History teaches us that ecclesial reform is a complex and conflictual issue. There is often tension between those who advocate for the primacy of spiritual reform and those who advocate for the primacy of structural reform. The synodal process Pope Francis initiated in 2021 attempts to hold in tension the spiritual and the structural, with primacy given to the former, allusions to the latter, all with the goal of addressing the fundamental question shared by all who seek reform: How does this enable the church to authentically and effectively proclaim the Gospel? The process of reform needs to draw from a range of ethical sources, and this essay will present three "onlooks"[1] into reform: a biblical text that

---

[1] See Richard M. Gula, *Reason Informed by Faith* (Mahwah, NJ: Paulist Press, 1989), 49: " 'Onlooks' provide not only a way of knowing the situation at hand but also an implicit commitment to behave in a certain way. In short, through onlooks 'deciding-that and deciding-to,' 'is' and 'ought,' come together. . . . Scripture and theological tradition provide an abundance of religious onlooks through parables, symbols and creeds. When religious beliefs form a great part of the framework within which the moral agent looks on experience, they become a powerful influence on moral character and action." Gula draws from Donald D. Evans's *The Logic of Self-Involvement* (London: SCM Press, 1963).

offers insight into a God of reform, a document of Catholic social teaching that challenges the church to internal reform, and the secular discourse of rights that can contribute to the broader consideration of ecclesial subjectivity that reform entails.

A God of Reform: Illuminating the Darkest Corners

Chapter 15 of Luke's gospel offers a reflection on the nature of God through parables about a lost sheep, a lost coin, and a lost son. The parable of the good shepherd (15:3-7) has shaped our pastoral and theological reflection on Christ and, by extension, on leadership and membership in the church. This parable is paired with a parable of a woman, the good housekeeper (15:8-10), both sharing similar structure and vocabulary. The second parable, perhaps because of its realism and domesticity, remains at the margins of our pastoral and theological imagination. Without wishing to diminish the beauty of the good shepherd image, it is clear that the revelations of recent years have shown us that an overreliance on shepherd leadership and flock-followers has brought great human damage and ecclesial corruption. What can we learn from the more neglected parable?

The momentum of the parable is that of knowing something is lost, lighting a lamp, sweeping the house, searching diligently, and then rejoicing with others when the lost treasure is found. It is only the woman in these parables of lostness who is described as seeking carefully. Domenico Fetti's painting of this parable depicts the woman tearing the house apart in her search, while Jacque Tissot's *The Lost Drachma* portrays the woman on the floor, lamp beside her, as she stretches into the darkest and least accessible corners of the house.

The Jewish New Testament scholar Amy-Jill Levine says, "If the shepherd of Luke 15: 3-7 is understood as God, so should this woman be."[2] This good housekeeper was frequently interpreted as a representation of God searching for lost humanity. Indeed,

---

[2] Amy-Jill Levine, "Luke: Introduction and Annotations," in *The Jewish Annotated New Testament*, ed. Amy-Jill Levine and Marc Zvi Brettler (Oxford: Oxford University Press, 2011), 133.

the theological tradition of the Latin West shows that "many Church Fathers, saints, and Doctors of the Church portrayed Jesus Christ as divine Woman Wisdom within their reflections on the parable of the woman seeking her lost coin."[3] This parable, like all parables, teaches both about God and about the indicative and imperative for ourselves that issues from knowing God in this particular way. God is the woman who seeks diligently for the lost and the mode of Jesus' telling of this parable challenges his listeners, who Luke describes as "grumbling" (15:2) because he ate with those regarded as sinners. Augustine, reflecting on this parable in the context of his discussion of memory in *The Confessions*, observes that "the woman who had lost her groat and, sought it with a light," could not have found it "unless she remembered it." He argues that if she—and we—had completely forgotten something, we would not be able to look for what is lost. Lost from sight, but not from memory, "its image is still retained within, and it is sought until it be restored to sight" (*Conf.* 10:18).[4] Memory is the place where God abides, and from the depths of memory God can show us a way out of forgetfulness. Luke's parable is a beautiful analogy of God's careful searching for, and extravagant joy at finding, the lost. Augustine takes this Lucan parable in a more Platonic direction, but he enables us to see in this good housekeeper both God and ourselves as the searcher.

The good housekeeper searches diligently in the darkest and least accessible corners of the house and illumines these spaces in order to find what has been lost. Some of the Franciscan reforms, fewer and slower than hoped for by many, can be seen as reaching into the darkest and least accessible parts of the *ecclesia*, illuminating these spaces, and searching for what is lost under the accumulated dirt of abuse, clericalism, and hierarchicalism. Among many Catholics, there is a profound sense of something lost—not Christendom but the *imago Christi* in our structures and systems. However, what is lost is, as Augustine teaches us, retained in

---

[3] Shannon McAlister, "Christ as the Woman Seeking Her Lost Coin: Luke 15:8-10 and Divine Sophia in the Latin West," *Theological Studies* 79 (2018): 9, https://doi.org/10.1177/0040563917745830.

[4] Augustine, *The Confessions of St. Augustine*, trans. E. B. Pusey (London: J. M. Dent & Sons, 1946).

memory. One way of interpreting the synodal process is as a dili-
gent search for some lost treasures, toward the recovery of what
the church is intended to be. The parable of God as the good
housekeeper reminds us that the recovery of memory of the forgotten, the finding of what is lost, and the hard, dirty work of
cleaning the house is primarily God's work. Our efforts at reform
are a participation in this. The parable concludes with a hopeful
promise of "joy in the presence of the angels of God" (Luke 15:10)
in response to repentance and reform.

Ecclesial Ethics: A Just Church

The Catholic ethical tradition—from the patristic texts to contemporary voices—is rich and resourceful. There is official church
teaching on a wide range of topics of personal and political life.
But there are also ethical perspectives, from implicit to more explicit, in the work of the great Catholic ecclesiologists, and there
are ethical implications, often insufficiently drawn upon, in the
models of church that emerged in the documents of the Second
Vatican Council. Yet the relationship between ethics and ecclesiology, specifically between the *character* of the church itself and its
capacity for moral proclamation, particularly on matters of justice,
is rarely tackled directly.

A tremendous amount of exemplary work has been done in
recent years on codes of practice within the church, specifically in
relation to the protection of minors and vulnerable people. This
is extremely important work, undertaken in response to the hor-
rific exposure of child abuse, but it does not mean that the church
has undertaken a critical analysis of its own processes and structures, its own ethic of being church. There is a lacuna of credibility
in relation to the institutional church, especially in Ireland. There
are individual Catholics whose lives are recognized as authentically Christian and Catholic organizations—for example, the
Society of St. Vincent de Paul—that are recognized as transparent
and incorrupt. There is also a recognition that at moments of profound tragedy in communities, the church often provides a sanctuary of love and support. However, to a large extent, these are
viewed as exceptions to rather than exemplars of the ethic of the
institutional church.

Since the initial dark revelations of abuse, there have been attempts by theologians to look at the question of church ethics, including interdisciplinary work with business ethics and organizational studies.[5] The empowerment of lay people in church governance emerges as a strong recommendation for restoration of confidence and prevention of further abuse. It could be argued, however, that without a deeper analysis of how power is operative in procedures and structures, the scope of ecclesial reform will be limited. Anna Abram argues persuasively for "ecclesial ethics" as a branch of moral theology which—while drawing from the usual sources of theology—is willing to engage with professional ethics, with the aim of developing a more participatory church. The areas that this ecclesial ethics would address include the development of good processes and practice at all levels of the church, "the handling of tensions and disagreements," and testing and applying "the Church's own teaching, such as Catholic social teaching, to the structures of the Church."[6]

One rare document that specifically addresses the relationship between the character of the church itself and its capacity to contribute to discussions related to justice, peace, and other matters of the common good, is the post-synodal document of 1971, *Justice in the World.*[7] This is one of the most significant documents of modern Catholic social teaching. There is an enduring relevance to *Justice in the World*, with its clarity and realism, its acknowledgement of structural injustice, its proclamation that action on behalf of justice is a constitutive dimension of the preaching of the Gospel, and its extension of the examination of justice to the church itself. The document directly addresses the relationship between the just ordering of the church and its capacity to speak about the just ordering of society and politics. In it, the Synod of Bishops wrote, "While the Church is bound to give witness to justice, she recognizes that anyone who ventures to speak to

[5] See Jean M. Bartunek, Mary Ann Hinsdale, and James F. Keenan, eds., *Church Ethics and Its Organizational Context: Learning from the Sex Abuse Scandal in the Catholic Church* (Lanham, MD: Rowman & Littlefield, 2006).

[6] Anna Abram, "From Moral Theology to Ecclesial Ethics," *Studia Nauk Teologicznych* Tom 15 (2020), 153. https://doi.org/10.31743/snt.9383.

[7] Synod of Bishops, *Justicia in Mundo* (*Justice in the World*), 1971, Catholic Charities of St. Paul and Minneapolis, https://www.cctwincities.org/wp-content/uploads/2015/10/Justicia-in-Mundo.pdf.

people about justice must first be just in their eyes."[8] It argues that the witness of justice is dependent on our modes of acting, possessing, and living, and it recommends an examination of these. Given the directness with which this document addresses the practice of justice in the church, one can only wonder about its near invisibility in official church documents for the following four decades and its complete exclusion from the Compendium of the Social Doctrine of the Church.

The explicit commitment to the practice of justice by the church is followed by a reference to the preservation of the rights of people within the church (see JW 41), and the following paragraph urges, albeit ambiguously, "that women should have their own share of responsibility" in church and society. It proposed the establishment of a mixed commission to undertake a "serious study" of the role of women in the church. Although Pope Francis established two commissions to study the specific question of the female diaconate, the broader commission recommended in 1971 has never been established. Half a century later, the raising of the issue of the full and equal participation of women in the church in synodal consultations on all continents is an incentive to action and a profound counterargument to those who suggest that only particular kinds of feminists in certain parts of the world are concerned with issues of gender and ecclesiology.

The recognition of the right of each person to "suitable" freedom of expression and thought specifies "the right of everyone to be heard in a spirit of dialogue which preserves a legitimate diversity within the Church" (JW 44). It could be argued that this right lay preserved on the pages of this text for half a century and has only been revisited with the initiation of the synodal process by Francis.

The term *credibility* is used twice in *Justice in the World*. Firstly, it appears in a reminder that the Christian message of love and justice will only gain credibility with people if it is effective through action (see JW 35). Secondly, the document states that the credibility of the church will be diminished if it appears to be located primarily among the rich and powerful (see JW 47). Two

---

[8] Synod of Bishops, *Justice in the World*, 40. Hereafter cited as JW.

of the eight main objectives of the 2023 synod outlined in the preparatory document directly link with the areas of ecclesial ethics addressed in *Justice in the World*, specifically the challenge of congruence between teaching about justice and the practice of justice *ad intra*, and the question of credibility. One objective refers to justice *ad intra*: "examining how responsibility and power are lived in the Church as well as the structures by which they are managed, bringing to light and trying to convert prejudices and distorted practices that are not rooted in the Gospel."[9] Another objective specifically addresses the question of being a *credible* witness to justice, using the unusual language of accreditation: "accrediting the Christian community as a credible subject and reliable partner in paths of social dialogue, healing, reconciliation, inclusion and participation, reconstruction of democracy, the promotion of fraternity and social friendship."[10]

The bishops gathering in 1971 could not have envisaged the diminishment of credibility that would ensue with the child abuse crimes and scandals. While there are many signs of hope and life in the contemporary church, the unprecedented extent of the diminishment of credibility makes attention to reform an imperative.

Ecclesial ethics necessitates the acknowledgment that:

1. The church is the first addressee of its own moral proclamation.

2. This calls for the conversion of heart and transformation of practice that the church's own ethical demands make of persons and politics.

3. This transformation of practice can be achieved by learning, with humility, from two sources: the victims of the sins of the church and those who work in the field of institutional ethics beyond the church.

---

[9] Synod of Bishops, *For a Synodal Church: Communion, Participation, and Mission* (September 7, 2021), §2, https://www.synod.va/en/news/the-preparatory-document.html.

[10] Synod of Bishops, *For a Synodal Church*, §2. Italics mine.

Justice *ad intra* is one of the church's most pressing responsibilities, not only to ensure that it is a credible subject and reliable partner working with all people of good will in matters related to the common good, but also because its very capacity for authentic proclamation of the Gospel is at stake.

Reformed Subjectivity: Dignity and Rights

A purely rights-based approach to reform is not in keeping with the nature of the church and its mission. Many divisive theological issues—for example, the ordination of women—cannot be solved simply by recourse to the language of rights. However, there can be no reform that bypasses an examination of the ongoing ambivalence of the Catholic Church toward subjective rights and obligations internally.

The full acceptance of human rights as a legitimate mode of ethical discourse was the major contribution of Vatican II to Catholic social teaching. This full acceptance was shaped by a number of factors, the most significant of which was the formal recognition of the right to religious freedom in *Dignitatis Humanae* (1965). Religious freedom, that neuralgic point in the relationship between the Catholic Church and Enlightenment liberty, was now held to be the primary freedom that secures other human and civil freedoms. The council stressed that a person may have duties to the truth, but the truth has no rights. The subject of rights is the human person, in truth or error, based on the dignity of that human person in their discernment and decision-making. Thus, the foundation of religious freedom in *Dignitatis Humanae* is the dignity of the human person, manifested in the gifts of rationality and freedom. The dynamic of freedom is one of movement from personal freedom to the freedom of the church. This tardy acceptance by the church of a basic principle of human rights—albeit one already recognized in civil law—enabled it to become a full participant in the human rights movement in the postconciliar period.

While the impact of *Dignitatis Humanae* was primarily on the church's engagement with rights *ad extra*, it is worth considering how this document could enable careful reflection upon and practical progress on human rights in the church: firstly, through its emphasis on the dignity of human discernment and decision-making; secondly, through its recognition that religious freedom moves from personal freedom to the freedom of the church; and thirdly, through the concept of progress in understanding the truth. Patrick Hannon suggests that the position of *Dignitatis Humanae* regarding religious freedom could be applied to the issue of moral freedom, arguing that people "should not be made to act against their consciences nor restrained from acting according to conscience—subject to the requirements of the common good."[11]

While the Christian does not stand before the church as the individual does before the state, fundamental rights founded on human dignity are not nullified by ecclesial membership, and the rights and obligations of the faithful are also specified in canon law. Many influences shaped the reflection on human rights in the church in the years between the ending of the council and the promulgation of the Code of Canon Law in 1983. These included the church's engagement with the Universal Declaration of Human Rights, the emphasis on human dignity and respect for each human person in the theological anthropology of Vatican II, together with the conciliar development of the church as the people of God.[12] There were canonists who advocated for greater clarity about and protection of subjective rights in the church. Canons 208–223 outline the rights and obligations of the faithful. Clearly, some of these rights have no parallel in secular conventions of human rights, for example, the right to celebrate liturgy according to one's own rite (canon 214). There are others, such as the right to freedom of opinion and the right to a good reputation and privacy (canon 212), that clearly mirror similar secular rights.

While the complexity of the legal foundation of rights within the Code of Canon Law is beyond the scope of this essay, Rik Torfs identifies two central questions that can illustrate some of the tensions inherent in the operationalization of these rights in the

[11] Patrick Hannon, *Church, State, Morality & Law* (Dublin: Gill and Macmillan, 1992), 3.

[12] See R. J. Castillo Lara, "Some Reflections on the Rights and Duties of the Christian Faithful," *Studia Canonica* 20 (1986): 9–10.

church that are relevant for the question of reform.[13] The first question pertains to the supremacy of fundamental rights. He argues that the Code omits to put the rights and obligations formulated in canons 208–223 in a framework that would have made them operationally relevant from a juridical perspective. In other words, "without formal superiority," these are not fundamental rights.[14] Torfs observes that in the two decades following the promulgation of the 1983 Code, the community of canon lawyers did not discuss the formal superiority of canons dealing with the rights and obligations of the faithful but focused more on the theological dimensions, so much so that he concludes "the theological beauty of canon law eventually eclipsed legal fairness."[15] This theological turn, together with the vulnerability of the subjective rights in canon law, were among the complex of factors that shaped the response to victims of child abuse, unjustly accused priests, and those charged with theological dissent. The same pattern is evident.

The second major question addressed by Torfs is whether the rights of the individual will always be eclipsed by concerns about the common good in the church.[16] His comparison of the case of freedom of expression is illustrative. According to the European Convention for the Protection of Human Rights and Fundamental Freedoms, the right to freedom of expression (art. 10.1) can be restricted for a number of reasons (including, for example, national security and public safety) but only as are prescribed by law and are necessary in a democratic society (art. 10.2). The Convention does not mention the "common good" as a restriction, as freedom of expression is seen as one of the essential dimensions of a democratic society. Torfs summarizes the difference thus: "According to the European Convention the common good is served by freedom of expression; according to canon 212 §3, freedom of expression is only permissible when it serves the common good. The two notions are squarely opposed to each other." He concludes

---

[13] Rik Torfs, "Human Rights in the History of the Roman Catholic Church," in *Human Rights and the Impact of Religion*, ed. Hans-Georg Ziebertz and Johannes A. van der Ven (Leiden & Boston: Brill, 2013), 55–74.

[14] Torfs, "Human Rights in the History of the Roman Catholic Church," 64.

[15] Torfs, "Human Rights in the History of the Roman Catholic Church," 67.

[16] Torfs, "Human Rights in the History of the Roman Catholic Church," 69–72.

that canon law cannot contribute toward a credible church "without solid human rights in the Church. Their formal superiority to other norms, as well as their legitimate position as part of, and not as enemy combating the common good, is a consequence of this idea."[17]

Greater attention to subjective rights internally will be fruitful for the reform and renewal of the church, enabling the dignity of the human person to be upheld in ecclesial procedures and structures. The church has a very high theological anthropology in its advocacy of human rights in the world. Its social teaching constitutes an attempt to discover and articulate the concrete implications of human dignity in interpersonal, social, structural, and international terms. Yet this rich theological anthropology and dignity-shaped normative approach do not find the same expression when the church discusses human dignity and human rights internally. When the church engages with rights *ad intra*, what is often operative is a "high" ecclesiology and a more reductive anthropology.

As well as focusing on the legal and theological nature of subjective rights, it is also useful to look at how the church, as an organization, embeds this approach to subjectivity in its systems and structures. Marie Keenan, in her analysis of sexual abuse within the Catholic Church and the responses to it, concludes that the mishandling of complaints by church hierarchy was systemic: "a systems failure of significant proportions, over and above the responsibilities of individual bishops . . . a failure of leadership and of the relational governance that went right to the top."[18] Rights were trampled underfoot or left to the whims of those who held the power, and all on a corporate level.

United Nations agencies and human rights bodies talk about a "human rights–based approach" (HRBA) to organizational reform. An HRBA approach to organizational reform has potential to facilitate cultural change, especially in situations where there is an imbalance of power or abuses of power, by undertaking a fundamental examination of their human rights practices. This approach enables duty-bearers to meet their obligations and rights-holders

---

[17] Torfs, "Human Rights in the History of the Roman Catholic Church," 74.

[18] Marie Keenan, *Child Sexual Abuse and the Catholic Church: Gender, Power, and Organizational Culture* (Oxford and New York: Oxford University Press, 2012), 214.

to claim their rights through a focus on participation, accountability, nondiscrimination and equality, empowerment, and legality. While the church is not like secular organizations, the systemic failures of recent years require a systemic approach to reform. The church can learn from approaches that put the human person at the heart of systems, structures, and processes, from analyses that critique the ethical abuses that can result from power differentials, and from approaches that maximize the capacity in organizations for participation, accountability, equality, empowerment, and legality.

While the kind of organizational reform referred to above is not yet evident, there are clear measures built into the synodal processes that may enable the maximization of participation and equality. Respect for the rights, dignity, and opinion of each participant is emphasized. Beginning with the consultation for the Amazon synod, we have seen the church engage in an unprecedented listening process. It is as if the beautiful opening words of *Gaudium et Spes* are now intentionally directed inward to the church: "the joys and hopes, griefs and anxieties" of the people of God, "especially those who are poor or in any way afflicted," are listened to.[19] All that is "genuinely human" has a place in this process, especially those who may consider that aspects of their humanity relegate them to the ecclesial margins. This reciprocal listening process, founded on the right to speak and the right to be heard, is indicative of a movement toward a reformed understanding of ecclesial subjectivity. There is the clear commitment to the ecclesial "we," the whole people of God as the subject of the synodal process. There is a personalist recognition of diversity of subjectivities, and there is a liberationist preferential option for peripheral subjectivities. It is a major step forward in terms of recognizing the rights and dignity of all the baptised. While rights cannot provide a fulsome understanding of ecclesial subjectivity, there can be no reform that bypasses the appropriate recognition of rights within the church. Rights remind us that hierarchy does not trump the radical human equality of the doctrine of the *imago Dei* nor the Christian equality conferred by baptism.

---

[19] See *Gaudium et Spes*, Pastoral Constitution on the Church in the Modern World (1965), §1, https://www.vatican.va/archive/hist_councils/ii_vatican_council /documents/vat-ii_const_19651207_gaudium-et-spes_en.html.

Conclusion

Reforming the church is an undertaking that has legal, spiritual, structural, and theological dimensions. The three "onlooks" outlined in this chapter touch on the variety of sources that can be drawn upon. The first, the parable of God as the good housekeeper, reminds us that the recovery of memory of the forgotten, the finding of what is lost, and the hard, dirty work of reform is primarily God's work. Our efforts at reform are a participation in this. The second, drawn from Catholic social teaching, reminds us that justice *ad intra* is one of the church's most pressing responsibilities in order to regain credibility and recommends the further development of the field of ecclesial ethics to enable a more accountable and participative church. The third "onlook," building on the secular discourse of human rights, is a reminder that there can be no reform that bypasses the appropriate recognition of rights within the church.

The synodal process offers insights into what is already possible and hints of the greater that might be possible, in terms of reform. To borrow a term from the field of international relations, the stated purpose of the synod is to exercise "soft power"—to plant dreams, allow hope to flourish, inspire trust, bind up wounds, learn from one another—in order to warm hearts and give strength.[20] However, unless this is matched with constructive, decisive, and imaginative action in response to needed ecclesial reforms, the validity and effectiveness of the synodal process as a *modus vivendi et operandi* will be diminished.

---

[20] Synod of Bishops, *For a Synodal Church*, §32. Here the Preparatory Document is citing Pope Francis, "Address at the Opening of the Synod of Bishops on Young People" (October 3, 2018).

Epilogue:
Reform and the Church of the Future

Kristin Colberg

While change and the need for reform exist as constants in church history, we live in an extraordinary time for both. Perhaps, because we are experiencing it, it can be hard to appreciate the distinctiveness of the current moment. Ecclesial reform is perennially difficult, but it seems especially complicated for a global church existing in a world facing unprecedented challenges. Some of the complexities confronting the church unfold differently throughout the world: for example, while certain communities struggle to manage rapid growth in members and vocations, other communities face hard decisions about closing or consolidating parishes due to drastic declines in numbers. Other challenges facing the church transcend locality, including the unspeakable tragedy of the abuse crisis, the ache of youth disaffiliating from the church, wounds caused by exclusive practices or failures in pastoral care, and perplexity over the church's seeming inability to speak meaningfully to certain contemporary issues. Problems also originate beyond the church's walls but nevertheless demand action: political polarization, conflicts such as the war in Ukraine, the widening gaps in income equality and opportunity, the looming climate crisis, and the persistent effects of the COVID-19 pandemic. All of these factors, individually and collectively, contribute to a sense of uncertainty about the future and make calls for renewal in the church both more complicated and more urgent.

How can a global church, faced with such complexity and so many challenges, achieve authentic reform? If we look around us for models of how to navigate the current situation, we see many national leaders promising easy solutions through efforts to draw clear lines of social, political, and ethnic demarcation. Rather than leading their communities beyond polarization, such leaders often stoke division, fear, and animosity as a way to consolidate power. Examples of leaders reacting defensively to chaotic or threatening situations should not surprise those familiar with church history, inasmuch as it includes countless instances of Christian leaders responding similarly. Given this historic pattern, it should amaze us that Pope Francis has chosen to respond to the complexities of our day with a call to listen to the Holy Spirit and to each other. In fact, he has responded with the most extensive exercise in ecclesial listening and discernment in the church's history. From its beginning, Francis has sought a maximally inclusive process where people are encouraged to speak freely (*parrhesia*) and one that carries no preconceived notions of its outcome. Amidst immense change and instability, Pope Francis is asking the people of God a simple question: "What is the Holy Spirit calling the church to in this time and place?" Amazingly, no topics are off the table. The process does not limit respondents to a list of options on a survey; rather it practices a fundamental openness to the voices of the faithful so that we might hear what the Holy Spirit "says to the churches" (Rev 2:7). Some people express that they have waited their whole lives for the Catholic Church to listen to their voices and address their most urgent concerns: that time is now.

To initiate this massive process of reform, Francis has invoked an ancient aspect of the church's identity: synodality. Problematically, few people know what synodality is and those who do know what it is know that its historical usage is insufficiently expansive to capture Francis's vision. A renewed theology of synodality is vital to meet this pivotal moment in the church's history. This volume performs an essential service in helping to illumine aspects of what this renewed theology of synod must look like. Drawing on the wisdom of the Second Vatican Council—not only on the council's theology but also on its style and methods—is crucial for advancing the work of synodality. The council's style differed from its predecessors in that rather than prioritizing precise and timeless language geared towards regulating observable behavior, it sought to promote renewed faith and interior conversion. Notably, Pope Francis is the first pope since Vatican II who was not a *shaper of* the council, but whose experience of the church was *shaped by* the council. He shares the conviction that true reform begins with attitudes and individuals before it focuses on structures. Vatican II's reliance on a dual program of *ressourcement* (a return to the sources) and *aggiornamento* (updating) also gives shape to a renewed theology of synodality. In terms of *ressourcement*, as these chapters describe, gathering in synod is an ancient aspect of the church; in fact, it is fair to say that the history of synods parallels the history of forming consensus in the church. These moments of collaborative decision-making in which leaders gathered as witnesses to pray, listen, dialogue, and discern ways forward stand out as major parts of the church's life for more than a millennium. Pope Francis wants to embrace essential aspects of this history of synodality; otherwise he would have employed a different term to describe the central effort of his papacy. Yet, as this volume underscores, historically, synods have not involved the participation of the entire people of God; they tend to accentuate the hierarchical decision-making nature of the church. So, while synodal gatherings throughout history involved listening and communal discernment, they did not typically engage these practices in the broad way that Francis seeks to cultivate. Here we need an *aggiornamento*, an updating, so that this constitutive element of the church's life can meet the needs of the current millennium. This type of updating is appropriate; as Shaun Blanchard notes, drawing on Congar, we are "called not to simply repeat past formulas but to meet new situations and challenges by thinking *with* and *in* the tradition."[1]

A renewed and expanded theology of synodality requires a more dynamic sense of who constitutes a witness and thus whose voices must inform the processes of decision-making. Vatican II powerfully conveyed that the people of God are not passive subjects; on the contrary, it called them to fulfil their vocation as active

---

[1] See p. 32.

agents who receive and transmit the word of God. As such, the entire people of God must participate in all processes of ecclesial discernment, planning, decision-making, and co-governance. While Vatican II retrieves and updates this powerful theology, it has yet to transform all aspects of the church's life. With the synod, Francis seeks to answer this question: What would the church look like if it took the theology of the people of God as a measuring stick for all of its structures, communicative dynamics, notions of authority—in short, for all the ways that it walks together? One answer is that such a starting point would eradicate a false distinction between an *ecclesia discens* and an *ecclesia docens* and instead illumine the church as one community of active subjects who are all called to fully participate in, and be co-responsible for, its mission. Accordingly, a renewed theology of synodality is one that maintains the ancient understanding of witnesses coming together to pray, listen, dialogue, and discern ways forward *and* dramatically expands our sense of who the witnesses are and how we hear them.

A renewed theology of synodality not only enlarges the number of participants in decision-making but also denotes a style that characterizes the church's life and mission. In the past, the word *synod* has been used primarily as a noun, but Francis is calling us to use it as an adverb and an adjective. The goal is not primarily to have more synods or to transform the execution of certain types of meetings; instead, synodality seeks a way of being church. Rafael Luciani captures this well when he says that what is needed is a "synodalization of the whole church."[2] The church as synodal is more global, dialogical, and participatory, one characterized by closeness, mercy, and listening, and one where authority is decentralized in order to gain involvement by people at the local level and on the peripheries. A synodal church recognizes authoritarian attitudes and clericalism as obstacles in the path of full participation and walking together. Instead, a synodal church seeks structures, relationships, and ways of walking that are expressions of Vatican II's teaching on the *sensus fidelium*. The synodality of the third millennium does not focus primarily on *what* synodality is but *how* it is lived.

---

[2] See p. 74.

The renewed theology of synodality demanded by the current moment remains in development, and it is also shaping the future of reform. The document prepared for the continental phase of the synod expresses this reality by its title: "Enlarge the Space of Your Tent." Released in the fall of 2022, it indicates the arc and process of synodal reform that lies ahead. This document emerges from a task force comprised of three people from every continent who came together to summarize the 112 national reports as well as reports from the Eastern Catholic Churches and from various Vatican dicasteries developed during the synod's diocesan phase. "Enlarge the Space of Your Tent" speaks to the question: "What did the listening church hear when it asked the people of God to speak?" Both the form and the content of this text are significant. Its form is expressed, in part, by what is not there: the text contains no quotes from Pope Francis, Vatican II, or any magisterial document. Additionally, it makes no efforts to theologize what the people of God said or why they said it, and it undertakes no technical descriptions of theological concepts such as the *sensus fidelium*, baptismal ecclesiology, or episcopal collegiality. Instead, the document conveys the voices of the people of God. It lifts up quotes that express deep love for the church as well as quotes that voice clear and firm convictions about needed change. It shares authentic cries for greater formation at all levels of the church, for the church to be more welcoming, for better homilies and more dynamic liturgies, and for new models of authority. As one of the authors of this text, I can affirm that our goal was to avoid merely repeating what the reports said and also to avoid a rush to problem-solving; instead, we wanted the people of God to recognize their own voices in these pages and to offer them as a tool for discernment. The expanded theology of synodality described here and throughout this volume is visible in "Enlarge the Space of Your Tent." The document accepts the entire people of God as witnesses by listening globally, holding up a decentralized vision of authority, embracing a dialogical style, and demonstrating genuine openness to the movement of the Spirit. This document does not theorize about becoming a listening church; it demonstrates a dimension of the church's capacity to listen. It seems significant to note that an effort in synodality could have unfolded differently. For example, the Vatican could have invited everyone to speak in a synodal process, facilitated listening sessions, and then not acknowledge what it heard. Such a process would leave synodality frozen in the past. "Enlarge the Space of Your Tent" illustrates that the synod process has become authentic and instantiated in a new way. By sharing the authentic testimony of people from throughout the world, the church is holding itself accountable to what it has heard. The first four words of the introduction to this text are: "The synod is on." These words demonstrate that the history of synodality and reform has entered a new phase: there is no going back as this is the way of reform and being church in the future.

Even as we are living in an exciting time in the history of the church and its efforts at reform, we must be patient. Reform within a synodal church can be slow, as it is rooted in individual conversion and careful processes of communal discernment. Synodality requires that we navigate creative tensions between unity and diversity, center and periphery, conservation and innovation, discernment and dialogue; it relies on the virtue of patient expectation for mature solutions to emerge. The synodal journey has thus far revealed that synodality is both the means of becoming the church that we aspire to be as well as the church we wish to become. In other words, it is both the content and the method. This volume is a key guide for the synodal journey that lies ahead. It illumines critical aspects of the path of synodality and what God expects of the church of the third millennium. It engages in the important work of *ressourcement* and *aggiornamento* so that we might become a church that truly walks together.

Notes on Contributors

Christopher M. Bellitto is professor of history at Kean University, where he teaches courses in ancient and medieval history. A specialist in the Middle Ages, church history, and reform, he is the author of ten books and over thirty articles and book chapters published in the United States and Europe. Publications include *101 Questions and Answers on Popes and the Papacy* (Paulist, 2008) and *The General Councils: A History of the Twenty-One Church Councils from Nicaea to Vatican II* (Paulist, 2002).

Shaun Blanchard is lecturer in theology at the University of Notre Dame Australia (Fremantle, Western Australia). A graduate of the University of North Carolina, Oxford University, and Marquette University, Shaun writes on a variety of topics in early modern and modern Catholicism. He is the author of *The Synod of Pistoia and Vatican II* (Oxford University Press, 2020) and coeditor, with Ulrich Lehner, of *The Catholic Enlightenment: A Global Anthology* (Catholic University of America Press, 2021). His most recent work, coauthored with Stephen Bullivant, is *Vatican II: A Very Short Introduction* (Oxford University Press, 2023).

Kristin Colberg is associate professor of theology at Saint John's School of Theology and Seminary, Minnesota. Her theological work is rooted in a desire to demonstrate the church's ability to speak meaningfully in the modern context. She is author of *Vatican I and Vatican II: Councils in the Living Tradition* (Liturgical Press, 2016). In 2021 she was named to the twenty-five-person theological commission assisting the Synod of Bishops, whose theme is "For a Synodal Church: Communion, Participation and Mission." She also has worked extensively with the Anglican-Roman Catholic International Commission.

Agnès Desmazières is maître de conférences in modern church history and systematic theology (ecclesiology and fundamental theology) at the Centre Sèvres, Paris. She was Robbins fellow at the University of California Berkeley in 2019. Her work focuses on the Catholic Church as it pertains to history, theology, and canon law. Publications include *L'heure des laïcs: Proximité et coresponsabilité* (Salvator, 2021) and *Le dialogue pour surmonter la crise: Le pari réformateur du pape François* (Salvator, 2019).

Massimo Faggioli is professor of historical theology in the department of theology and religious studies at Villanova University. His areas of expertise include the papacy, Vatican II, the Roman Curia, liturgical reform, new Catholic movements, and Catholicism and global politics. He is a contributing writer for *Commonweal* and a columnist for *La Croix International*. Publications include *The Liminal Papacy of Pope Francis* (Orbis, 2020), *The Church in a Change of Era: How the Franciscan Reforms are Changing the Catholic Church* (Twenty-Third Publications, 2020), and *Joe Biden and Catholicism in the United States* (Bayard, 2021).

Francis Gonsalves, SJ, is president of the Pontifical Institute of Jnana-Deepa Vidypeeth, Pune, India. He has lectured in Seoul, Korea, and Berkeley, California. He is the author of seven books, the latest of which is *Saint Romero and Pope Francis: Revolutionaries of Tender Love* (Pauline, 2019). He is executive secretary of the Conference of Catholic Bishops of India.

Julia Knop is professor of dogmatic theology at the Catholic Theological Faculty of the University of Erfurt, Germany. In April 2021 she was elected to the Central Committee of Catholics whose current major project is the synodal path in Germany, for which it is responsible and which it is shaping together with the German Bishops' Conference. Publications include *Beziehungsweise: Theologie der Ehe, Partnerschaft und Familie* (Pustet, 2019) and *Heute christlich glauben: Der Leitfaden für die Ökumene im Alltag* (Herder, 2019).

Rafael Luciani is a Venezuelan layman who holds a doctorate in theology from the Pontifical Gregorian University and has done postdoctoral research at the Julius Maximilians Universität, Germany. He is professor at the Universidad Católica Andrés Bello in Caracas and extraordinary professor at Boston College School of Theology and Ministry. He currently teaches ecclesiology, Latin American theology, Vatican Council II, and synodality in the church. He serves as an expert of the Conference of Latin American Bishops (CELAM) and as a member of the Theological Advisory Team of the Presidency of the Latin American Confederation of Religious (CLAR). He coordinates the Iberoamerican Theology Project, is a member of the Intercontinental Seminar Group Peter & Paul for the reform of the Catholic Church, and serves as an expert of the theological commission of the General Secretariat of the Synod of Bishops. Publications include *Pope Francis and the Theology of the People* (Orbis, 2017) and *The Emergence of Synodal Ecclesiality: A More Complete Definition of the Church* (Paulist, 2022).

Declan Marmion is professor of systematic theology at St. Patrick's Pontifical University, Maynooth, Ireland, and a former dean of the Faculty of Theology. Previous publications include *The Cambridge Companion to Karl Rahner* (Cambridge University Press, 2005), *An Introduction to the Trinity* (Cambridge University Press, 2011), *Remembering the Reformation: Martin Luther and Catholic Theology* (Fortress, 2017), and *Models of Priestly Formation: Assessing the Past, Reflecting on the Present, and Assessing the Future* (Liturgical Press, 2019). He was editor of *Irish Theological Quarterly* from 2013 to 2023.

Vincent Long Van Nguyen, OFMConv, STL, DD, born in Vietnam, is Bishop of Parramatta, Australia. He has been a leading light in the process of synodal renewal currently underway in Australia.

Ethna Regan teaches theology and ethics at Dublin City University. She was previously a lecturer at the University of the West Indies, Trinidad, where she lived for over a decade. Her teaching and research have been shaped by the experience of working in the Caribbean, particularly her involvement with the Credo Foundation for Justice. She also worked for five years in Samoa in the Pacific Islands. Her doctoral research at the University of Cambridge was on human rights and theology. Publications include *Theology and the Boundary Discourse of Human Rights* (Georgetown University Press, 2010) and "The Bergoglian Principles: Pope Francis' Dialectical Approach to Political Theology," *Religions* 10, no. 12 (December 2019) .

Salvador Ryan is professor of ecclesiastical history at St Patrick's Pontifical University, Maynooth, and has published widely on various aspects of the history of popular belief from the Middle Ages to the twentieth century. Among his most recent publications are (with Laura K. Skinnebach and Samantha Smith) *Material Cultures of Devotion in the Age of Reformations* (Peeters, 2022), (with James E. Kelly and Henning Laugerud) *Northern European Reformations: Transnational Perspectives* (Palgrave, 2020), and *Material Religion, Popular Belief and Catholic Devotional Practice in the Age of Vatican II (c. 1948–c. 1998): Global Perspectives*, which he edited as a special issue of the journal *Religions* (2021). In 2019 he published (with Declan Marmion and Michael Mullaney) *Models of Priestly Formation: Assessing the Past, Reflecting on the Present, and Imagining the Future* (Liturgical Press). He is reviews editor of *Irish Theological Quarterly* and a member of the editorial advisory board for *British Catholic History*.

Pedro Trigo, SJ, is a Venezuelan Jesuit of Spanish origin. He studied literature and philosophy at the Catholic universities of Caracas and Quito and received a doctorate in theology at the University of Comillas (Madrid). He is a full professor on the theology faculty of the Universidad Católica Andrés Bello in Caracas and a member of the Centro Gumilla, the research and social action center of the Jesuits in Venezuela. He has accompanied grassroots communities for more than thirty years. Known throughout Latin America for his contribution to liberation theology, he is the author of more than fifty books and articles on theology and is a frequent participant in conferences and seminars throughout the world on liberation theology.